Policy for Open and Dist Learning

Policy for Open and Distance Learning considers the questions that planners and policy makers in open and distance learning need to address at any level of education.

Starting by analysing the range of purposes for which open and distance learning is used, the book places the issues in context and examines experience in both the public and private sector. As well as discussing in detail new agendas set by new information and communication technologies, the book covers:

- Inputs – in terms of learners, staff and resources.
- Processes – organisational structures, technologies, globalisation and governance.
- Outcomes – benefits set in the context of costs.

The editors, Hilary Perraton and Helen Lentell, have drawn together an international team of contributors who have examined the varied roles of the new technologies as well as low-technology approaches to open and distance learning throughout the world.

This book will be invaluable to policy makers in education and those planning or managing open and distance learning programmes. It will also be of interest to students and teachers of education and anyone concerned with comparative education.

Hilary Perraton has worked in international education and in open and distance learning for many years. He was the founding director of the International Research Foundation for Open Learning. **Helen Lentell** is an educational specialist in training and materials development at the Commonwealth of Learning.

World review of distance education and open learning
A Commonwealth of Learning series
Series editor: Hilary Perraton

Higher Education through Open and Distance Learning
World review of distance education and open learning: Volume 1
Edited by Keith Harry

Basic Education at a Distance
World review of distance education and open learning: Volume 2
Edited by Chris Yates and Jo Bradley

Teacher Education through Open and Distance Learning
World review of distance education and open learning: Volume 3
Edited by Bernadette Robinson and Colin Latchem

Policy for Open and Distance Learning
World review of distance education and open learning: Volume 4
Edited by Hilary Perraton and Helen Lentell

The World review of distance education and open learning is published on behalf of the Commonwealth of Learning.

The Commonwealth of Learning is an international organisation established by Commonwealth governments in 1988. Its purpose is to create and widen opportunities for learning, through Commonwealth cooperation in distance education and open learning. It works closely with governments, colleges and universities with the overall aim of strengthening the capacities of Commonwealth member countries in developing the human resources required for their economic and social development.

Policy for Open and Distance Learning

Tony Dodds

Dec. '03

World review of distance education and open learning: Volume 4

Edited by Hilary Perraton and Helen Lentell

RoutledgeFalmer
Taylor & Francis Group

LONDON AND NEW YORK

THE COMMONWEALTH *of* LEARNING

First published 2004
by RoutledgeFalmer
11 New Fetter Lane, London EC4P 4EE

Simultaneously published in the USA and Canada
by Routledge
29 West 35th Street, New York, NY 10001

RoutledgeFalmer is an imprint of the Taylor & Francis Group

Selection and editorial matter © 2004 Commonwealth of Learning (COL);
individual chapters © 2004 the contributors

Typeset in Palatino by
Keystroke, Jacaranda Lodge, Wolverhampton
Printed and bound in Great Britain by
Antony Rowe Ltd, Chippenham, Wiltshire

British Library Cataloguing in Publication Data
A catalogue record for this book is available from the British Library

Library of Congress Cataloging in Publication Data
A catalog record for this book has been requested

ISBN 0–415–26306–9 (hbk)
ISBN 0–415–26307–7 (pbk)

Contents

Illustrations

Contributors

Szarina Abdullah has been involved in teaching and research in the fields of distance education, e-learning, information and library science. She pioneered the e-learning programme for the Universiti Teknologi MARA in Malaysia in 1998 and initiated the establishment of the Malaysian Association of Distance Education, of which she was elected the first President during 2000 to 2003.

Neil Butcher works with the South African Institute for Distance Education, where he specialises in educational planning and use of technology. He has conducted financial planning for several universities and other distance-education organisations in South Africa, as well as supporting educational planning and implementation for government departments, the public broadcaster, international donors and private providers, both in South Africa and other parts of Africa.

Glen Farrell has had a long career in distance education and the management of innovative organisations. He is now involved in international consultancies on change and reform in education systems and the use of technology, and is the author/editor of several reports on the development of virtual education systems.

Andrea Hope was the education specialist for higher education at the Commonwealth of Learning, with a particular interest in quality assurance and credit mobility. Her career in the administration of open and distance learning began at the Open University in Britain and took her to Hong Kong, where she was appointed Registrar of the Open University of Hong Kong in 1990. She has been involved in the process of institutional upgrading and quality process review as Associate Vice-President (Development) at Lingnan University of Hong Kong and, since January 2003, as Associate Academic Vice-President of Shue Yan College in Hong Kong.

Janet Jenkins is a freelance consultant in open and distance learning and has most recently been working on an extended assignment in

Uzbekistan. In a long career in this area she worked in Britain for the National Extension College and International Extension College and for the (then) Open Learning Foundation. She is also a former staff member of the Commonwealth of Learning.

Colin Latchem is an Australian-based international consultant in open and distance education. He was formerly Head of the Teaching Learning Group at Curtin University, Western Australia, and he is a past President of the Open and Distance Learning Association of Australia. He has written and lectured extensively on distance education and educational development.

Helen Lentell is an educational specialist in training and materials development at the Commonwealth of Learning. Before she joined COL she was head of higher education and professional studies at the National Extension College. Prior to this she worked at the Open University in Britain in a number of roles, including staff tutor in the social science faculty and assistant director for regional academic services. She has been a visiting scholar at Deakin University, Australia.

Kurt Moses is Vice-President of the Academy for Educational Development and Director of the Systems Services Center. He is a specialist in learning technologies and in educational planning, and has had extensive consultancy experience in Africa, Latin America and Asia.

Santosh Panda is a professor of distance education and staff development at the Indira Gandhi National Open University in India. Previously, he was Director of its Staff Training and Research Institute and also Director of Research at the Association of Indian Universities. A well-known educator and researcher from the developing world, Dr Panda practises, consults and researches in distance education, teacher education, student learning, and online learning and research. Currently, he is a Fulbright Visiting Scholar at the University of New Mexico, USA.

Hilary Perraton was the Founding Director of the International Research Foundation for Open Learning. He is a former member of the Commonwealth Secretariat with long experience in international education and distance learning, and was made an honorary Fellow of the Commonwealth of Learning in 2002. He has been managing editor of this series since its inception.

Reehana Raza is a political scientist and economist who is currently a research Fellow in higher education at the International Research Foundation for Open Learning. She has extensive consultancy experience, especially in South Asia, on education and development.

Bernadette Robinson is an independent consultant working internationally in open and distance learning and Special Professor of comparative education at the School of Continuing Education, University of Nottingham. She is also a research associate of the International Research Foundation for Open Learning.

Nicky Roberts is an educationist, with experience of teaching in Britain and South Africa, specialising in the use of media and technologies. She is currently employed by the Liberty Foundation in South Africa as the Education Director for Mindset, an educational satellite delivery system making use of print, broadcast and web technologies to target disadvantaged communities in Southern Africa.

Greville Rumble is an independent consultant working in the field of the planning, management and costs of open and distance learning. From 1970 to 2002 he worked for the Open University, latterly as Professor of Distance Education Management. He is based in Sussex, England.

Yoni Ryan is Associate Professor in higher education and deputy Director of the Centre for Learning and Teaching Support at Monash University, Melbourne, Australia. She has extensive experience in staff development and educational design and development with new technologies in Australia and the Pacific, and consults for state and federal governments on education policy.

Foreword

In a world whose vigour and well-being depends in good measure on expanding knowledge, provision for lifelong education is no longer an option for a few but a necessity for all. Universal provision entails reforming educational systems so that education and training can reach out to people wherever they live, work, socialise and rest. Many nation states have already embarked on such educational transformations while others are still considering them. Those falling into the former category are mostly the high- and middle-income countries and those in the latter category are mostly in the developing economies.

Distance, open and flexible learning is not a new phenomenon. In one way or another some form of organised distance education has been in existence for well over a hundred years. However, contemporary distance and open learning differs considerably and in a variety of ways from the historical version. In some countries, specialised single-mode institutions have been created to deliver education at a distance; in others, departments of external studies have taken on the task, and in yet others, ministries of education or their departments have been mandated to offer open-learning programmes. The past few years have seen the emergence of for-profit organisations and entrepreneurs embarking on online and virtual learning. Some of these ventures, such as the open universities of Britain, India, South Africa and Hong Kong, have been extremely successful, while many others have not yet matched their promise. At the heart of success or failure are sound and clearly defined policy frameworks at national and institutional levels.

This volume of the World Review of Distance Education and Open Learning recognises the expanding role of distance education and considers through its thirteen chapters the policies and structures of governments and organisations that are making it possible. The purpose of the exercise is to highlight those arrangements that work, to enable distance and open learning to progress, and also to identify factors that are likely to impede the system's development. Readers will note that, despite the three to four decades of contemporary distance education, many institutions and many of their governments are still struggling to design supportive and enabling policy frameworks. It is our hope that this series, and this volume in particular, will assist decision and policy makers by enabling them to benefit from the experience of others. The contributors, all with experience as practitioners or researchers, are drawn from different locations, cultures, sectors and agencies. There is richness in their collective wisdom.

This volume has benefited from the thoughtful and considered guidance of the international editorial board of the series and its Managing Editor, Dr Hilary Perraton of the International Research Foundation for Open Learning. To all of these persons as well as to the expert contributors, I record my sincere thanks and appreciation on behalf of the Commonwealth of Learning.

Gajaraj Dhanarajan
President and Chief Executive Officer
The Commonwealth of Learning

Acknowledgements

The editors wish to acknowledge the assistance received from the Commonwealth of Learning and its Editorial Advisory Group in the development of the plan of the book.

We are grateful for permission to use material in chapters 6, 8 and 9. Tables 6.1 and 6.3 are reproduced with their permission from UNESCO publications. Table 8.1 was originally published by the Department for Education and Employment and is © Crown copyright material which is reproduced with the permission of the Controller of HMSO and Queen's Printer for Scotland. The first part of Chapter 8 is based partly on an article by Hilary Perraton on 'Choosing technologies for education' originally published in *Journal of Educational Media* (25:1. pp. 31–8, March 2000) and is reproduced with permission from Taylor & Francis, publisher of the journal, whose website is at http://www.tandf.co.uk. The second part, by Kurt Moses, is reproduced with permission from the January to March 2002 issue of *TechKnowLogia*, Copyright © 2002 Knowledge Enterprise, Inc. *TechKnowLogia* is an international bimonthly journal of technologies for the advancement of knowledge and learning, available free on the internet at http://www.TechKnowLogia.org. Material in Chapter 9 by Glen Farrell, Andrea Hope and Yoni Ryan is taken with the consent of the Commonwealth of Learning from their web-based publication *The changing faces of virtual education* (ed. Glen Farrell 2001) which is available at http://www.col.org/virtualed.

Helen Lentell is indebted to Richard Freeman and to participants in workshops they ran together in Durban and the Caribbean for discussions that fed into the final chapter, Chapter 13. As with previous volumes in the series, we are grateful to Keith Harry who has compiled the index.

NOTE

Throughout the book, editorial material introducing parts of the book, and introductory material printed on a grey background, is the responsibility of the editors, while the actual text of chapters is that of the individual authors.

Part I

The policy agenda and its context

Chapter 1

Introduction

Planning open and distance learning

Hilary Perraton and Helen Lentell

Planning has a bad name, apparently standing against the individuality that education ought to foster and echoing to the collapse of the planned, command-led economies of the old second world. Yet in practice we – educators, managers, policy makers and citizens – need to allocate resources between educational alternatives and to do so rationally. The purpose of this book is to help that process, looking in particular at open and distance learning.

Effective planning matters, and matters beyond the confines of a small handful of planners in open universities, because of the growth and growing variety of uses of open and distance learning. In India, for example, distance education has been given the major role in expanding higher education. In Britain, the government has embraced open learning through its University for Industry as a tool for improving the skills seen as necessary for economic growth. Worldwide, Ford, Cisco, British Aerospace and others are beginning to use open and distance learning for the professional development of their own staff. The expansion of open and distance learning has forced it to the attention of institutional, national and international planners, provoking questions about its legitimacy and its methodology: Does it work, and if so what policies are needed to make it work effectively?

The authors of the following chapters try to answer those questions, drawing widely from international experience. They do so both factually, examining and describing the policies that have been adopted, and analytically, identifying the policy issues that demand the attention of planners. Their aim is to elucidate decisions that need to be taken in the management of open and distance learning in order to suggest when it may, and may not, be an appropriate solution to an educational problem.

In identifying policy issues, authors have looked at education in both developing and industrialised countries, at all levels of education, and using a variety of technologies. There are merits in looking at industrialised and developing country experience side-by-side, not least because the distinctions are becoming blurred. Rich countries can now recruit distant students in the south while the computer skills around Bangalore show how that part of India is within the industrialised world. While open and distance learning has gained most publicity through the activities of open universities, its use for basic education and for vocational education and training demands as much of our attention. As technologies are changing, and many programmes of open and distance learning use more than one of them, it makes sense to look widely at their variety and potential.

In order to maintain their focus on quality, the authors have kept away from three staples of the literature. First, there is no evangelism as they are not proselytising for (or against) open and distance learning. Second, this is not a toolkit. Its purpose is to identify policy options and their strengths and weaknesses, not to provide didactic prescriptions. Third, and closely related, it is not a management guide on the internal details of running open and distance learning. There has long been ample literature, for example, to guide internal, institutional decisions about the design of materials or the tutoring of students. Rather its purpose is to examine the prior decisions about when, if at all, to use open and distance learning and to frame those decisions within thinking about the educational service as a whole. The book is about policy for education, not just about policy for open and distance learning.

In order to review policy we look first at the purposes for which open and distance learning has been used. We then examine inputs in terms of purpose, learners, staff and resources. As the processes of open and distance learning are different from those of conventional education, we go on to examine the organisational structures available for open and distance learning, its technologies, the influence of globalisation, and measures to deal with quality and accreditation. We then look at outputs, examining the achievements of open and distance learning and its costs. The final chapter draws together the threads of the argument about inputs, process and outputs to relate these back to global educational needs and hopes.

Two themes run through much of the analysis in the following chapters. The first is about a kind of maturity in open and distance learning and its new place at the world's educational tables. Until the British Open University was established in 1969, open and distance learning belonged at the fringes of educational and political thinking. It was dominated by the private sector, and rightly coruscated for its shoddy quality (*Which* 1963, Mitford 1970, Noble 1999). Australasian and Soviet experience was mentioned occasionally but barely known. In the 1960s the efforts of Wedemeyer in America, Young and Jackson in Britain, and Lefranc in France began to get it attention but as an experiment, on a modest scale, and for narrow and often disadvantaged audiences (Young 1963, Wedemeyer and Najem 1969, Lefranc 1971, Perraton and Jenkins 1980). The success of the Open University, in attracting students and producing graduates, made it a model for the rest of the world, and stimulated a process of convergence between distance and conventional education. That process has been reinforced by changes in technology, and by the effect of those changes in conventional education. If a student is studying electronically it may no longer be sensible to ask if this is study on-campus or off-campus, or if this is to be regarded as comparable to conventional education or comparable to distance education. This convergence means that questions about the inputs, process and outputs of open and distance learning cannot be separated as easily from similar questions about conventional education as was the case even a decade ago.

The second theme concerns the role of the state and its formal institutions. The widespread acceptance of the neo-liberal agenda has eroded a consensus that governments, or their institutions, should provide, fund, monitor and accredit education and play the lead role in doing so. These functions are now more likely to be shared among a number of stake-holders, with the process of sharing influenced and probably complicated, by globalisation. The move away from central control or guidance is reflected in decisions about funding, technology and accreditation: changed expectations about funding mean that students in many jurisdictions have to meet more of the costs of their education; access to communication technologies for education is changing where central control of broadcasting is falling away; globalisation and a new kind of competition between universities point up the limitations of existing accrediting structures in protecting the student interest.

These centrifugal moves, dispersing control and influence, are shaping the policy of many educational institutions. They have a particular significance for open and distance learning since, more often than not, it rests on a partnership between different institutions. One may prepare teaching materials, another offer broadcasting, perhaps a third offer tutoring. The nature of these partnerships is shifting in relation to changing state roles and public-sector institutions are having to re-examine their relationship with the private sector. In Thailand, for example, educators in its open school can no longer expect free access to broadcast time in a privatised system. As computer-based or e-learning grows, so new questions are being framed about the partnerships needed for effective teaching. Good policy-making never could be insular; analysis of where it is going in open and distance learning takes us into questions of partnership, and of shifting institutional roles, which recur throughout the following chapters.

In order to define a framework for identifying policy options we begin by looking at the purposes for which open and distance learning has been used. In Chapter 2, Perraton looks at the varied uses of open and distance learning in the developing and industrialised world, examining in turn basic education, schooling and tertiary education. He goes on to identify the main forces that have driven its development and then to set out the main policy options open to the various stakeholders. In a coda to the chapter he asks how far the development of e-learning presents new issues to policy makers, or forces them to look at old policy decisions in a new light.

In the light of that discussion of purposes, the four chapters in Part II look at inputs, beginning with two chapters about learners. In an international overview Jenkins illustrates the variety of students attracted to open and distance learning and their reasons for using it. She contrasts experience in Britain and India – among other examples – before discussing how a profile of learner characteristics needs to feed into the planning process. In a case study of Asian students, Abdullah goes on to identify some of the similarities and contrasts found among students, mainly in higher education. She looks at the implications of her findings for the curriculum and goes on to propose policy recommendations designed to help support students.

In Chapter 5 Panda discusses the staff needed for open and distance learning, pointing out that its methods demand a different kind of division of labour from that needed in conventional schools or colleges. He examines the new type of role required of staff and goes on to draw distinctions between the jobs of full- and part-time staff, and those working at the centre or in decentralised jobs. He ends by examining the human resource development and management polices needed for effective open and distance learning.

Chapter 6 moves the discussion from people to finance in examining the resources needed for open and distance learning and possible sources of funding. Perraton notes that institutions tend to rely increasingly on a variety of sources of funding so that total reliance on state funding is becoming more unusual. Institutions are now drawing funds from government, from learners or their families, from community support, from the private and NGO sector, and from international funding agencies. The policy maker needs to look at the trade-offs required in favouring one source of funding over another. The chapter identifies the kinds of expenditure needed for open and distance learning, distinguishing between one-off and continuing costs, and sets these against a range of possible sources.

Part III moves from resources to process, asking how open and distance learning is working, about the policy decisions needed here, and examining in turn organisational structures, technology, governance and quality assurance, and the impact of globalisation. Rumble and Latchem introduce the section with a discussion, in Chapter 7, of the organisational models that have been adopted for open and distance learning. They contrast large- and small-scale approaches to open and distance learning, and look at the comparative strengths and weaknesses of single-purpose institutions, such as open universities, and dual-purpose ones, such as universities that teach both face-to-face and at a distance. The two approaches are seen as merging, partly as a consequence of the increased use of information and communication technologies and e-learning within conventional institutions. These new approaches are causing issues of inter-institutional cooperation to move higher up the policy-maker's agenda.

Several kinds of decisions about technology are discussed in Chapter 8. Planners need to choose between the different technologies that may be available to them, balancing educational and economic advantages and disadvantages. These will have an impact on students and on tutors whose roles are likely to change as technologies change; the adoption of e-learning, for example, has major consequences for tutors and for programmes to brief and train them. The chapter concludes with recommendations for the process of choosing between technologies.

Globalisation, and its impact on education, affect policy decisions in open and distance learning which are examined by several authors in Chapter 9. It looks at the changing institutions and structures which are now playing a part, especially through cross-border enrolment and the development of inter-institutional collaboration, themes already identified in Chapter 7. The chapter analyses policies needed for organisational development, for student support and for quality control as governments and distance-teaching institutions respond to globalisation.

Issues of governance, examined in Chapter 10, concern both the internal management of institutions and national or international policies about accreditation and quality control. Robinson analyses the structures that have been developed as the emphasis of state activity has generally shifted from control to supervision. She looks at the changing patterns of governance and at the mechanisms that have been developed for internal quality control and for external accreditation and supervision of open and distance learning, identifying the principal actors involved in both processes.

Part IV moves from process to outcomes and outputs, looking first at the available evidence on the effects of open and distance learning and then at costs and effectiveness. To put the discussion of outcomes in context, Raza begins Chapter 11 by setting out the practical and conceptual difficulties involved in measuring the benefits of open and distance learning. She then reviews the available evidence on its use at various levels of education, picking up the distinctions between them made in Chapter 2. Conclusions about the impact of open and distance learning are drawn from the literature generally and from two detailed studies carried out in Britain and India.

Butcher and Roberts, in Chapter 12, make the case for strong financial planning and set out recommendations for ways of achieving this. They provide a framework for financial decision making, based on sound analysis of the different categories of costs that are involved for open and distance learning and within that framework examine the logic of distance-education costing and the evidence on its comparative cost-effectiveness.

In the final chapter Lentell draws together the argument from this analysis in terms of inputs, process and outputs. She identifies the critical areas in which policy makers need to choose between options, at institutional, national or international level, if they are to provide an education that will meet the needs of their learners. Her balanced appraisal suggests how open and distance learning can meet many of its expectations while proposing guidance on good practice, based both on international experience and an understanding of the conditions for success in the many and varied forms of contemporary open and distance learning.

REFERENCES

Lefranc, R. (1971) 'Radio and television programs for teacher training'. *Educational Media International* 2: 18–25.

Mitford, J. L. (1970) 'Let us now appraise famous writers'. *Atlantic Monthly* 226, 1: 45–54.

Noble, D. F. (1999) *Digital Diploma Mills, part iv: Rehearsal for the Revolution*, http://communication.ucsd.edu/dl/ddm4.html (accessed 9 December 2002).

Perraton, H. and Jenkins, J. (1980) *The Invisible College: NEC 1963–79*, Cambridge: International Extension College.

Wedemeyer, C. A. and Najem, R. E. (1969) *AIM: From Concept to Reality: The Articulated Instructional Media Program at Wisconsin*, Syracuse: Syracuse University Press Publications in Continuing Education.

Which (1963) 'Correspondence courses', October.

Young, M. (1963) 'Announcing the National Extension College'. *Where?* 14: 16–17.

Chapter 2

Aims and purpose

Hilary Perraton

The twentieth century brought the world revolution, war, disease and education, all in unprecedented measure. By 2000, although 120 million children were still out of school, another 600 million were enrolled. Teaching had become the largest profession. The expectation that all children should go to school, already the dominant orthodoxy in the north in 1960, had moved from being a political aspiration to a cultural norm in most of the south by 2000. Education had expanded as dramatically at other levels. In 1960 there were six universities south of the Sahara; forty years later there were over a hundred (Domatob 1998: 87, Hinchliffe 1987: 29). Economics came to buttress politics in the expansion of education so that it was seen increasingly as a prerequisite for prosperity and economic growth as well as a means of personal empowerment. Technological changes played their part in this process, creating new demands for workforce training and for schooling that would lay the foundations needed for this. One set of technological changes, in communications, had a dual influence on the process in creating new jobs with attendant educational demands and in enabling educators to do their job in a different way. The growth of open and distance learning forms part of that story of educational expansion.

This chapter asks three questions about the story. First, what has open and distance learning been used for? Second, what has driven its development? Third, what does the experience identify as the critical options for the various stakeholders?

THE VARIETY OF USES

We start at the most basic and work up, looking at open and distance learning for basic education, for schooling, for tertiary education and for vocational education and training, including the education of teachers.

Basic education

In Jomtien in 1990 and in Dakar in 2000 the world reviewed its progress towards education for all. On both occasions communication technologies and distance education were seen as having potential for the expansion and strengthening of basic education, but, each time, they were seen as being peripheral rather than central. The reports of world experience brought to the meetings found few examples of technology-based approaches to basic education for children. For good reason, since the new technologies:

> are of limited relevance to children in the poorest schools where a trained teacher, a few books and a blackboard rightly take precedence over more advanced technologies. And, while there has long been an expectation that it might be possible to offer a technology-based, nonformal, alternative to primary schooling, there is little record of success to guide us here.
>
> (Perraton and Creed 2000: 81)

While open and distance learning may have an indirect role in expanding and strengthening the teaching force, it has not generally been perceived as a way of offering basic education.

The exceptions to this are telling. The most important have been in Latin America. From a small beginning in Colombia in 1947, radiophonic schools were established in most countries of Latin America as nongovernment, church-based institutions offering basic education to both children and adults. José Joaquín Salcedo, then a village priest and later a Monsignor, set up the first radio school Acción Cultural Popular (ACPO) in Colombia in the belief that education was fundamental to human development and the struggle against poverty. They used radio programmes and printed materials which were addressed to small, and often family-based, groups of learners. The schools employed a force of rural animateurs who visited and supported the learner groups. Initially at least, the Roman Catholic Church provided strong backing to the schools. They offered a curriculum, some of which was equivalent to the formal school curriculum, some targeted more closely to the needs of adult, poor and rural audiences. Children and adults studied together. The largest of the schools, ACPO, grew from 3600 students in 1950 to a maximum of over 240,000 in 1965, with numbers remaining between 100,000 and 200,000 in the 1970s to fall again and for the school eventually to close in 1987.

Both the rise and the fall of the radio school movement need to be seen within the political and cultural context of Latin America. They were able to set up radio stations because, in contrast with post-colonial Africa and Asia, broadcasting was not seen as a state monopoly. With severe limits on state activity in the countryside, the church was in a position to play a role in offering schooling. Their church backing gave them a degree of strength and measure of independence. Some moved from offering an education that was intended to be liberating to one that was designed as empowering campesino students to challenge the power of the plantocracy and the state. Most walked a tightrope between offering relevant education and being closed down as being dangerously revolutionary. Hernando Bernal, ACPO's director of planning and programming, contrasted two views of its work:

> That ACPO slogan 'Development is in the mind of mankind' was dangerous. Some people on the left took it as being ingenuous and lacking revolutionary fervour. In fact, there was a leftist guerrilla's movement called M-19 that accused Salcedo of betraying the peasantry by not fomenting revolution. . . . For other people the ACPO slogan had the flavour of an obvious and irrefutable truth, but one that made them uncomfortable, because it was threatening to the status quo.
> (quoted in Fraser and Restrepo-Estrada 1998: 160)

During the 1980s, their position became ever more precarious. In Colombia, the crippling effects of the recession meant that campesino students could not afford even the modest fees charged by ACPO. At the centre, where it seems never to have enjoyed more than tolerance from the state, it now lost the support of both state and church. Accusations of the misuse of funds, and the withdrawal of support from the church authorities led to the formal closure of the organisation in 1987 (Fraser and Restrepo-Estrada 1998: 158–9).

At their peak the radio schools demonstrated that their combined technologies of radio, print and supported group study could be effective in offering a basic education to children and to adults. In both Colombia and the Dominican Republic, where figures are available, they were doing so at costs that compared reasonably well with those of conventional schooling. (Probably few other schools matched their modest costs.) (Perraton 1984: 170, 2000: 121–2.) Some of the radio schools are continuing to use their well-tested methods for basic and secondary education, but the conditions that led to their flowering – of a pluralist tradition, a powerful and adequately staffed church influenced by libertarian theology, and a dramatic shortage of rural school places – are particular to Latin America of that period and contained within themselves the seeds of the schools' decline. Little in this experience suggests that there is a model that could be translated to the countries of subsaharan Africa and South Asia where large numbers are still out of school.

Secondary education

In contrast with these accounts of work at basic level, open and distance learning has solid records of achievement, and grand claims of potential, at the level of secondary education. In many parts of the south, the expansion of primary education has led to a demand for secondary schooling that outstrips the expansion of conventional schools. In the north, there are smaller numbers of adults who missed some of their secondary education, or did badly at it, and large numbers of children seen as a potential market for technology-based education. In a sense, distance education began here with private-sector colleges in both Europe and America and a small number of public-sector universities in America developing secondary-level correspondence education programmes. Today, we can distinguish three models.

We can label the largest model *the open school* although not all the institutions concerned use this as their title. In Africa, Latin America and Asia open schools have been created to offer junior- and sometimes senior-secondary education to adolescents for whom there are no conventional schools, for reasons of geography and economics. The largest and most well-established institutions are in Latin America, and include Telecurso in Brazil and Telesecundaria in Mexico. Telesecundaria uses broadcast television programmes to reach rural students who work under the supervision of a monitor. The structure has made it possible to reach students where government has argued that it is uneconomic to build small secondary schools. With thirty years of history, and an annual enrolment of 750,000, Telesecundaria is an established part of the formal education system. Its scale has made the use of television economically viable and its costs are now around the same as those of conventional schools (Perraton 2000: 34–5).

Variants of the open-school approach are on a more modest scale in Africa and Asia. The governments of Malawi, Zambia and Zimbabwe set up *correspondence centres*, where students came together to study centrally produced correspondence lessons under the guidance of a monitor. Television was not an option here and early experiments with the use of radio fell away. While the centres were working on a relatively large scale, with more students enrolled with the Malawi College of Distance Education, for example, than in regular schools, their results were modest and they were regarded as a poor second-best alike by parents and governments. In Asia, open schools have been established in South Korea, India and Indonesia with plans to extend them to reach millions of students. While Korea and Indonesia have made some use of broadcasting, much of their teaching is dominated by print. In all these cases the aim has been to make up for a shortfall of places in formal secondary school while also making it possible for young people in work to study part-time. It seems that the Asian open schools are continuing to receive government support as an alternative form of schooling whereas this model is in decline in Africa. The Malawi centres, for example, have been redesignated as community schools. But, in much of the south, there remain demands for an alternative approach to secondary education.

By contrast, the second model is concerned with the needs of individual and scattered students who cannot get secondary education even where this is virtually universal. The New Zealand Correspondence School, for example, offers teaching on the same syllabus as conventional schools to isolated children in scattered farms. From the early years of the twentieth century, its teaching was based firmly on correspondence lessons with some use of radio. It demands a considerable investment of time and support from the parents of school-age children who are following the primary or secondary curriculum. Similar schools were set up to meet the same social demand in other rich countries with low population densities, such as Australia, Canada and, to a lesser extent, the United States. With imagination and a sense of what was to come, the French government established a school on somewhat similar lines in 1939 to meet the needs of children who were being evacuated. It has changed its name, to become the Centre National d'Enseignement à Distance (CNED), and extended its range of work so that it runs from primary to degree level, but remains an integral part of the formal system of education.

The third model is designed to meet the needs of adults, or sometimes adolescents, who went through the school system but did not gain the qualifications they needed. This audience was the mainstay of commercial correspondence colleges which dominated the area in much of the world until the 1960s, while a number of American universities offered secondary-level courses for much of the twentieth century. In Britain, the National Extension College, established in 1963 as a pilot for the Open University, set out to meet this demand for General Certificate of Education courses from adults. In its early years it attracted students whose schooling had been disrupted by the war, but as time has gone on it has continued to attract adult students wishing to study at home for school-level qualifications. In a variant of this and the previous models, some of these institutions have also provided courses to isolated and small schools in order to extend their curriculum. The same pressure from rural voters that led to the development of the second model also prompted American rural high schools to seek help from their land grant universities; distance-teaching methods filled the gap where there were not enough children to justify the employment of a particular specialist teacher.

Thus, at secondary level, a range of open and distance learning approaches have been developed to meet demands from young people and adults that are not being met by conventional schooling. While this work is less honoured and less sung than that of the world's open universities, it remains a significant part of public-sector distance education in the south and of private, NGO and public-sector activity in some countries of the north.

Tertiary education

Open and distance learning is best known today for its work not at secondary but at tertiary level. It has a long pedigree. Some American universities were offering degree courses off-campus in the first half of the twentieth century as, in a modest way, was the University of London through its unattractively named Commerce Degree Bureau. In 1946 the University of South Africa was re-formed so that it became what would now be called an open university. Much of this was small-scale and un-noticed, although the experience of the Soviet Union in external education was picked up by the Robbins Committee that reviewed British higher education in 1961 to 1963. This was all to change with the establishment of the Open University in Britain in 1969, designed from the outset to attract students in large numbers (initially 20,000 a year) and to attain parity of esteem with conventional universities. Its foundation rested on a number of principles: that residence was not an essential part of university edu-cation; that a variety of technologies should be used to teach and would together overcome the disadvantages of distance; that the distant elements of any course should be integrated with occasional face-to-face study; that students should receive individual support from tutors or counsellors; and that the strength of these methods justified its being established as a university, awarding its own degrees, comparable with those of its conventional sisters.

Scepticism about all these heresies was normal among educators, but rare among the Open University's first students, whose success out-witted the critics. It survived a change of government two years after its establishment and rapidly attracted wide international interest. 'By 1975 open universities of one kind or another had been set up in Canada, Germany, Iran, Israel, Pakistan, Spain, and Thailand: the idea was adopted alike by secular democracies and fading autocracies, by states that were rich, middle-income and poor. By the late 1990s there are over thirty open universities while a far larger number of conventional universities have established open-learning programmes, with students numbered in tens or hundreds of thousands' (Perraton 2000: 84). As conventional universities began to expand their off-campus work, offering courses through open and distance learning, so they became, in the jargon, dual-mode universities. In Australia, for example, where there was a long tradition of off-campus teaching, most universities became dual-mode and successfully resisted suggestions that Australia needed a separate, free-standing, open university.

Within the industrialised world this movement has been part of a general expansion of tertiary education, seeking to provide alternative routes for students, generally older than conventional university students, who cannot study full-time. Within the developing world, in contrast, many open-university students are enrolling at this kind of university simply because there is no room for them within the conventional system. For their part, governments have seen open universities as a means of expanding higher education for post-school entrants, working on the assumption that the costs will be lower. In India, for example, the Planning Commission set out proposals to expand higher education 'in an equitable and cost effective manner mainly by large-scale expansion of distance education system and increased involvement of voluntary and private agencies' (Planning Commission 1992, vol. 1: 11). India hoped to increase the proportion of students studying through open and distance learning from 11.5 to 16.5 per cent. Some developing countries have exceeded these figures; Thailand had over 50 per cent of their university students working in this mode in 1985 while Turkey had over a quarter some ten years later. Figures of between 10 and 20 per cent are more common while, within industrialised countries, the proportions are usually between 7.5 and 15 per cent.

As university open and distance learning has grown so there is evidence of some convergence between it and conventional education. Within Britain, for example:

> on the one hand 'conventional' institutions are increasing access by moving towards modular degrees which can be taken in a variety of ways, part-time, full-time, resource-based, classroom-based and through distance learning. On the other hand the traditional approach to distance education, based on correspondence materials, broadcasts and video/audio tape supplemented by face-to-face and telephone teaching and counselling is rapidly being augmented by access through communication technology to other students and staff from home.
>
> (Mills 1999: 84)

At the same time, there are limits to the convergence. In India, for example, while it is possible for students of dual-mode universities to switch from distance to face-to-face study, students cannot usually transfer from an open university to a conventional one.

Recent changes in technology may stimulate the process of convergence. Over the past decade both universities and the private sector have been experimenting with computer-based learning. In doing so they have found that this demands a high level of investment but also that teaching is distributed more easily. There are therefore pressures to maximise student numbers, either by offering the same material to existing students both on- and off-campus or by seeking new groups of off-campus students. As it develops, and if it does so on any significant scale, e-learning may therefore bring down the barriers between different modes of teaching.

The dramatic growth of open learning based on print and broadcasts, and the new fascination with e-learning, demonstrate that universities and governments on the one hand, and large numbers of potential students on the other, see open and distance learning as having a significant role to play in the expansion of higher education. While there are differences in the audiences, and the purposes, for which open and distance learning is provided, it is becoming part of the mainstream educational system, and therefore raises inescapable policy issues for educational planners.

Vocational education and training

With the exception of teacher education, the use of open and distance learning for vocational education has attracted less attention than the work of open universities. While this makes it difficult to assess its scale, vocational courses have been offered by specialist teaching institutions, as part of the work of open and dual-mode universities, and by employers. The specialist institutions have included, for example, the external polytechnic institutions of the former Soviet Union that provided diploma and degree-level courses to scattered students working in heavy industry throughout the Union. (I was impressed, on visiting them in 1978, to find they were teaching nuclear power-station maintenance but Chernobyl made me rethink.) In Latin America the National Apprenticeship System of Colombia (SENA) works with companies to develop distance education to deal with problems arising from technological change (Ruiz 1992: 39). Courses for updating and for continuing education have been a mainstay of universities teaching at a distance in both the north and the south. Elsewhere, vocational education has dominated the work of an institution. The National Technological University, for example, which teaches by television, satellite and computer, came into existence to offer postgraduate courses, mainly in engineering, to students throughout North America. Employers, as well as teaching institutions, have seen open and distance learning as having particular advantages for providing inservice education for scattered staff members. British Aerospace has announced plans for creating a virtual university for its staff, following in the footsteps of the Vatican which began using distance education to update the priesthood in Italy after Vatican II.

In terms of numbers, the use of open and distance learning for teacher education probably outstrips all other vocational education. Africa, where the demand for teachers has for more than a generation often exceeded the supply from teachers' colleges, provides a set of examples. Soon after independence, Botswana and Swaziland ran inservice, distance-education courses for untrained teachers in their schools with the once-for-all intention of creating a fully trained profession. Nigeria, Tanzania and Zimbabwe all launched major programmes of teacher education at a distance in order to provide enough teachers for universal primary education. Tanzania and Zimbabwe used one-off intensive programmes while Nigeria launched a unique, monotechnic, National Teachers' Institute to run teacher education at a distance for the foreseeable future. After the fall of apartheid, teacher education expanded in South Africa so that, in 1995, nearly 130,000 teachers were studying at a distance (Gultig and Butcher 1996: 84). Outside Africa, courses for teachers are a mainstay of the open universities in India and China. Within the industrialised world, teachers seeking to improve their own qualifications have always sought opportunities to study part-time; a high proportion of the British Open University initial students were trained teachers without a degree who wanted to raise their status, improve their promotion prospects and gain additional increments, as well as to learn. More recently the university has run a targeted programme for a postgraduate certificate in education; this is the other way round, offering a formal teaching qualification to graduates rather than an academic degree to qualified teachers. (Recent experience is reviewed in Creed 2001, Perraton *et al.* 2001, 2002 and forthcoming.)

Across both developing and industrialised countries we can distinguish three kinds of activity here. First, open and distance learning has been used to provide initial training to teachers either for trainee teachers before they start work or for unqualified teachers already working in the schools. These programmes have typically tried to ensure that study at a distance was linked with measures to supervise, guide and assess teaching practice. Second, open and distance learning has been used for the continuing education of qualified teachers in schools. In Pakistan, for example, courses for teachers were linked to curriculum reform and aimed at a high proportion of all primary school teachers. Burkina Faso has used distance education to train headteachers. Third, as we saw, many teachers use open and distance learning programmes as a means of self-education, enrolling individually – and usually paying their own fees – as opposed to participating in a centrally managed upgrading programme.

To sum up: while there are many exceptions, open and distance learning in the south, both at secondary and tertiary level, has generally been used as a means of expanding education for students who could just as well have studied conventionally. In the north, however, its main use has been for audiences who for reasons of age, occupation or location prefer to study at home; it has expanded as a way of reaching new audiences. Much vocational education shows something of the same pattern, with Latin American institutions, for example, enrolling students who would follow a more conventional path in the north. With the exception of teacher education, the expansion of vocational education at a distance seems to be a function of economic development. Advanced and high-tech industries have made the running in developing e-learning in the north which is aimed at learners with a good formal background education and a need to keep up with their subjects.

DRIVERS OF DEVELOPMENT

Why has all this happened? The process has been driven mainly by a desire to widen access, by an intention to strengthen education in the interests of the economy, by technological opportunities, and by the hope of containing costs.

Improving access to education has been a dominant theme of many of the formal statements about the development of open and distance learning. The planning committee, set up to establish the Open University, made the case at the beginning of its report:

> In the past limited opportunities for education, determined by social, economic and political factors, have resulted in a low educational attainment on the part of a vast number of individuals.

> For long regarded as a privilege of the few, the opportunity to engage in higher education is at last becoming widely accepted as a basic individual right.
>
> (Venables *et al.* 1969: 2)

The report went on to identify as the first task of the university to meet the needs and aspirations of the 'substantial, though slowly diminishing proportion of people able enough to enter higher education who were born too soon to reap the benefits of increasing educational opportunity' (ibid.). Only after a discussion of the numbers of individuals who had missed earlier opportunities of higher education did the report go on to discuss the university's role in providing updating courses demanded by 'the changes in, and the increasing rate of change within modern technological society' (ibid.: 4). Access in the interest of equity came first.

We hear the same theme at other levels of education and in other parts of the world. At the level of basic education, the demand for access to primary education has driven the expansion of distance education for teachers. At secondary level, the main purpose of Telesecundaria in Mexico has been to provide access to rural students who could not otherwise get to school. (Unusually it has not been expected to operate at lower unit costs than conventional schools; as long ago as 1972 government was meeting more of its costs than it was for conventional schools (Perraton 2000: 187).) Moving back to tertiary education, the first open university established in India – the Dr B.R. Ambedkar Open University – defines its main aim in terms that are familiar in many other open university charters:

to promote equality of educational opportunity for as large a segment of the population as possible including all adults who wish to upgrade their education or acquire knowledge in various fields through distance education whether employed or not, and particularly including housewives and other women.

(ICDL 1997)

Geography as well as polity has led to the use of open and distance learning for access. In both the South Pacific and the West Indies, the regional universities have adopted distance education programmes in order to provide access to higher education to small islands without a university campus.

Arguments based on economics are nearly as common as those based on access. Both Indonesia and Thailand, for example, adopted an open-school approach to widening junior–secondary education because of a desire to meet the demand for educated labour as industrialisation went ahead. In higher education many of the Asian open universities have

had explicit economic and developmental ends. In Turkey, as the open university got under way, the largest single group of students were doing degrees in economics and business, presumably seen as contributing to economic development. The Payame Noor Open University in Iran seeks first to promote science and culture and then 'to provide skilled manpower in areas critical to national integration and development'. Its first courses were in chemistry, education, mathematics and Persian to be followed by biology and geology. The first objective of Sukhothai Thammathirat Open University in Thailand is 'to provide and promote university and professional education so as to enable the people to raise their educational standards in response to the needs of society'.

(Perraton 2000: 90)

Economic arguments have been important to international and funding agencies too. The European Union launched a series of activities to explore the use of advanced communication technologies within education and training in the interests of European competitiveness. The DELTA project, one of the European Commission's early ventures into the use of communication technology, had, according to its evaluation,

two main strategic goals: to improve access to learning in Europe through the provision of new flexible tools, and systems, and to improve market competitiveness in learning technologies. Underlying these strategic goals are wide strategic policy orientations, such as the promotion of European economic and social cohesion, and improving European competitiveness in international markets.

(Cullen *et al*. 1992: 30)

It is more difficult to assess the significance of technology in driving the development of open and distance learning. Going back to the foundation of the British Open University, the planning committee began its chapter on the 'general approach to open university education' with the surprising words: 'It is no longer necessary to argue that the broadcasting media, when imaginatively used, are efficient means of instruction, since this has now been established by an adequate body of research' (Venables *et al*. 1969: 6). With passing references to correspondence and hardly any to student support the chapter went on for its remaining seventeen paragraphs to discuss broadcasting. Between around 1965 and 1975 there was an expectation that television would transform education. In America, the Mid Plains Airborne Television Instruction project had been beaming television programmes to schools from a circling aircraft; in Côte d'Ivoire, El Salvador and American Samoa alike (perhaps only in this?) educational television projects were set up to revolutionise education; Britain had its specialist Centre for Educational Television Overseas. Open learning became credible in part through faith in broadcasting.

There are eerie parallels between the claims for television then and for computer- and internet-based learning now. Before disappointment set in, educational television projects were set up in Africa, Asia and Latin America in the expectation that 'ETV would serve as a catalytic agent for overall educational reform – upgrading the quality of instruction, reaching larger numbers of students, equalizing educational opportunity, and reducing unit costs of instruction' (Arnove 1976: xi). In Côte d'Ivoire, for example, the government's five-year plan justified the national television project by quoting

the pedagogical advantages (presentation of concrete and not merely verbal elements, good visual and auditory models, an opening to the outside world, constant updating of content and methods); the advantages of a centralized production system (the need for a limited number of staff, the unifying quality of the teaching, the integration of the different subjects taught); the advantages of a modern telecommunications system (rapid delivery, a theoretically infinite number of reception sites); its role in the permanent education and updating of teachers; its role in reducing regional disparities in the quality of teaching, and in increasing a sense of national unity.

(Kaye 1976: 149)

Thirty years later, one of the background papers for the British government Imfundo project on technologies for education in Africa argues that

> Information and Communication Technologies (ICT) can support learning in a number of ways. It can facilitate communication, increase access to information, provide greater access to learning for students with special educational needs, model and simulate a range of scientific phenomena, and generally motivate students, develop problem solving capabilities and aid deeper understanding.
>
> (Selinger 2001)

Technology has driven open and distance learning through three mechanisms. The first is opportunity: educators have seized the chance to use technologies to meet perceived educational needs. Just as the inventors of university extramural work used the railway in the nineteenth century, so their successors used television in the twentieth. Both television and computer-based technologies have been seen as a way of transforming education and so as meriting investment for that main reason. Second, enthusiasts are important. In studying the cost-effectiveness of various technologies in European higher education, the International Research Foundation for Open Learning found, repeatedly, that technologies were chosen because an individual liked the idea of using them and could find soft finance to meet the bill. Third comes financial interest. It would be naive to explain the whole of open and distance learning in terms of a desire to expand the sales of advanced technology. But this has played a part: Japanese aid has been used to fund the purchase of communications technology and broadcasting equipment for education; the United States has funded projects designed in part to demonstrate that there is a market for the private sector; and telecommunication companies stand to gain if there is increased use of their systems through education.

Moving to economics as a driver, open and distance learning has been widely sold as a good bargain. In an overview of the economics of open and distance learning, Rumble reports that:

> governments have come to see distance education as a means of enrolling large numbers of students at a lower capital cost than traditional institutions. . . . Numerous distance teaching institutions have been set up with the specific intention of reducing the unit costs of education. . . . The planners of the Andhra Pradesh Open University in India, the Universidad Nacional Abierta in Venezuela and Everyman's University in Israel all specifically hoped that the use of distance teaching methodologies would lower the unit costs of higher

education. Industry too has seen open learning as a way of reducing the per capita cost of training.

(Rumble 1997: 2)

In practice, while open and distance learning sometimes offers the possibility of reducing the unit costs of education, it does not always do so. While the manufacture and distribution of teaching materials make economies of scale possible, student support costs tend to rise with the number of students and can eat up all the savings made. But the perception that open and distance learning will lower unit costs has been all important in attracting governments to its support. They have in some cases done so with a concentration on the cost per student – often looking quite good – well before there is information about the cost per successful student – a more demanding measure where comparisons between conventional and distance education are seldom as stark.

We cannot easily weigh the significance of access, economic development, technology and cost-saving as drivers of the growth of open and distance learning. For the policy maker they suggest a set of questions about the interaction between them. The key issues are about the compatibility between the various forces: widening access may compete for funds with the demands for workforce development; technology choice may be constrained by cost or by the limited opportunities some students will have of using certain technologies; there are potential contradictions between containing unit costs and providing a learning system with enough support to benefit disadvantaged or remote students.

These various drivers have operated differently on the various stakeholders concerned with open and distance learning, among them learners, governments, the private sector, and teachers and their institutions.

It seems likely that the possibility of widening access to education has been most significant for learners and for governments. Both of these groups, too, have an interest in keeping down the cost of education – particularly important where learners have to bear most of the costs through student fees. Governments and the private sector alike have been influenced by the possibility of using open and distance learning for educating and training the workforce, as have learners if they see personal advantage in doing so. The scale of investment needed for advanced technology means that both governments and the private sector may be involved in promoting its development – television in one generation, computer-based technologies in another. Private-sector interests here may bear directly or indirectly on educational decisions: one of the drivers of the early television projects, for example, was the availability of funding for equipment from Japan. Today, concern about the digital divide is pushing governments both to support investment in communications technology and to support education for workforce training in relation to it.

Teachers' attitudes to the various drivers tend to be ambivalent. On the one hand, some are enthused by the possibilities offered by new technologies and interested in exploring new ways of working. Open and dual-mode universities and open schools would not work without the enthusiasm of their staff. But, on the other, many teachers are concerned that the introduction of open and distance learning, or of new teaching technologies, may add to their workload or, even worse, be used by educational managers as a way of reducing staffing levels. The technological driver is seen in this case as operating against the long-term interest of a profession and of the values it upholds.

The actions of the various drivers and the behaviour of the stakeholders together influence the choice of options in terms of management and organisational structure.

OPTIONS FOR MANAGEMENT AND ORGANISATIONAL STRUCTURE

The organisation and management of open and distance learning is necessarily more complicated than running a school; the complexities are examined further in Chapter 7. At its simplest, the work of a school is confined within its walls: knowledge in the heads of the teachers, communication by chalk and talk, accreditation as a rite of passage. Open and distance learning has brought a new division of labour into education and, with it, a set of options for stakeholders about the location of the separate functions of recruiting students, of developing, producing, reproducing and distributing teaching materials, of teaching and supporting students, and of awarding credit. Many of these functions may be undertaken by a single agency, if a distance-teaching institution has wide powers and functions. But they are often shared between partners, as shown in the examples in Table 2.1. If functions are divided between different agencies, then questions arise about the limits of their responsibilities and about the financing of each activity.

The answers to those questions are in part a function of the level of education for which open and distance learning is being used. Distance-teaching institutions may work at any level, may be in the public or the private sector or a partnership between the two, and may be in single- or multi-purpose institutions. At one extreme, a single-purpose, public-sector, distance-teaching institution, such as the National Teachers' Institute of Nigeria or an open university, has an autonomy and authority that means it can itself recruit students, teach them with its own materials, and award its own degrees and diplomas. Similarly private-sector corporate universities, offering continuing education and training to the staff of a single company, may not need to look outside their virtual walls in meeting

Table 2.1 Location of functions for some models of open and distance learning

Functions	Open University, Britain	NEC Company degree (CCSB)	OLA, British Columbia	University of the West Indies
Materials development	OU, but for broadcasting shared with BBC	NEC	OLA with freelance writers	Regular faculty members with Distance Education Centre (DEC)
Distribution	OU except for broadcasts	NEC	OLA either to individual students or to colleges within Province System Broadcasting by OLA through dedicated channel	Students collecting materials or attending sessions at university tutorial centres
Student recruitment	OU	Company	Both OLA and colleges	Responsibilities shared between DEC, campuses, and tutorial centres
Tutoring and counselling	OU	NEC with Bradford University	OLA for students enrolled directly; colleges for students they recruit	Shared between faculty members and resident tutors in non-campus countries
Student records	OU	All three parties need records	OLA for own students; colleges for theirs	Shared between DEC and campuses
Assessment or accreditation	OU	Bradford University	OLA can award its own school graduation equivalency certificates and degrees	University responsibility but with delegation to campuses

their company and learners' needs. This may slightly exaggerate their autonomy. Some corporate universities look to the formal education sector for accreditation, while, in the public sector, the autonomous Open University nevertheless looks to the BBC for its broadcasts.

Where open and distance learning is one function of a university that is also teaching conventionally, the picture is likely to be more complicated. In dual-mode universities, for example, questions arise about the responsibilities of academic staff and of the staff of specialist distance-teaching units. Some such units have been limited to an organisational role which consists essentially of reproducing and distributing teaching materials and arranging tutorials with little responsibility for educational or pedagogical issues. In other cases, units have skills in educational technology which give them a recognised role in the educational design of teaching materials or planning of tutorials. In yet another model, off-campus teaching has its own academic staff. The University of the West Indies, for example, moved over the years from the first of these positions to the second, but might, with advantage, have opted for the third (see Box 2.1).

Box 2.1 The University of the West Indies

The University goes back to 1948 when it was set up as a university college on a single campus in Jamaica. One of its main initial purposes was to train the small administrative cadre that would be needed as the countries of the region moved towards independence. It has expanded over the years so that it now has three campuses, 24,000 students, and university centres throughout the fourteen territories it serves, from Belize in the west to Trinidad and Tobago in the south-east.

For much of its history it was the only university to serve its archipelago region of small states and has tried various strategies of doing so. It became a fully fledged university in 1962, under the leadership of the Nobel Prize winner Sir Arthur Lewis, who was then its vice-chancellor. He set the University on the road to expansion, seeing that the region needed more than a handful of administrators, and opened university centres in seven of its non-campus territories, which have become a vital part of the educational and cultural life of the region. The vice-chancellor's successor in the mid-1990s, Sir Alister McIntyre, carried the process further, pressing the needs and interests of the smaller territories, and justifying expansion by noticing how the region lags behind the Asian tigers in its production of graduates.

Geography suggests that distance education should play a part in higher education among territories with a population of less than 100,000, a common language, cultural similarities, and the separating sea. The University began by experimenting with telephone links between its campuses and with its non-campus centres. In the early 1980s the United States agreed to fund a 'University of the West Indies Distance Teaching Experiment' (UWIDITE) which got under way in 1982. It provided telephone links, with loudspeaker telephone classrooms, which allowed lecturers on any of the three campuses to teach remote students, by audio, throughout the region. The system has continued to be used, both for teaching and for administrative exchanges between university staff, and has been upgraded in quality as time has gone on.

In 1991 the University commissioned a report from the Commonwealth of Learning on how it should develop its work in distance education. It recommended an expansion, to move away from the principal dependence on audio teaching that marked UWIDITE, and to integrate the University's distance teaching with its on-campus work. It rejected suggestions for setting up a quite separate institution to look after distance education as impractical for a total population of less than five million. In response, the University raised a loan from the Caribbean Development Bank – much of it to upgrade the UWIDITE hardware – and went on to establish a Distance Education Centre, with a director of professorial status as its head, and announced an expanded programme of work off-campus. The fundamental purpose was to widen educational opportunity in the non-campus territories with the hope of reversing a trend that saw these students taking a declining pro-portion of places on the campuses as compared with students from the three campus countries.

The most difficult issues to be resolved in this expansion were about the relationship between off-campus and on-campus teaching. First, over the years, the university had decentralised much of its decision-making, including, by the early 1990s, responsibility for curricula at first-degree level. But this was the point where the new distance-education team wanted to develop teaching materials that would be common across the whole university. Second, as ever, most of the loan funding was for hardware and not soft-ware. Third, UWIDITE had set a strange precedent. It was set up as an experiment, with limited funding and organisationally responsible to the principal of one campus, who had raised the funds and driven it ahead. Academic staff were invited to 'teach on UWIDITE' and were paid a modest extra fee to do so. Most gave lectures, comparable to those they gave on campus, and only limited teaching materials were produced. Fourth, perhaps most important of all, the University's role was shifting. As other tertiary institutions were being developed within the region, so they were beginning to offer courses at the level of the first two years of university teaching. There was an inbuilt contradiction then between the economics and purposes of distance education – maximise the audience by working at the lower levels – and the culture of the University and the direction in which it was moving.

All these difficulties influenced the university decisions about the courses it should offer at a distance and the organisational location of distance education. Its initial plan was to move on two main fronts: developing sub-degree courses in business and administration and to develop a raft of courses at first- and second-year level, so that students would be able to do two-thirds of a degree off-campus and come on to the campus for the third year. This involved a change of culture for on-campus staff, who for the first time were asked to take on a significant load of course development for distance teaching, and for off-campus part-time staff, who would have to provide a new kind of face-to-face support for students of distance-education courses.

Various organisational models are possible for this move to dual-mode activity. In the interests of parity of esteem, and in an attempt to build distance education into the regular work of the faculties, the initial policy was to make distance education firmly the responsibility of faculties, with the distance education centre able to call on them for writers to an agreed programme. The laudable aim of getting faculties to adopt a sense of owner-ship over the distance-education programme ran up against the reality that faculties could not find staff time for materials development. The University seems, in consequence, to be moving to a quite different model, of creating a fourth virtual campus, which would run in parallel with the existing three, but would buy in services from any of them or from elsewhere.

The University of the West Indies is unique. But its problems, of reconciling new developments in distance education with the conventional culture of on-campus teaching, and of finding the right location for distance education within its system, are common to many institutions, north and south, as they change their modes of teaching.

In developing, or reshaping, an organisational model for a particular purpose the planner is likely to choose between some of the options discussed in Chapter 7 and to be particularly concerned about strategies for collaboration and about three related issues that affect students' interests – funding, technology and quality.

Strategies for collaboration

Much open and distance learning, at all levels of education, has been built up on collaboration between different partners. In the Latin American radio schools, for example, materials were developed centrally while local support was the responsibility of local animateurs and the parish priest. This division of responsibility among nongovernment partners is relatively unusual. A university-level programme in Britain, in contrast, shared responsibility between a private-sector company, an educational charity and a university. As described in Box 2.2, Coca-Cola Schweppes Beverages worked with the University of Bradford and the National Extension College to offer a part-time degree programme to employees.

Box 2.2 Coca-Cola Schweppes Beverages, the National Extension College and the University of Bradford

This programme was designed to give junior sales staff working for Coca-Cola Enterprises throughout Britain the opportunity to study for a BSc (Hons) in business and management while also gaining four and a half years' work experience in a commercial environment. The programme was developed and delivered in partnership between three parties: the company, the University of Bradford and the National Extension College (NEC).

The company recruited students directly on to the degree programme, usually from school or college. They had to have university entrance qualifications and enough application to work and study at the same time. They were funded by the company to study on a supported degree programme of the University of Bradford Management Centre which was developed and managed by the NEC. Students studied the University's regular modular undergraduate programme over a period of four and a half years using distance learning and teaching methodologies, while working a thirty-five-hour week for the company with a further full day a week designated as a study day. The teaching and student support were planned, organised and administered by the NEC.

Each partner had different aims and functions. The company wanted to recruit potential managers and meet their training needs. The programme helped solve a recruitment problem; whereas most of the staff in this category left after a year and a half, this group tended to remain for the full four and a half years. Coca-Cola Schweppes wanted an innovative programme consistent with its company image, but did not wish or attempt to control the curriculum. NEC sees its mission as to widen access to learning opportunities through innovative open and distance education and was therefore interested in the programme both because of its purpose and in order to experiment with new approaches to work-based learning. The University's management centre had a long tradition of collaboration with industry and the professions so that a sponsored off-campus programme fitted its approach to higher education. Responsibilities were shared between the parties so that the University had responsibility for the curriculum content and the examination process while the NEC was responsible for the delivery of the programme, including the development of distance-education materials, providing tuition and student support, organising residential schools and record keeping. University staff members worked with the NEC as tutors and writers. The company had the normal responsibilities of an employer, provided its staff with time to study as well as an income, and met all the costs.

The students' day job was to be at the front line of the company, selling and delivering products to local shops, newsagents, restaurants, service stations and other outlets. They were expected to put in a minimum of twenty hours of study time per week at the first of three stages of the degree programme and then up to thirty hours for the two remaining stages. The company allocated additional study time near examinations for revision and preparation and released staff for residential schools.

The programme ran for ten years from 1994 to 2003; as the partnership refined its methods of working the successful completion rate went up from 25 per cent for the first cohort to 73 per cent for the third, in which withdrawals from the programme were for work or personal, not academic, reasons. It meant that students could work in regular employment, study for a degree without incurring debt and, after four and a half years, have gained both solid work experience and a management degree.

Source: adapted from Lentell 2001

Collaborations are fraught. While educational institutions have a long tradition of cooperation in research, there is little culture of cooperation in teaching. It is worth identifying the level of complexity involved in cooperation:

> In an ascending order of complexity and institutional risk, collaborative projects may include exchanges of information, experience and consultants; collaboration on development, adaptation and evaluation of learning materials; establishment of credit-transfer arrangements; and creation of new management structure, both within and among institutions.
>
> (Moran and Mugridge 1993: 3)

The greater the complexity, the greater the risk that one or other of the stakeholders will decide that the costs exceed the benefits. Decisions are likely to be influenced by the extent to which functions are shared or divided. In some cases several members of a partnership may be capable of carrying out a particular function, such as developing materials, but decide to share it. In others members may have different capacities – perhaps one in materials development and one in accreditation – and their functions are necessarily divided. The sharing of functions is inherently risky; one partner may at any time decide they can do a better job.

International experience suggests a number of conditions for success:

1   High-sounding rhetoric is a waste of time as is a vague desire to collaborate.
2   The smaller the initial group of participants, the greater the chance of success.
3   Objectives of collaboration have to be clearly defined and probably not too ambitious, at least at the outset.
4   There has to be something in it for every participant.
5   There must be people in every institution who want and are in a position to make it work.

(Mugridge cited in Daniel *et al.* 1986: 9)

A set of guidelines for effective cooperation is set out in Box 2.3.

The difficulties of developing and sustaining cooperation point up the varied interests of stakeholders in open and distance learning. In the Coca-Cola Schweppes example the learners were at once employees of the company, students in need of support from the college, and examinees of the university in its role as a degree-granting institution. Stakeholder interests were bound to diverge. We may expect learners to favour collaborative structures where these improve access to learning, and for governments and funding agencies to favour them where they see possible economies. Private-sector institutions welcome cooperation where it provides them with a service, such as accreditation, that they cannot themselves provide, or one that they can buy in more cheaply or with more limited commitment of resources, through outsourcing. For the most part educational institutions have been more guarded in their attitude, especially where they are in principle themselves able to provide a service that is available from a partner.

Funding

Education and training are generally funded from one or more of five sources: the learners themselves or their families; governments; the private sector, often as an employer; international agencies; and charities and foundations (discussed more fully in Chapter 6). Open and distance learning has drawn its funding from the same sources but often in different proportions from those that mark conventional education. As it can be used by part-time learners, managers have often assumed that students are in paid employment and can therefore themselves meet a higher proportion of the costs. Open-university degree students in industrialised countries, for example, tend to be mature students, with an individual or family

Box 2.3 Cooperative structures: international experience on how to make them work

First, there need to be clear goals and a clear statement of purpose. (One of the reasons for the failure of the Open College – a government-funded project to offer vocational education and training at a distance that absorbed funds but recruited few students – was fuzziness about its aims and about the comparative importance of offering education to unemployed people or to those in work.)

Second, there need to be significant roles for administrative and academic staff in all member institutions. Some partnerships have been created because funding agencies required it, but in practice action has remained almost entirely with a single institution; open and distance learning projects funded by the European SOCRATES programme provide examples. Staff playing an active part have to be at the right level in the organisation: one organiser of a company degree programme commented that the scheme could not have worked without the support of a senior manager with the willingness to find a way around university procedures and the status to carry proposals through the necessary committee. Support at the top or bottom alone is not enough.

Third, there needs to be a governance and funding structure that fits the purpose. An analysis of American educational consortia which failed found that a governing body of academic presidents did not work because they lacked both time and commitment. In Britain an Open Tech project gave all the emphasis to production and none to distribution or marketing; little distribution took place. The funding arrangements need to be such that the partnership can continue – if its job still needs to be done – once pump-priming is no longer available.

Fourth, members of a partnership need to see that they have complementary roles and that there are benefits to all. It seems likely that partnerships where functions are divided, so that members do not have the capacity to undertake each other's functions, as in company degrees, are more stable than those where functions are shared. Traditions of academic autonomy, for example, mean that there has been a great reluctance for institutions that can each generate teaching material to share this.

Fifth, effective partnerships are likely to seek a commitment of resources from all partners. Some of these resources may be in kind, as in the preliminary work done by academic institutions in preparing for a company degree, while others may be by means of a subscription.

Source: adapted from Perraton and Hülsmann 1998

income, which makes substantial fees possible. The British Open University fee for a one-year, one-module, social science foundation course (one-sixth of a degree) was £405 (US$590) in 2001, or about a quarter of the average monthly wage. This is not always the case. Many Asian open-university students are school leavers, while those at the Chinese Central Radio and Television Universities study full-time at a distance. At secondary level students of institutions such as the Mexican Telesecundaria are adolescents and full-time students, not employees with an income.

In many cases funding comes from a mixture of sources. As we saw above, the wish to contain educational costs has been one of the drivers of open and distance learning. However, while it may have cost advantages over conventional education, the economic structure of open and distance learning means that there are potential or actual conflicts between the social and economic interests of the various stakeholders. An educational provider, wanting to contain costs and maximise revenue, will seek to hold down student support and maximise the total number of students, in order to spread the fixed cost over the larger number. The student, on the other hand, may want to maximise student support and have the widest choice of options in terms of different courses.

There are two conflicts here for the educational planner. The first is between economy and equity. The more heavily dependent an institution is on student fees, rather than public funding, the more difficult it is to reach the poorest students: they cannot afford to pay. The Indian National Open School, for example, under pressure to become self-financing, charges fees that necessarily exclude the poorest students. Conventional secondary education is free. The second conflict is between equity and quality. The quality of open and distance learning depends partly on the quality of the teaching materials and the logistics but, in large part, on the quality of arrangements for student support, that part of the system where economies of scale are not possible. Another dimension of quality is relevance to individual learners and their environment, achieved through local support and adaptation to local circumstances and not through market maximisation. Institutions – especially when underfunded – have to strike a difficult balance between their concerns for economy and for quality. For their part students may well bring pressure to minimise fees, even against their long-term interest in quality education. Funding policy needs to reflect the purposes for which open and distance learning is being used but has not always done so.

Technology

The technological options share some characteristics with those for funding with trade-offs between numbers, costs and quality. The experience of open and distance learning suggests that teaching is more effective if a variety of educational media are combined; print and broadcasting, for example, are likely to be more effective than either by itself. For their part teachers and course designers often welcome the opportunity to teach in a variety of media, seizing the opportunity to use computer-based approaches, or television, or to set up video-links with their students. But each increase in sophistication is likely to come at an increased cost. Students may then be priced out of their education, or it may make unreasonable demands in terms of access to communication.

In some cases enrolment levels are such that the cost can be justified. Radio is used to reach schools in South Africa at a modest cost per student. Educational television programmes in China are part of the regular work of the radio and television universities and are reaching students in such large numbers that the cost per student is acceptable. Computer conferencing was used by the Open University in Britain to link scattered students on a teachers' certificate course with costs that were an acceptable proportion of the total, externally funded, expenditure. But these are almost the limiting cases; in many other cases print has been chosen as the dominant technological option not just because of its convenience but also because of its modest cost. The pursuit of educational variety, and possibly quality, is likely to conflict with the search for wide access and increased equity.

Quality

Two general policy issues face the decision maker in considering quality. First, do the structures for quality assurance, often developed for the conventional sector, fit the particular circumstances of the external student? Second, how do systems of quality assessment work across borders where the legislation, or arrangements for due process, that control the activities of a teaching institution do not apply? We come back to this issue below in looking at e-learning and examine it further in Chapter 10.

Arrangements for the assessment of quality and for accreditation are usually a function of organisational structure and of arrangements for collaboration between partners. They lie on a continuum from self-regulation to external control. At one extreme, an open university with the appropriate status may monitor its own quality and award its own degrees without further outside control beyond peer pressure or the deployment of external examiners. At the other extreme, some jurisdictions have formal systems to control the work of distance-teaching institutions backed by legal sanction. Somewhere between these extremes the work of institutions is constrained by the activities of funding agencies and apex institutions. In India, for example, the Indira Gandhi National Open University is both a teaching institution and an apex body, with funding, advisory and regulatory powers, in relation to other open universities and university correspondence departments. Measures of control in the interests of learners, professions and the effective use of public funds mean that no institution can be an island in the sea of quality.

There is a case for pressing the claims of learners here, against those of other stakeholders. Market forces will not work in the learner's interest: it is usually impossible to tell whether an advertised course comes from a bona fide institution or a bogus one. If the bogus institution is cheaper but more enticing a Gresham's law may operate with bad institutions driving out good. (Titmuss showed the weakness of the market in the social sector long ago in his classic demonstration of the superiority of free over paid donations of blood; more recent events have tragically demonstrated how right he was (Titmuss 1970).)

Questions of quality cannot be separated off from the other organisational issues. For open and distance learning to be effective, and to meet the purposes for which it is being designed, it needs an organisational structure that fits the realities of students' lives while respecting the interests and integrity of academic staff. Structures of collaboration need to work effectively and sensitively. Funding arrangements and the choice of technology need to be designed so that they fit both student and purpose.

CODA

In the early twenty-first century open and distance learning is, perhaps, being reborn as virtual learning. The process is acclaimed variously as the long-awaited educational revolution and dismissed as improbable hype, welcomed as a new way over educational barriers and denounced as a tragedy that follows the farce of the earlier 'distance education craze' (Noble 1999). As a coda we can look at the same issues about the purposes of open and distance learning as they are illuminated by the new technologies.

Two parallel studies commissioned by the Committee of Vice Chancellors and Principals (now renamed Universities UK) in Britain and the Department for Education Employment Training and Youth Affairs (DEETYA) in Australia have drawn a map of recent international developments. The British study distinguishes between two main sets of actors: traditional universities and new providers, many of them in or linked with the corporate sector. Their map is reproduced as Figure 2.1. At one pole they see conventional universities which are either continuing to operate inde-

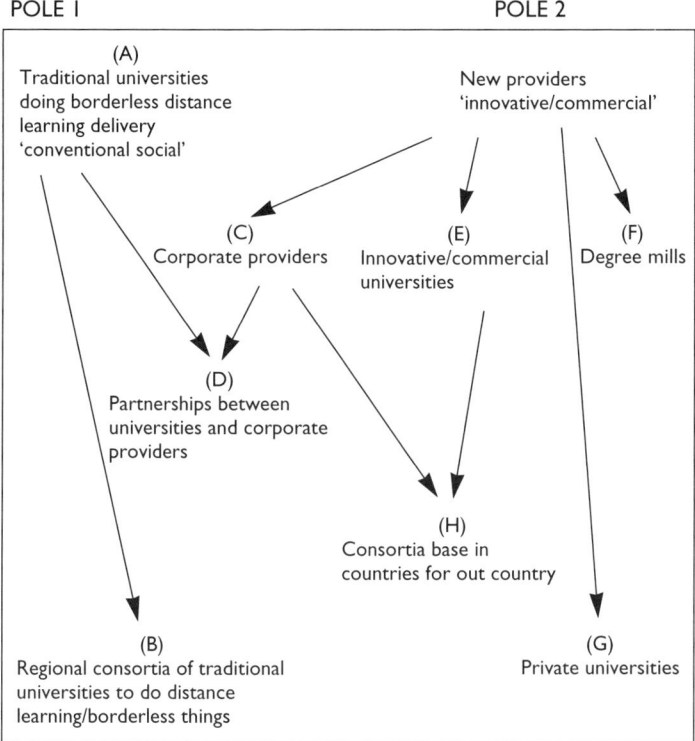

POLE 1   POLE 2

(A)
Traditional universities   New providers
doing borderless distance   'innovative/commercial'
learning delivery
'conventional social'

(C)   (E)   (F)
Corporate providers   Innovative/commercial   Degree mills
                       universities

(D)
Partnerships between
universities and corporate
providers

(H)
Consortia base in
countries for out country

(B)   (G)
Regional consortia of traditional   Private universities
universities to do distance
learning/borderless things

Figure 2.1 The providers of borderless education (CVCP 2000: 96)

pendently, or working within consortia (category B) or cooperating with the corporate sector (category D). At the other pole the non-traditional providers

> are characterised by highly innovative approaches, and a strong core reliance on communication and information technology for main-stream activity. Category E is based on innovative distance learning universities set up within state systems but with missions which are substantially different to traditional universities. . . . Another brand of non-traditional provision is that of the private university (category G); these are not part of state systems but nonetheless are subject to some of their regulatory requirements. The huge expansion of higher education in the last decade has spawned the growth of small-scale private providers with a narrow subject range, the so-called 'degree mills' (category F) especially in Central and Eastern Europe. Whilst catering for an undoubted market need, they are often perceived to be of dubious quality. This cannot be said of category C, which are large

corporate providers that have set up substantial educational divisions, primarily for the development of their own employees, but later diversifying provision for employees within their supply chains. . . . The alliances between these category C providers and traditional universities (category A) into partnerships (category D) constitute a potentially major organisational form of higher education in the 21st century.

(CVCP 2000: 95)

One significant difference between these and the earlier development of distance education is that many of the e-learning plans are deliberately international. Leaders among the corporate sector have, for example, been companies such as Ford and Microsoft with worldwide labour forces. In some cases they have had a dual interest: to meet their own training needs and, building on that foundation, to develop information technology software in the company's interest. For their part, while universities have edged into computer-based teaching for their on-campus students, publicity about the expansion of e-learning has been very much in terms of attracting international audiences. The University of Southern Queensland, for example, seeing itself as a 'regional university with an international mission', had 15,000 off-campus students in 1999 of whom nearly 3000 were studying abroad (CVCP 2000: 133).

Institutions of these kinds, in the university and corporate sectors, are not the only drivers. Several international agencies have also promoted this new kind of distance education. In its White Paper on education and training of 1995, for example, the European Commission argued that 'information technologies are making significant inroads into production-related activities and into education and training, thus bringing the "learning system" and "producing system" closer together'. In the south, the World Bank has made and supported an array of different activities about e-learning and promoted and funded the African Virtual University, using both video-conference and computer links between northern and southern universities.

Most of the debate – like this discussion so far – is about higher education, but e-learning is also beginning to be significant for schools. With support from both industry and a range of different agencies that include the World Bank and the Canada-based International Development Research Centre, schools have been experimenting with the use of computer links both for access to the web and for linking schools. At the same time, publishers and technology companies have begun to make teaching material available both on the web and through television for schools in Britain. Within the United States both computer companies and broadcasters have been at the fore of moves to provide software of various kinds to schools. (The market is significant: in the mid-1990s schools were spending more on technology than on books with annual expenditure rising from $4 billion to $7.8 billion per year (Schiller 1999: 181).) In contrast with higher education, and with the exception of school-to-school computer links, the promotion of e-learning at school level seems to have been dominated by the corporate rather than the public sector.

To put these developments in context, and to compare them with the earlier development of print-based open and distance learning, we can ask why the various drivers have been promoting e-learning and how significant their activities are.

The international agencies' interest has been mainly, though not entirely, economic. Thus the European Commission, in discussing how to build the learning society, sets out three reasons for its new approach: first, because 'giving priority to quality in education and training has become vital to the EU's competitiveness'; second, because of increasing demand for education and training; third, because 'social exclusion has reached such intolerable proportions that the rift between those who have knowledge and those who do not, has to be narrowed' (Commission of the European Communities 1995: 49). Elsewhere, much international concern has been about the significance of education for economic growth, and the potential of the technologies to support this. The World Bank's support for the African Virtual University springs from its concern with the weakness of sub-Saharan higher education as one of the props of economic development.

At the same time, multilateral and bilateral agencies have been concerned to explore ways of overcoming the digital divide, between the information-technology rich and poor, for reasons of equity. The British government's White Paper on *Eliminating world poverty* is concerned about the 'real risk that poor countries and poor people will be marginalised, that the existing educational divide will be compounded by a growing digital divide' (Secretary of State for International Development 2000: 40). Among the agencies, at least, the conventional reasons for promoting open and distance learning, of economics and equity, remain significant for e-learning.

Within the university sector, e-learning has been pushed by three groups. First, both open and dual-mode universities have seen e-learning as a new technology that may help them in their existing task of finding appropriate technologies for reaching off-campus learners. Second, and often in those same institutions, individuals have been keen to exploit a new way of teaching out of a personal interest in the technology. Third, universities have seen the new technologies as a way of expanding their recruitment at a time when they have felt the need to compete for students and for resources. In Australia, for example, federal funding for universities fell from 90 per cent of income in the early 1980s to below 54 per cent in 1997 with a consequent pressure to recruit international students and then to seek new ways of teaching them (CVCP 2000: 131). E-learning has been seen as a way of expanding student numbers while holding back costs.

As suggested above, the corporate sector has been motivated partly by its own training needs and partly by the desire of the communications industry to move further, and profitably, into education. Alongside the industry, the for-profit educational sector has also been making the running in e-learning. Its public acceptability marks a change. It would be surprising today to hear counsel for the American Federal Trade Commission's Bureau of Deceptive Practices arguing as he did to Jessica Mitford that 'There's a basic contradiction involved when you have profit-making organizations in the field of education. There's pressure to maximise the number of enrollments to make more profit' (Robert Hughes quoted in Mitford 1979: 169). Today, an institution such as Phoenix University, for example, is welcomed as existing legitimately alongside public and nonprofit institutions.

What is the new policy agenda and how is it different from the old? Managers of e-learning are still faced with allocation decisions about expenditure on different kinds of technology, and on the balance between central expenditure on materials development and decentralised expenditure on student support. We have few studies of the costs to guide them here. Estimates suggest that moving from print- to computer-based teaching will increase materials development costs while the cost of student support may rise even more dramatically. In an overview of the issues Rumble has suggested that the costs of online support are likely to dwarf other costs in applying computer-based technologies to education (Rumble 1999).

The new agenda redefines some of the issues about the allocation of functions between partners working in open and distance learning. In particular, the promise that information, even teaching materials, will be widely available on the internet prompts questions about who will do the teaching – for any learners other than committed autodictats who successfully decide they do not need it. Three other specific questions get a new prominence. The first is about the new kinds of partnership, whether involving the private or the public sector or a combination of the two, which are made possible or even necessitated by the new technologies. The possibility of reaching global audiences, coupled with the high costs of developing materials, means that e-learning is giving a new impetus to partnerships between previously independent stakeholders. Second, for very similar reasons, e-learning may fuel the moves to integrate conventional and open and distance learning. Computer-based learning of various kinds oncampus may at the same time meet the needs of off-campus students. Again, the cost of developing materials in computer format is likely to drive the process. Third, both because of the growth of private-sector involvement in e-learning and because it goes so easily across frontiers, issues of regulation and accreditation are firmly on the new agenda. Some private-sector companies exploring the option of setting up a corporate university have deliberately sought a partnership with a conventional university in order to gain recognition for the qualifications awarded.

The e-learning experience casts a narrow beam across this analysis of the purposes for which open and distance learning is being used. It illuminates the landscape of higher education more brightly than that of schools. Perhaps deceptively so: the heavy involvement of the private sector, coupled with the scale of the school market, suggests that e-learning may produce its pay-off through programs and links for schools. Then, too, e-learning is shining more brightly in some areas of adult education and training than in others. While much earlier distance education has concentrated on general educational needs at secondary and tertiary levels, e-learning has responded to a different demand: first for narrow and specific vocational courses, often in the computer technologies, and then for high-value courses such as MBAs. The process has been driven in part by the search for markets, as universities have become more competitive, in part by economic justifications for vocational education. The idea of widening educational participation in the interests of equity has played little part in the growth of e-learning.

CONCLUSION

There is, then, a continuity in the agenda from the old forms of open and distance learning to the new. The record of its use, in both forms, for a wide range of audiences and purposes makes it possible to draw some conclusions about the options it presents to the planner. This chapter has argued that the planner faces key choices in terms of organisation (see also Chapter 7), of funding (Chapter 6), of technology (Chapter 8) and of quality (Chapter 10), while these same issues are reshaped by the new technologies and by globalisation (Chapter 9). At the same time, the way the planner reacts to the issues is a response to the interests and commitments of students and staff (Chapters 3, 4 and 5).

REFERENCES

Arnove, R. F. (1976) *Educational television: a policy critique and guide for developing countries*, New York: Praeger.

Commission of the European Communities (1995) *Teaching and learning: towards a learning society (White Paper on education and training)*, Brussels.

Committee of Vice-Chancellors and Principals (CVCP) (2000) *The business of borderless education: UK perspectives* (Case studies and annexes), London: CVCP/HEFCE.

Creed, C. (2001) *The use of distance education for teachers*, Cambridge: International Research Foundation for Open Learning (Report to the Department for International Development).

Cullen, J., Kelleher, J. and Stern, G. (1992) *Delta pilots and development projects and their evaluations*, London: Tavistock Institute.

Daniel, J. S., Mugridge, I., Snowden, B. L. and Smith, W. A. S. (1986) 'Cooperation in distance education and open learning' (Paper presented to Commonwealth Secretariat Expert Group on Commonwealth Cooperation in Distance Education and Open Learning).

Domatob, J. K. (1998) *African higher education policy: a survey of subsaharan Africa*, San Francisco, CA: International Scholars Press.

Fraser, C. and Restrepo-Estrada, S. (1998) *Communication for development: human change for survival*, London: I.B. Tauris.

Gultig, G. and Butcher, N. (1996) *Teacher education offered at a distance in South Africa*, Braamfontein: South African Institute for Distance Education.

Hinchliffe, K. (1987) *Higher education in sub-saharan Africa*, London: Croom Helm.

International Centre for Distance Learning (ICDL) (1997) *Distance education database* (CD-Rom), Milton Keynes.

Kaye, A. (1976) 'The Ivory Coast educational television project', in Arnove 1976.

Lentell, H. (2001) 'Earning and learning: issues from Coca-Cola's frontline degree programme' (Paper presented at workshop *Raising the standards in work based learning*, 23 May).

Mills, R. (1999) 'Diversity, convergence and the evaluation of student support in higher education in the UK', in A. Tait and R. Mills (eds) *The convergence of distance and conventional education: patterns of flexibility for the individual learner*, London: Routledge.

Mitford, J. (1979) *Poison penmanship: the gentle art of muckraking*, New York: Knopf.

Moran, L. and Mugridge, I. (1993) *Collaboration in distance education*, London: Routledge.

Noble, D. (1999) *Digital diploma mills, part iv: rehearsal for the revolution*, Downsview: York University Division of Social Science (http:\\www.communication.ucsd.edu/dl).

Perraton, H. (1984) *Costs and effects of mass media for adult basic education: a study in comparative evaluation*, unpublished Ph.D. thesis, University of London.

Perraton, H. (2000) *Open and distance learning in the developing world*, London: Routledge.

Perraton, H. and Creed, C. (2000) *Applying new technologies and cost-effective delivery systems in basic education* (Thematic study for Education for All 2000 Assessment), Paris: UNESCO.

Perraton, H. and Hülsmann, T. (1998) *Planning and evaluating systems of open and distance learning*, Sheffield: Department for Education and Employment.

Perraton, H., Robinson, B. and Creed, C. (2001) *Teacher education through distance learning: technology, curriculum, evaluation, cost*, Paris: UNESCO.

Perraton, H., Creed, C. and Robinson, B. (2002) *Teacher education guidelines: using open and distance learning*, Paris: UNESCO.

Perraton, H., Robinson, B. and Creed, C. (forthcoming) *Case studies of teacher education through distance learning*, Paris: UNESCO.

Planning Commission (1992) *Eighth five-year plan*, New Delhi: Government of India.

Ruiz, M. M. (1992) 'Expanding distance learning through technology transfer to employers in Colombia', in G. Rumble and J. Oliveira (eds) *Vocational education at a distance*, London: Kogan Page.

Rumble, G. (1997) *The costs and economics of open and distance learning*, London: Kogan Page.

Rumble, G. (1999) 'The costs of networked learning: what have we learnt?' (Paper to Sheffield Hallam University FLISH Conference)
(http://www.shu.ac.uk/flish/rumblep.htm (accessed 23 March 2000)).

Schiller, D. (1999) *Digital capitalism: networking the global market system*, Cambridge, MA: MIT Press.

Secretary of State for International Development (2000) *Eliminating world poverty: making globalisation work for the poor (White Paper on international development)*, Norwich: HMSO (Cm 5006).

Selinger, M. (2001) 'Communication technology in schools', available at http://www.imfundo.org/papers/cit_in_s.doc (downloaded 9 May 2001).

Tavistock Institute of Human Relations (1987) *The Open Tech Programme development review: final report*, London.

Titmuss, R. M. (1970) *The gift relationship*, London: Routledge & Kegan Paul.

Venables, P. *et al.* (1969) *The Open University: Report of the planning committee to the Secretary of State for Education and Science*, London: HMSO.

Part II

Inputs

Education can – even should – be more than a factory-like activity with inputs, a process which uses or changes them, and outputs. But the analogy is a convenient one which leads us to begin an analysis of open and distance learning in terms of inputs of students, of staff and of resources. The planner's key decisions are about the deployment of these three types of input.

We begin with the students, looking at some general questions about them in Chapter 3, and then illustrating those questions by means of a case study in Asia in Chapter 4. Between them they analyse the evidence in relation to three themes: about knowing our audience, about the variety of audiences, and about support for them.

In order to design an effective educational programme, the planner needs to know about the potential audience; Chapter 3 illustrates some approaches to doing this. There are particular difficulties for new programmes of open and distance learning. As the method of teaching affects the recruitment of students, so we cannot simply extrapolate from conventional to distance education. Programmes that deliberately seek new audiences, in the interest of equity or of a new style of workforce education, cannot assume that the new audience, attracted by the convenience or even glamour of distance education or web-based learning, is similar to the old. It will sometimes be possible to extrapolate from existing distance-education audiences to new ones; students in one academic area may be similar to those in another. But often, as planners develop new types of work, they will need to undertake small-scale pilot projects or carry out action research in order to learn more about a potential audience.

Chapters 3 and 4 both stress that there is unlikely to be a single audience for open and distance learning. Its methodology is likely to attract an audience that is more heterogeneous than those attending a conventional class, either at school or college level. World experience reinforces this expectation, and Chapter 3 illustrates some of the varied audiences served by open and distance learning and the different demands they will make on planners. Recent developments have probably been making audiences more heterogeneous. The 1980s and early 1990s were dominated by the growth of open universities, successfully seeking students in large numbers, with many following the most popular courses. Similarly, large teacher-education projects offered the same curriculum, from a single institution, to students in their thousands. More recently, a larger number of institutions around the world at a variety of levels have been developing more specialist programmes, aimed at students in their scores or hundreds rather than thousands. This process has been particularly marked in higher education. British universities have, for example, offered programmes in financial management and in Japanese studies at master's level. Specialist courses, from niche providers, make it dangerous to base planning on the assumptions or achievements of the larger open universities. And, of course, it would be wrong for the planner to assume that an adult working on a secondary-level course needed an identical approach to that used at tertiary level.

The planner needs to go beyond knowing who the students are and how to recruit them. Good planning demands a sensitivity to the way students learn, examined in Chapter 4, and to draft and implement plans that fit students' educational background and culture. In teacher education, for example, recent literature in the north is insistent on developing trainee teachers' capacity to be reflective practitioners, able to reflect on and strengthen their own professional practice. But it is an open debate as to how far this is realistic for teachers who have themselves a very limited educational background. A sensitivity to the needs of learners will also affect the deployment of teaching media and technologies, the theme of Chapter 8.

There is an extensive literature on the development of student support services. Three general points are important for the planner. First, the nature and extent of student services need to be based on an understanding of students, their circumstances and their needs: institutions need to undertake the type of analysis illustrated in Chapters 3 and 4. Second, despite distance educators' and distance-teaching institutions' search for parity of esteem, the students attracted to open and distance learning are often from modest educational backgrounds with a limited record of success: the most successful students still tend to go to the more privileged conventional institutions. In consequence there is a particular onus of responsibility on distance educators to plan effective systems of student support based on an understanding of their needs. Third, individual student support is relatively costly and will not show the economies of scale that are possible for the large-scale development or distribution of learning materials. (We come back to this point in looking at resources in Chapter 6.) Again, the planner will be able to discharge responsibility for effective student support only when plans are based on a good understanding of students' own circumstances.

Chapter 3

Students in open and distance learning

Janet Jenkins

This chapter aims to guide the policy maker in considering the suitability of open and distance learning for a particular audience and educational need. Distance education stands or falls according to the learning that results. This in turn depends on the participation of learners. With a very few exceptions, distance education is used for teaching and learning in post-compulsory or non-formal settings. Most distance learners participate on a voluntary basis, many turn to distance education as a more convenient alternative to traditional learning methods, and completion is not compulsory. Relations between learners and providers in distance education are thus quite different from those between pupils and teachers in schools.

WHY DO YOU NEED TO KNOW ABOUT STUDENTS?

These differences mean that, in planning distance education, basic research is essential to determine whether there are potential learners – people as opposed to statistics – and to explore their nature, characteristics and circumstances. Such investigation can make a significant difference to success, if taken into account in planning. Knowledge about the distribution of potential students provides a good example. In Guyana an inservice training programme for teachers used information from school mapping to design a delivery system that uses different arrangements for face-to-face tutorials in order to accommodate differences in terrain and population distribution. In densely populated coastal areas trainees meet every two weeks, but in remote inland areas they attend a week's residential course at the beginning, and then gather in school-cluster study groups from time to time. Some 65 per cent successfully complete the programme. This compares with 32 per cent success in an inservice training programme for government employees in another developing country. Here, the same tutorial arrangements were used in every region, regardless of distribution of learners; some had to travel two days on horseback to a tutorial, and understandably attrition was high (Thomas 2000: 24–31).

Another aspect to investigate is learning need. Learners, particularly adults, tend to learn with a purpose. Often the curricula of formal education need to be adapted to meet the need of distance learners. Educational background and personal circumstance may influence choice of content. Recent experience suggests that it can be beneficial to involve potential learners in the design of learning. Motivation and retention are guiding factors.

The number of learners is critical to cost-effectiveness, but not easy to determine in advance. Once the total potential market for learning is estimated, it is then necessary to consider what proportion will take up the opportunity for distance learning. In some cases a distance-education route, such as a university degree programme, competes with other traditional opportunities. In others, such as some inservice teacher education schemes, it is the only opportunity available, but not every potential learner will want to take up the opportunity. Some, for example, may be approaching retirement age. Some courses may be sponsored or heavily subsidised; others may entail fees too high for many of the intended market to bear, resulting in disappointing uptake.

It is thus necessary to go beyond quantitative data to look more closely at students, their learning needs, their characteristics, circumstances and environment. Such investigation properly forms part of planning distance education, and applies both at the macro level of policy makers and at the level of the individual course or programme. It can usefully be seen as one element of a systems approach (Jenkins 1981: 36).

WHAT KINDS OF STUDENTS ON WHAT KINDS OF COURSES ARE USING OPEN AND DISTANCE LEARNING?

There are no obvious limits to kinds of students and courses. The examples of distance learners that follow give an indication of the variety on both counts, at the same time illustrating the main themes that will be developed in this chapter.

A mature postgraduate student

Frances is an African woman in a senior managerial position. She is already well educated, with a PhD, but sees it as important to continue her own self-development and also to develop her competence as a manager. She felt she would benefit from a better understanding of economics and enrolled for a postgraduate diploma as an external student of London University.

It has taken her two years to complete all the courses, although she has not yet taken all the examinations. She worked on the material –

printed course units with accompanying textbooks – in her spare time, at home. She found some aspects of the course more difficult than she expected, and that the assignment work always took more time than predicted. She intends to complete the diploma but may not proceed to the master's level, as she feels that she has already gained her objective.

Frances lives alone as her family is already grown up. While she has plenty of time to study, she found the distance study altogether more demanding than she expected. In her case, based in Africa, she was unable to benefit from face-to-face tutorials or meetings with other students. Her contact with her tutor is through traditional correspondence.

A young Indian woman completes school

'Nineteen year old Lakshmi is physically handicapped and moves with the help of crutches. She enrolled for the Class 10 Secondary course offered by the National Open School [in India] after completing her eighth standard [in a special school]. Simultaneously, she was trained to become a watch mechanic in a vocational training unit.

Today Lakshmi has not only completed her 12th grade/Senior Secondary from National Open School but is also employed as a mechanic at a watch servicing and repair centre in Delhi. Full of enthusiasm and courageous, she travels daily to work, a distance of about 20km on her motorised bicycle.

Her dear mother and loving brother have been a source of inspiration. Her firm determination has also helped her come a long way and become completely independent. Lakshmi does not plan to continue with her education but has certainly been able to make her life meaningful.'

(National Open School 1997: 8)

University study

Abdul is 19. He stays with his uncle in the capital of an Asian country. His parents sent him from his small home town up-country when he finished high school. They wanted him to attend the state university, but his marks were not good enough to get a place. He is doing open-university courses instead, and has finished the first two semesters. His uncle pays – his parents don't have that kind of money. He tries to study full-time, but he has to work a bit too, sometimes helping his older cousin with his business, sometimes working as a driver for his uncle's company. He is studying business subjects – economics, accounting, management, computer. He says the courses are OK. He likes the computing best. He does not have a computer, nor do any of his friends; much too expensive. But he goes to the internet café. He goes to his study centre quite often – at least he goes when there is a test due, but not much otherwise.

A new career for Sara

Sara lives in a village in Essex, England. It is a quiet place, off the main road and quite a journey from the nearest town. She is married with three children. After the first baby arrived, she stayed at home to look after the children and the house. Before that she had worked in house-keeping and catering, which she had studied at basic level at college after leaving school. She finished the college course when she was 18. When the youngest child was 18 months old, in 1998, Sara started to help at the village playgroup for pre-school children. She realised that she wanted to continue working with children, and she felt it was time to think about returning to work on a permanent basis. If she was going to make this her new career, she needed qualifications.

This was something of a problem. The other workers in the play-group had got qualified by day release. This meant taking a whole day off work each week to travel to college in town and attend classes. For Sara that would be awkward, because she would have to find someone to look after the baby all day and the older children after school. Her husband could not help as he worked long hours. Distance learning seemed an interesting possibility so when she saw an advertisement in a magazine for a course leading to the diploma in pre-school practice she sent off for details.

Her colleagues at the playgroup thought it was a strange way to get qualified, but they encouraged her, and were ready to discuss the course. She got a lot of encouragement from her tutor and enjoyed receiving feedback and marks on her correspondence assignments. She particularly liked doing the observation activities that formed part of the course, as she could follow through practically with the play-group. She completed the course without any major problems.

With her qualification, Sara soon found a part-time job at a nursery for young children. She feels too that the period of study has given her more than a job. Her horizons have broadened, she has more to think about and is more outgoing.

As well as illustrating the great variety to be found among distance students, these four examples between them show a number of common characteristics.

First, while there is a range of ages represented, it is usual for distance learners to be on average a little older than their peers taking similar courses in regular institutions. The exception is the young university student. The age of learners is relevant to those who plan learner support. In some countries, in particular the large population countries of Asia, open universities have become a means of providing greater access to higher education for school leavers. But youngsters lack the maturity of older learners and, in order to benefit fully from the opportunity, may need a more supportive learning environment than that offered by open universities. The youth of students could be one factor in the disappointing performance of some open universities. Open schools and some other school-level schemes aimed at young candidates such as Lakshmi provide support for their younger students through optional class tutorials in learning centres.

Second, distance education is sometimes assumed to be a good way of involving more women in learning. While it is no accident that three of the four examples are women, there is no evidence that distance education is naturally attractive to women. And, while women participate in as wide a range of learning as men, the proportion choosing traditionally 'male' subject areas can be low (Carter and Kirkup 1991). If distance education is intended as a means to improve opportunities for women, special measures may be necessary to encourage participation.

One factor influencing female participation may be the educational background of learners. Sara, for example, had left school and college with only basic educational qualifications. Initially nervous, she quickly gained confidence as 'the course material looked interesting, drew her in, and made it easy to get started'. Imagine a Sara in Bangladesh or Sudan taking the same course. Although they would have studied English at school, they would no longer remember enough to cope with the course. They might do well if they also did a preparatory language revision course, but they probably finished school at age 13 or 14, so their basic education might be too weak. People – men as well as women – may be similar from country to country, but differences in their educational background affect their chances of success with distance learning.

Such difference may also affect whether or not, as adults, they take part in learning. In England, a recent study of adult participation in learning reported that 61 per cent of those who continued in formal education to age 21 engaged later in more learning, compared with 28 per cent of those who completed full-time education at 16: 'the age at which people finish their formal initial education does appear to be very influential on their learning patterns in later life' (Hillage *et al.* 2000: xii and 55).

The above case studies also illustrate how distance learning opens doors to those who are disadvantaged in the face of traditional education. Sara, for example, has family responsibilities, lives in a rural area with no local access to learning opportunities, and has no significant independent income. Lakshmi, with her physical disability, is perhaps a recognisably typical candidate for distance education. Policy makers are right in assuming that distance education is a valuable tool for providing learning to those who are otherwise excluded. But equally it is a tool for providing a wider range of opportunity to all – inclusive in the broadest sense.

The notion that distance education is the best option for the disadvantaged can be misleading. Poor people do not own computers, sick people cannot travel, working mothers lack spare time – there are numerous ways in which economic, social or personal disadvantage can present barriers to participation even in distance learning. Such barriers may be overcome but often entail special measures on the part of the distance-education provider. The flexibility of distance education is an important factor in addressing disadvantage. For example, a variation in arrangements in a distance inservice programme for high school teachers in Papua New Guinea made it possible for women who were single heads of households to participate. Six one-week residential sessions replaced a single six-week session. Women who could not have left their families for the longer periods necessary could now attend (Simpson 1990).

The traditional view is that distance education attracts those, like Sara, who do not have a local opportunity to learn. But in practice the distribution of distance learners tends to reflect that of the population in general, with the majority in urban areas. The location of learners is all the same an important factor, since much distance learning involves some face-to-face or residential sessions, as in the case of the Papuan teachers. Such components are costly, with some costs falling on the provider, some on the learners. One of the biggest challenges in distance education is to organise face-to-face sessions in a way that gives value for money.

The Papuan teachers are typical of distance learners in that they have both family and work responsibilities alongside their learning. This pattern of multiple roles is perhaps the major distinctive feature of distance learners, at least in higher education. Distance learning is often more convenient for working people, because of the flexibility it offers. The experience of institutions in many parts of the world confirms that, often, up to 90 per cent of distance students are in full-time employment and up to 75 per cent married. The numbers not only highlight differences between distance students and their counterparts on campus but also help to explain the appeal of distance education's flexibility and convenience for adult students of these kinds. The removal of many of the constraints of place and timing brings considerable advantages to adult learners as they try to balance their multiple roles and responsibilities.

To sum up: typical students may be young or old, but are generally older and more mature than their peers in regular learning; almost all older students are employed, and most are married or have family responsibilities; they may be of either gender, but women may not participate in sufficient numbers unless they are specifically targeted; educational backgrounds will vary, and extra help may be necessary for those with weaknesses in prior attainment; they may include people in disadvantaged categories or people from a variety of environments, and study arrangements need to support their inclusion.

There is little to differentiate such people from other mature learners. The difference may be sharper when we look at personal characteristics. Recent research – so far inconclusive – has attempted to discover how far personality type and preferred learning style affect attitudes to and success in distance education. Perhaps the most important personal characteristic is motivation.

STUDENTS AND MARKETS: A DEVELOPED ENVIRONMENT

In order better to grasp the potential range of students and courses, this section looks more closely at Britain, a country where distance education is highly developed. British universities today realise the value of distance education as a tool for retaining and expanding markets and reaching new ones. As recently as the 1980s, it was very different. Other universities saw distance education as the business of the Open University, but by 1994 over 50 per cent of around a hundred UK universities offered at least one programme by distance learning (Jenkins 1994a). Today, few do not have any distance education.

The Open University is still the largest provider of distance education, and by far the largest university in Britain. Today it has over 200,000 people studying its courses. Of these, 125,000 are working towards a BA or BSc degree, and 40,000 are studying for postgraduate degrees. While students outside Britain – notably in Europe – may enrol, the majority of students are in Britain. Nearly 80 per cent are in paid employment, the largest proportion is aged between 25 and 45, and over 6000 have some kind of disability. Undergraduate courses are open to all, regardless of educational background, and, over the university's lifetime, about one-third of those who have graduated had started without the normal minimum entry requirements for traditional university (Open University 2001).

The distance students of traditional universities are drawn from a different pool. Most study at postgraduate level. The main exception is the London University external programme, which attracts those who are looking for an opportunity for a specialist degree or a single honours programme. While the external programme enrols many from overseas, a significant number of students are based in Britain. The external programme also offers a number of postgraduate programmes, such as the economics programme chosen by Frances.

The overall total of distance students from other British universities is not available, but is unlikely to equal that of the Open University. Students differ in that most are looking for continuing professional development rather than a second chance for a first degree. The 1994 analysis found that most students were employed, most in mid-career, and gender balance tended to reflect the gender balance of those employed in the profession concerned (e.g. more men on management courses). The variety of provision was wide:

> Many programmes are small, with annual intakes that sometimes barely touch double figures. But 10 students annually, though small for distance education, could be a normal departmental intake for a face-to-face course, and could be a satisfactory justification for distance education for a highly specialist course where demand is limited and course candidates widely dispersed. A small intake also means small, manageable, interactive tutor groups. . . .
>
> Those who have recruited in greater numbers include Durham University. It has just over 600 students on its distance DBA/MBA. This is by far the single largest degree course offered by the university, and it would be impossible for them to envisage so many students registering even on a part-time basis if regular attendance were required.
>
> Some programmes, particularly the bigger ones, have a substantial proportion of overseas students. Heriot Watt University offers an MBA programme that has about 2,000 registered students, of whom only 20 per cent are in the UK. It has recently conducted a student evaluation of the course, which reveals a high level of satisfaction amongst this mixed group of home and overseas students. The feature of the course that is most highly valued is its flexibility.
>
> (Jenkins 1994a: 16)

These examples illustrate the increased use of distance education in the British university sector. Universities have continued to expand their range of distance education, in part stimulated by the possibilities of online learning that have emerged since the OECD study. Distance learning is also used extensively in Britain for non-university learning – for general education, vocational and technical training, and in a number of professions – through a range of specialist organisations, colleges, professional institutes and corporate bodies, some long established. The range of learning material associated with these bodies is huge: a recent report suggested, 'There are probably 20,000–25,000 commercially available packages of which 5,000 are computer-based' (Hillage *et al*. 2000: 81).

Britain is not alone in wide-ranging use of distance education:

> The increased use of distance education is common to all [OECD] countries, but the form it takes differs from one to another. Differences

derive partly from national needs and the socio-economic environment, from the extent of government involvement, national structures for education and training, the communications infrastructure, and resource availability. They also derive from history, culture, personal preferences and academic and intellectual traditions. The result is a range of what are, to some extent, indigenous models of distance education. . . . For example:

- In New Zealand a long tradition of government planning in education, including the provision of distance education at all levels and for all subjects, has led to a relatively smooth transition to mixed mode integrated post secondary education and training
- In Denmark the heritage of a strong tradition of adult education, the Folk High School movement, has meant on the one hand the late development of national distance education strategy and on the other the evolution of a form of distance education which builds on the tradition of the learning group
- In Japan broadcasting was dominant in early distance education activities and remains so, in the new University of the Air. Similarly, television is widely used in the USA. Audio conferencing is widely used in Canada and New Zealand, and little used in other OECD member countries.

(Jenkins 1994b: 26)

Such developments suggest that distance education is reaching new markets. However, there is as yet no evidence that the students who take up the new opportunities have different characteristics from those attending traditional classes.

Undoubtedly the most significant recent development is online teaching and learning. It is certainly driving the expanded use of distance education, and possibly reducing dependence on print and traditional media and means of communication. In Britain it has led to two new developments at national level: the e-university and Learndirect. The e-university was announced in early 2000 and is being established as a consortium of universities to offer the best of British online university distance learning worldwide. Learndirect (formerly the University for Industry) is a government-backed initiative to provide easy access to lifelong learning for all, with online learning a principal means of delivery.

Online learning offers learners both pluses and minuses. On the positive side is potential for a better learning environment, with benefits such as enhanced interaction between teachers and learners and among learners, and access to more information and resources. But there are many problems. As teachers and educators, we are still feeling our way. We are still exploring how best to use new technology applications in our materials, how to improve our teaching and learning systems, and identifying the new skills our teachers and tutors need to acquire. For the present, there is a risk that some online courses will not pass the quality muster.

Then, we know little about the impact on learning and learners over the longer term of substituting computer communications for face-to-face interaction. It would be dangerous to assume that enhanced quality of learning material does away with the need for tutors. A recent survey of people who had tried e-learning in England found that 96 per cent felt a clear need for learning support; while most liked the method, those who had less prior education were not as positive (Campaign for Learning 2000). It seems also that would-be learners need special preparation for online learning. A recent study in the USA has identified twenty-four benchmarks for success in internet-based distance education (Phipps and Merisotis 2000). Student readiness figures strongly:

> Before starting an online program, students are advised about the program to determine if (1) they possess the self-motivation and commitment to learn at a distance and (2) if they have access to the minimal technology required by the course design.
>
> (ibid.: 3)

Further benchmarks elaborate on the need for orientation and training in the methodology of online teaching and learning of both learners and faculty.

But the most critical issue is computer access. While access to the internet is increasing rapidly, in Britain today still under half the population – 49 per cent – has access. But access is concentrated heavily among younger better-off people in richer parts of the country; only 21 per cent of the poor or unemployed have access (*Guardian*/ICM poll, 24 January 2001). We can reasonably conclude that if international distance education is to be of value, not only should content be relevant but also teaching and learning support processes need to be fitted to the needs of learners in each different environment. In the foot and mouth epidemic of 2001, many farm children in infected areas were confined to home. Their teachers sent them their lessons by mail, not over the internet (*Guardian*, 25 March 2001).

The emphasis on preparing participants for distance learning and on providing adequate support has important implications for costs. Distance education attracts providers and users alike because of its apparent value for money. But it also requires considerable investment if it is to operate to acceptable standards, and the level of investment is likely to be very high if computer-based technologies are used. The 79 per cent of poor and unemployed people in the UK who do not have access to the internet are unlikely to be able to afford their own computers and the extra telecommunications charges for connectivity. Should distance-education providers offer courses with alternative technology options, even if it costs providers more? Will poorer people be excluded from some distance-education opportunities? Will governments be prepared to invest in a technological infrastructure that supports free or low-cost public access?

These are difficult questions, particularly in an environment where all too little is known about the costs and effects of technology-based distance learning. A recent study of Canadian online distance education reported considerable potential pedagogic benefits for learners, but stressed the need for careful cost analysis. 'Cost structures are different from both face-to-face and print-based distance learning' (Bartolic and Bates 2000: 7). As in the US study, they stress the need for students to be 'psychologically ready and financially able' to take part in online learning. They further suggest that cost-saving through online learning is unlikely, but 'if the organization values collaborative learning, increased access for lifelong learners, and the internationalisation of the curriculum, then an online program may be of value'. But they also stress that not all courses and course material should be put online: 'young students without good independent study habits will find an online course particularly challenging' (ibid.: 16).

With the addition of online learning technology to the distance-learning toolbox, policy makers face difficult decisions. In richer countries, as in Britain, attention is now focused on e-learning and its potential. Poorer countries too would like to explore the benefits of new technology in their distance education. Online distance learning is of limited use when few potential learners have access to connected computers. But so far we know very little about student response to online learning and conditions in which it works well. We need to know more in order to justify heavy investment in online distance education.

LEARNERS AND LEARNING: A DEVELOPING ENVIRONMENT

But can the same distance education work for learners in different environments? In particular, are there differences between rich and poor countries? With increasing globalisation in all aspects of our lives, it is important to ask whether there are any longer significant differences between distance learners in rich and poor countries. (In this context Chapter 4 looks at experience in Asia.)

Distance learning continues to attract increasing interest in less developed countries. Much of the interest is technology-driven, the exciting potential of access to world class learning via the internet, coupled with the notion that new technologies can help to make good education more available widely within countries. However, as we have seen, even in rich countries access to online facilities is likely to be restricted to those who are already better off and probably better educated, while potential learners need help to prepare for online learning and demand support while they learn. Technology is not a cheap solution.

But it is not simply a matter of bridging the digital divide. A number of factors constrain participation and affect success in traditional distance education in the poorer parts of the world. Many of these stem from a basic difference in the purpose of distance education. In rich countries, which have a developed national education system, distance education tends to have three main purposes: to provide a second chance for adults, to cater for those who are excluded by circumstance from the formal system, and to provide opportunities for adults for lifelong learning, whether for economic or social objectives. These purposes also apply in developing countries, but there is usually a more important primary purpose: to provide a fuller range of educational opportunity for all.

To take India as an example, where the expansion of primary and secondary education still leaves large numbers of children outside but creates an unsatisfied demand higher up the system, it is hardly surprising that distance education is enshrined in national education policy as a means to enhance participation. It has a national open university, the Indira Gandhi National Open University, which enrols 300,000 students a year, a National Open School with more than 200,000 learners, as well as an array of state open universities and open schools, correspondence departments at universities, and private and specialist distance-education institutes.

Distance education is used in India on a massive scale, as in other developing and emerging economies with large populations. Daniel has identified eleven 'mega-universities' with over 100,000 students. All used distance learning and, not surprisingly, seven were in developing or emerging economies, six in Asia and one in Africa (Daniel 1996). Such huge institutions are difficult to manage and quality is easily compromised. Student support is particularly vulnerable.

In smaller developing countries it is equally important though used on a different scale. In Mauritius, for example, distance education is a means of training teachers in the face of limited capacity at the national Institute of Education, the multi-country University of the West Indies uses distance learning as a means to provide learning to students from island countries too small to support their own campus, and in Botswana the government has recently established the Botswana College of Distance and Open Learning (BOCODOL) with the provision of secondary-level qualifications as one of its major objectives.

Botswana has a relatively well-developed education system, with ten years of education now available for all young people. But many do not complete the whole cycle, whether through drop-out or failure. Then there is a serious shortage of school places at senior secondary level; government plans envisage 50 per cent progression from junior to senior secondary levels by 2003. Such factors informed the decision to create the new college (Government of Botswana 1993).

In all these settings, learners tend to be those who fail to obtain places in formal schools and universities. Distance learning is their only option, not a deliberate choice. While there will undoubtedly be many highly intelligent and excellent students among them, the less academically successful get distance education, the cream get the traditional institutions. Accordingly, many will need a high level of learning support, but this may be very difficult to provide if, as often happens, there is a shortage of qualified tutors.

Further, in these countries where education systems are less developed, distance education must be ready to cater for a large proportion of learners with a low level of basic education: the Indian girl Lakshmi had ten years of schooling; some of the Botswana students drop out even before that. Without appropriate measures, limited educational background can in turn limit success in distance education. In the GUIDE programme mentioned above, for example, special introductory courses in English language and mathematics were added to address learners' difficulties in these subjects (Thomas 2000: 27).

Age is another factor. Abdul and Lakshmi are both very young. Graduation rates at Asian open universities tend to be low; where comparative figures are available they are often less than half the rate at conventional university (see also Chapter 11). Youth may be a factor: when students are young or their educational background is weak, good support makes a difference. Group learning and interaction with a teacher are often crucial.

Unfortunately, for many learners such support is out of reach. Like Frances and Sara, most do not have access to a local tutor or study group. Most, like Sara, Abdul and Lakshmi, do not own a computer. Many do not even have a telephone connection at home, many have no reliable electricity supply, and many live in places where postal communication is slow and unreliable. Shortage of human resources, poor communications and limited technology access conspire to make learning at a distance difficult.

Economic constraints compound the difficulty. Distance-education institutions usually require learners to pay part of the cost of learning, even when formal education is free. In terms of local salaries the fees can be quite considerable, and it is remarkable how much quite poor people will invest in learning. But learners expect value for money. Some early drop-out may be because the initial courses do not live up to expectations, or because people cannot afford to continue. Time itself is costly. Many students cannot find enough of it unless they take time off paid work. Few can afford unpaid leave, few employers will agree to paid leave. Then there are costs of study materials, of communications, of travel to tutorials, of nights spent away from home at tutorials or residential courses. The costs tend to lie heaviest on the more remote and isolated learners who are often the most disadvantaged.

IDENTIFYING THE MARKET AND ANALYSING NEEDS

Information about potential students is crucial in deciding whether or not distance education will work, and in what circumstances it is likely to work well. How then is the task of gathering such information best approached?

The first step is to review information available and as far as possible estimate the size and nature of the potential market. Educational statistics are a good source of information, as is labour-market information, which can help educators match the provision of education to potential employment possibilities. From such figures it is possible to estimate the total market for education or training in a particular category. The next step is to estimate how many are likely to take up distance education. To take the case of Botswana quoted above, 50 per cent of each cohort finishing junior secondary education will be denied a place in a senior secondary school, making it easy to calculate a total potential market. But of these some will enter vocational training, some will seek work, and so on. The actual market for distance learning will be only a proportion of the total.

The case of unqualified primary schoolteachers in Uzbekistan demonstrates the difficulty of making accurate predictions. The government has announced recently that teachers should become qualified at bachelor's level if they wish to continue in the profession. Some 60,000 teachers – around one in seven – fall into this category, many in remote rural schools. The government proposes to provide upgrading through distance education, but of these 60,000 teachers around 10,000 are known to be already studying for a university degree by correspondence. Some others are already approaching retirement age, yet others may not wish to continue as teachers. While figures are available giving the number of unqualified teachers in each province, they do not provide sufficient information to predict how many are likely to take up the opportunity. Further, degree programmes have to offer specialist subject options, and data by province are lacking on teacher preferences and prior qualifications. In some subjects, there may be little demand for training. The necessary detail has to be gathered as part of a school mapping exercise prior to detailed planning of the programme.

In the university sector, distance education can stimulate a shift from supply-driven to demand-led provision. In central and eastern Europe distance education has been welcomed as a means to assist the transition

to a market economy, with forty distance-education centres being established with European Community help in eleven countries in the early
1990s. In small countries, a single national university cannot easily provide
the range of subjects and sufficient places to cater for growing demand. In
Namibia, distance education is seen as playing a crucial role:

> Distance and open learning can in the very near future offer the majority
> of Namibian adults the most economic, effective and available
> opportunities to seek tertiary level qualifications. Limited financial
> resources, family and professional responsibilities, and geography
> make other alternatives unaffordable or inaccessible.
>
> (Republic of Namibia, Ministry of Higher Education 1998: 68)

But in-depth information about demand is necessary to determine
learners' interests and priorities. In Mauritius, for example, detailed studies
to prepare for distance education were undertaken in the early 1990s. The
master plan for education set out a clear policy for distance education,
which would be used to improve the quality and range of education and
training nationally and to provide access to education for new groups. As
a starting point for implementing this strategy, educational statistics were
carefully examined. In addition, a detailed survey of demand took place.
Information supplied by the Mauritius Examinations Syndicate showed
that about 2500 people sat the examinations of foreign universities and
professional bodies annually, suggesting a total enrolment of several
thousand on foreign distance-education courses. A questionnaire survey
of a structured sample of employed people found that 70 per cent of respondents had engaged in some learning during their employment, indicating
a high level of commitment to learning, while over 90 per cent indicated
they would be interested in distance education. The most popular subject
would be management. A further interview survey, of housewives,
took place, which again revealed a high level of interest – 80 per cent – in
further learning. It also gave good information about the range of subjects
that would interest them. The data were used to complement Ministry of
Education statistics in developing national strategy in distance education
(Tertiary Education Commission 1994).

Further detail about students' circumstances is also needed for policy
decisions on the form and methods of distance education. For example,
the choice of media and technology depends on student access not only to
the technology itself but also to the necessary services. Does the student
have electricity at home? Or a telephone connection? Such data may be
gathered through developing profiles of typical students. The University
of Botswana developed a detailed profile of unqualified primary teachers
when planning its inservice training course. It covered personal data,
educational background, work patterns, economic circumstances, attitudes

and aspirations, study habits and environmental factors, yielding a summary of twenty-two characteristics which could be used as a basis for a wide range of management and educational decisions. The part of the profile on housing was as follows:

> A number live in single dwelling units – mainly hired, especially in rural settings:
>
> • Most with no electricity or fluorescent lighting facilities
> • No running water within the dwelling unit
> • Some areas in the western part of the country have desert conditions
> • Pit latrine is mostly used
> • Water is in the yard or at a stand-pipe nearby
>
> Some in rural and urban areas live in multi-dwelling units with electricity and/or running water – some privacy is possible
>
> • Density of occupancy depends – in some cases possibly more than one person
>
> Some have access to radio/radio-cassette player and television.
>
> (Kamau 1997)

Such data may come as a shock to educational planners in an external agency or even a capital city. It sets clear limits to media and technology options.

The next step is to interpret and use information to design a programme that meets student needs. Delivery of a course on a trial basis may be used as a tool for analysis of data.

Another method of interpreting students' needs is through a participatory approach to programme design. The School-based Teacher Development Programme in Kenya, an inservice training programme for primary teachers, took this approach, involving all stakeholders, including the teacher-beneficiaries, in consultations throughout the planning and development of the distance programme (Pontefract *et al.* 2000). Such an approach can help avoid misunderstandings in interpreting data about students as well as generating a sense of ownership among all parties from the outset.

Distance-education programmes that meet known demand and are honed carefully to match need have a better chance of resulting in high participation, learner satisfaction and good learning outcomes over the long term. Market research and needs analysis are critical in a type of education in which most participate on a voluntary basis.

THE GLOBAL MARKET

One of the drivers for expanding distance education today is the potential for economy and efficiency through international delivery – the idea that one course fits most, if not all (see Chapter 7). But the above examples underline the specificity of different learners and environments. They suggest that it is not easy to use the same distance education in different countries. In what circumstances, then, is global distance education likely to meet learner expectations?

International distance education seems to work reasonably effectively at university level, in cases where students have the maturity to cope well in an international setting. Weakness of feedback and tutorial support can be a problem and generally it is not possible for isolated international students to participate in face-to-face events, although as e-mail becomes more widespread it may alleviate the situation for some.

At lower educational levels, distance education is likely to need adaptation. Often the delivery system needs as much attention as the content. The Ministry of Education in Mauritius, for example, set up a scheme in 1994 to provide courses in senior secondary subjects (A levels) to under-qualified teachers in secondary schools (Jenkins 1997, Thomas 2000). Course materials were purchased from a British institution and adapted slightly. Delivery arrangements were changed more radically. The Mauritian teachers were offered more support than British distance students, including regular face-to-face tutorials. In Mauritius:

> The style of learner-centred tutorial support was new. . . . Tutors responded well to the idea, valuing the amount of contact. They recognised that these arrangements gave the new system the edge over traditional correspondence education. But the arrangements were more of a challenge to the Ministry of Education who had to cover the cost. It was difficult for them to accept that without such services the distance education would not be of adequate quality.
>
> (Jenkins 1997)

Adaptation of the system was a crucial factor of success for the students. In another African country, where British courses were also used, neither courses nor delivery system were initially adapted to student needs. Although the students were employed in similar situations to their British peers, for whom the courses were designed, their personal backgrounds, experience and circumstances were very different. Their success in study was adversely affected by factors such as difficulty in relating the content to their environment, adapting to a learner-centred approach, keeping to a timetable in their very demanding work environment, or travelling long distances to tutorials. Singly, these factors might not have been significant;

cumulatively, they had a strong impact on completion and pass rates. Student profiling at the outset and appropriate adaptation of the delivery and support system, together with some localisation of the materials, could have avoided much disappointment and failure.

The internet has brought new possibilities for international teaching and learning. We know little as yet about how international classes work, but one case demonstrates the sensitivity to difference required of participants in multinational learning groups. A course was offered online simultaneously to students at a Canadian and a Mexican university. The course was the first to be developed in a postgraduate certificate in technology-based distributed learning. The students were treated as a single group.

> Students benefited from the highly diverse nature of fellow students due to the collaborative components of the course (international discussion groups and collaborative assignments). . . . Culture may also affect the success of online courses or programs. It was found, for example, that the Mexican students . . . were very outgoing in spite of their difficulty with the English language. Some of the Asian students, however, whose grasp of the English language was quite good, rarely participated in the online discussions and collaborative assignments. This warrants further research.
>
> (Bartolic and Bates 2000: 7, 14)

We may reasonably conclude that if international distance education is to be of value, not only should content be relevant but also teaching and learning support processes need to be fitted to the needs of learners in each different environment.

CONCLUSIONS: WHEN WILL IT WORK?

To end with a plea for research is appropriate. It is not possible to specify what form of distance education will work with what learners. In a situation where the audience for distance learning continues to expand and change, investigation of potential students and sensitivity to their situation is necessary in each different environment.

However, some generalisations are possible and useful:

- Media and technology that are accessible to learners should be chosen.
- The financial cost to learners should be affordable.
- Time requirements should be realistic.
- Study arrangements should take into account educational background; the less educated the learner, the more learner preparation and tutorial support is likely to be needed.

- Programme and course design should take into account educational culture.
- Learning support should be accessible to all on a regular basis.
- Learning systems should cater for different learning styles, taking into account cultural factors.
- Student motivation – influenced by students' values and aspirations – is an important factor in participation and completion.

Gathering sufficient information about students to inform policy decisions is vital. When the Open University was set up in the 1970s there was a lot of counting and classifying of students. The availability of these data was crucial for the development of the university. For example, it was not only possible to say how many students lacked minimum entry requirements for a traditional university, it was also possible to determine whether targets were met for attracting such students, to monitor their performance in comparison with others, and to analyse and use the data as a basis for action to adjust or improve the system.

Others have been less thorough. To some extent this is understandable. In the early years of a distance-learning enterprise, there are other priorities. At Indira Gandhi National Open University, for example, in the early 1990s the evaluation of an initiative to increase women's participation was hampered by lack of systematic data according to gender and course (Ladbury 1993). Similar situations are all too frequent. Without the benchmarks of baseline data, inappropriate decisions may be made; without comprehensive student records, little can be learned from the past. Quality is elusive.

In researching this chapter the absence of published reports analysing students and their needs is notable. It is somewhat ironic that distance education, the flagship education methodology of the information society, is bedevilled by poverty of information. But today, with an increasingly pervasive stakeholder culture and emphasis on learner-centred learning, the situation is perhaps changing. New questions are being asked and new research is under way so that the poverty of data on students reflected in this chapter may soon be a thing of the past.

REFERENCES

Anzalone, S. (ed.) (1995) *Multichannel Learning: Connecting All to Education*, Washington, DC: Education Development Center.

Bartolic, S. and Bates, T. (2000) *Investing in Online Learning: Potential Benefits and Limitations*, Vancouver: University of British Columbia.

Campaign for Learning (2000) *Attitudes to e-learning: A National Survey 2000*, London: Campaign for Learning/Southgate Publishers.

Carter, R. and Kirkup, G. (1991) 'Redressing the balance: women into science and engineering', *Open Learning* 6 (1): 56–8.

Daniel, J. S. (1996) *Mega-universities and Knowledge Media*, London: Kogan Page.

Government of Botswana (1993) *Report of the National Commission on Education 1993*, Gaborone.

Hillage, J., Uden, T., Aldridge, F. and Eccles, J. (2000) *Adult Learning in England: A Review*, Brighton: Institute for Employment Studies/Leicester: NIACE.

Jenkins, J. (1981) *Materials for Learning*, London: Routledge & Kegan Paul.

Jenkins, J. (1994a) *State of the Art Distance Learning in UK Universities*, Report prepared for OECD, October 1994, as part of a study of the Impact of Information and Communication Technologies on Post-secondary Education for International Conference on Learning Beyond Schooling – New Forms of Supply and Demand.

Jenkins, J. (1994b) *Technology-assisted Distance Learning in Post-secondary Education: State of the Art in OECD Countries*, Summary prepared for OECD, December 1994, International Conference on Learning Beyond Schooling – New Forms of Supply and Demand.

Jenkins, J. (1995a) 'Indian distance education for women in an international frame', in A. S. Kanwar and N. Jagannathan (eds) *Speaking for Ourselves: Women and Distance Education in India*, New Delhi: Manohar.

Jenkins, J. (1995b) *Producing Gender Sensitive Learning Materials: A Handbook for Educators*, Vancouver: Commonwealth of Learning.

Jenkins, J. (1997) 'A case of adoption: distance education at the Mauritius College of the Air', *Open Praxis* 1: 40–1.

Jenkins, J. and Sadiman, A. (2000) 'Open schooling at basic level', in C. Yates and J. Bradley (eds) *Basic Education at a Distance*, London: Routledge.

Kamau, J. W. (1997) 'Characteristics of distance learners', University of Botswana Centre for Continuing Education, reprinted on Southern Africa pages of World Bank Global Distance Educationet.

Ladbury, S. (1993) *Increasing the Participation of Women on IGNOU Study Programmes*, unpublished study.

Moon, B. (2000) 'Reconceptualising teacher education: open, flexible, and moving to embrace the digital age', *Open Praxis* 2: 4–7.

National Open School (1997–8) *Profile*, New Delhi.

Open University (2001) Website http:\\www.open.ac.uk.

Perraton, H. (2000) *Open and Distance Learning in the Developing World*, London: Routledge (Table 5.4, p. 101).

Phipps, R. and Merisotis, J. (2000) *Quality on the Line*, study prepared for the Institute of Higher Education Policy, April, Washington, DC: Blackboard Inc/National Education Association.

Pontefract, C., Kanja, C., Karukungu, J., Limozi, J. and Sankale, J. (2000) 'Towards a national model of in-service: improving teaching and learning through distance education', *Open Praxis* 2: 38–45.

Reddi, U. and Dighe, A. (2000) 'Literacy and adult education through distance and open learning', in C. Yates and J. Bradley (eds) *Basic Education at a Distance*, London: Routledge.

Republic of Namibia, Ministry of Higher Education (1998) White Paper on higher education.

Simpson, N. L (1990) 'Combining distance education with residential instruction to upgrade secondary teachers in Papua New Guinea', in M. Croft, I. Mugridge, J. S. Daniel and A. Herschfield (eds) *Distance Education Development and Access*, Caracas: ICDE.

Tertiary Education Commission (1994) *Distance Education in Mauritius: The Present and the Future*, Port Louis, Mauritius.

Thomas, D. (2000) 'Guyana In-service Distance Education (GUIDE): promise and performance', *Open Praxis* 2: 24–31.

Warr, D. (1992) *Distance Teaching in the Village*, Cambridge: International Extension College.

Chapter 4

Students in distance and open learning

The Asian experience

Szarina Abdullah

This chapter focuses on students in distance and open learning in Asia, the region reported to have the world's largest student enrolment in open and distance education. The topic has been given prominence as the theme 'The Asian distance learner' at the Asian Association of Open Universities twelfth annual conference hosted by the Open University of Hong Kong on 4–6 November 1998. Asian students so far have not included many of the special population: those who are physically disadvantaged/handicapped, minorities – aborigines, socially and legally disadvantaged – prisoners, housewives/homemakers and special children who are home-bound. Asian students mostly discussed are mainstream working adults who cannot leave their jobs to attend full-time on-campus education. They come from various backgrounds of work experience and socio-economic status. In spite of their differences, many studies on distance learners seem to indicate certain characteristics common among them. These traits include:

- the majority are in the age range of 20 to 30 years;
- male outnumber female students (except for Japan where the number of females is 60.5 per cent (Yoshimoto 1998: 443);
- most have a job in middle or lower management, technical or clerical level;
- most perceive distance learning as a way to improve their qualifications for promotion or better career prospects;
- most have little or no idea about distance learning;
- most have little self-confidence and low self-esteem;
- most have a poor academic background;
- most cannot get into the conventional education system;
- most are passive learners whose major concern is passing exams;
- most are inclined towards pragmatism, not interested in theories;
- most possess relevant experience;
- most are often pressured by time, finance, family and job commitment;
- teachers outnumber other professions among distance learners.

The above characteristics contribute to a phenomenon common among distance learners: high attrition and low graduation rate.

They are not, however, universal. In Singapore, for example, students entered three degree programmes jointly operated by the Singapore Institute of Management and the British Open University with two A-level qualifications (a requirement in Singapore higher education) and graduated in expected record time. Weekly tutorials/meetings with instructors were held throughout the period of their study. The programme may be seen as an innovative way of taking advantage of the well-designed learning packages and the learners' support to fulfil the need for higher qualifications among Singapore's citizens and, on a narrow definition, might not be classified as open or distance learning.

STUDENT NEEDS AND LEARNING STYLES

In an attempt to understand students' various needs, many studies have been conducted and reported, notably in the conference papers of the Asian Association of Open Universities (AAOU). They generally reflect a preference for face-to-face learning. Among studies done, those on Chinese students, in particular in Hong Kong, outnumber other nationalities. Biggs and Watkins (1996) said: 'Hong Kong students tend to have good receptive skills, listening and reading, but poor expressive skills, speaking and writing.' Hills' study (1998) of students in Hong Kong, Malaysia and Singapore found that most students did not choose distance learning as their preferred mode of study: 'they preferred full-time, class-based situations in which the teacher would cover the concept, direct them to specific sources and tell them what information to look for and be there to provide immediate feedback to questions.' Niu Jian *et al.*'s (1998) study of Chinese students at the China Radio and Television Universities found that 86 per cent of students felt they had 'bad self-study effect'. At Nanjing University, it was mentioned that 'meticulous arrangement of face-to-face tutorial is very popular among students' (Chunxin 1998). As such, the tutorials make up two-thirds of total credit hours for each course. Hong Kong students are also reported to rank as their preferred style of learning 'tutors lecture to the whole group' (Fung and Carr 1998), and among their reasons for attending tutorials, rank first and second 'receive guidance from tutors on assignments', and 'listen to the tutor explaining the course materials', while students in Malaysia are posing a great challenge to instructors, since most of them reportedly do not read or study the materials before attending the face-to-face seminar sessions (Abdullah 2000). They expected seminar sessions to be like lectures delivered in traditional classrooms. Such behaviour is in consonance with the findings from a national survey on the reading habits which were found to be lacking among university students (Abdullah *et al.* 1994).

Hormozi (1998) conducted a study among students at Payame Noor University, Iran, and found that successful students are those who possess a positive self-concept as compared to the unsuccessful students, who have a lower self-perception. The results of the study suggest that academics, counsellors and tutors can play a significant role in empowering, building self-confidence and boosting morale in distance learners. The study seems to indicate similar findings about students' achievement in relation to their self-concept to those found by previous authors about Iranian (Delavar 1994, Rohani 1980) and Pakistani students (Ismail 1992). In India, Kumar (1998) has conducted an investigation of open university distance learners' self-concepts, study habits and attitudes. Based on the findings, several recommendations have been put forward, suggesting that learners' needs are varied. Among them are the need to develop positive attitudes towards distance education and about themselves, and to be highly motivated in order to complete the study. The sentiment in India is also apparent that learners' varied needs have not been adequately met, as the paradigm among education administrators has not changed in accordance with the changing needs of students (Murugan and Savithri 1998).

Students in Malaysia have been the subjects of a recent qualitative study by Roy (2000) who found that successful students are those who strike a balance of three main elements, namely learning strategies, teaching strategies and learner's locus of control. She called this model of success a 'Transaction Model'. Roy's findings are similar to those observed by Ibrahim (Ibrahim and Silong 1998) whose students reportedly need support from staff, family members and instructors' feedback to get through. 'Getting in touch' with instructors and other students and knowing that somebody cares to see them progress motivates students to stay on. Even though they are separated by physical distance, they cannot be left alone; they want to be in touch with someone who understands their situation. The challenge for the planner is to build in arrangements for this kind of support.

SOCIAL PERCEPTIONS OF DISTANCE LEARNING

The tradition of getting an education by going to school and university still has a strong hold in Asian society. It is rare to see social recognition bestowed upon individuals who study on their own part-time. Only a few graduates from distance education speak proudly of themselves as being a 'distance learner'. This situation is contrary to what one experiences in the United States, Britain, Canada or Australia where students choose to learn at a distance and parents speak proudly of sons and daughters who are working and continue to learn part-time, under their own efforts. The Accreditation Board of Malaysia, which evaluates programmes of study at private universities and colleges in Malaysia, for example, does not recognise the fact that individuals can study on their own (without face-to-face classroom contact with instructors) and acquire 'quality' education. It also does not recognise 'open' entry into any programme that leads to a qualification. Certain professional bodies, including the Malaysian Engineering Council, the Legal Profession Qualifying Board and the Medical Council, have not recognised distance learning as a mode for professional qualifications (Moreira 1998).

Thus despite the many benefits and advantages of distance and open learning for the productivity and economic development of nations, the general perception about distance education in Asia has not been entirely positive. Boshier and Pratt (1997), in their study about open learning in Hong Kong, mentioned a stigma attached to open learning, seen as education for the second best (those who are not accepted into university in the first instance). Such negative perception is also felt in Malaysian and Thai society. Most school leavers whose grades are not good enough to get into university need to get a job and, having left education for a few years, find it difficult to tune themselves into learning again, especially when they have to depend more on learning materials than on teachers. This situation, and high attrition and failure rates, leads to a perception that distance education is of no or low quality. A testimony to this view is reflected in the fact that by the year 2000 Malaysia and Singapore still did not have an open university that implemented an open entry system: all distance-education programmes in Malaysia are operated within the context of the mainstream, on-campus programmes: dual-mode universities. Although the Open University of Malaysia, established in 2000, accepted its first batch of students in 2001, its policy on entry requirements still applies for candidates entering degree programmes. Likewise, Singapore Institute of Management which collaborates with the Open University of the UK in three degree programmes requires two A-level entry qualifications like any other conventional university. This practice is necessary in order for the graduates' qualifications to be recognised on a par with other graduates from conventional universities.

SUCCESS RATE

It is a commonly known fact that the success rate among students of distance education is lower than that of the conventional education system. Attrition rate is high and completion is poor by comparison with that of on-campus education. In Africa, 50 per cent often drop out early in the programme. At UNISA and TSA, 10 to 17 per cent of those in undergraduate programmes graduate over a period of nine years (Dodds *et al.* 1999: 103). In India, completion rate ranged between 22.5 and 34 per cent. At the Korea National Open University, the range was 14.5 to 34 per cent.

Thailand's open university reported a completion rate of 9.8 to 24.8 per cent, while the Open University of Indonesia had only 0.7 per cent completion rate (Hülsmann 1999: 79).

In Japan, the average graduation rate of correspondence courses at twelve private universities is 10.5 per cent (Yoshimoto 1998) and the graduation rate at the University of the Air ranged from 5.7 per cent in 1989 to 25.6 per cent in 1995. The more positive figures seem to be those of Korea's Air and Correspondence High School Education, where the graduation rate ranged from 46.3 to 58.1 per cent (KEDI 1993) between 1977 and 1993. In China, where the Nanjing TV University enrolled 490 students under open learning, almost 40 per cent of students majoring in financial accounting passed the exam, compared to almost 83 per cent majoring in English language (Chunxin 1998: 449). In order to improve the situation, the university has imposed some preferential entry requirements by 'selecting the best' from among the many applicants, and by providing tutorial hours amounting to two-thirds of total credit hours for each course.

IMPACT OF DISTANCE LEARNING

In the final analysis of the performance of any educational system we can look at graduates as the outcomes of the system and their contributions to society. If we can gather evidence to show that graduates of open and distance education contribute to the social, economic and political development of nation building, we should be able to convince sceptics of open and distance education. However, systematic research into this area is rare. Most studies on the effectiveness of distance education focus on technology in androgogy or on the management of distance-education systems. Very few studies touch on the effectiveness and impact of distance learners. The three volumes of the conference papers of the twelfth Asian Association of the Open University having the theme 'The Asian distance learner' have only one paper (out of sixty-two) that discusses careers of Japan's University of the Air's graduates (Yoshimoto 1998). Apart from this, the study of graduates' success after distance education is mostly done by the way, not in purpose-built design research into this area. Such studies are rare, such as Douglas (1996) and Yates (2000). While Douglas found that graduates of a master's programme on campus and by distance are comparable in getting promotion, and playing a leading role in their career, Yates reported employers' satisfaction with graduates from the mixed mode of teacher education. Evidence is scarce to show how well graduates of distance education in Asia perform when compared with their counterparts on campus.

Where resources are limited and allocation is based on performance, the poor impact of distance learners has to be addressed. More evidence needs to be collected to impress upon policy makers and administrators that investment in distance learners is justified by their performance. At present, although open universities are generally supported by government grants, the allocated sums are smaller in comparison with those allocated for conventional universities (Daniel 1996:31). With the exception of the United Kingdom, where the government has shown conscientious support for lifelong learning and has allocated £12 million (*Open House* 1999a) to universities that operate continuing education programmes for adults, we have yet to see governments in other parts of the world following this path. In Thailand, for example, the government covers 80 per cent of the cost of education at conventional universities, but only 4 per cent of the cost of the open university (Daniel 1996:190). In Iran, where Payame Noor University comprises 31.7 per cent of student enrolment in the country, the government provides less than 20 per cent of its budget (Alimohammadi and Zohoor 1998: 4). In Malaysia, educational loans are available only to full-time on-campus students; distance education is operated on a cost-recovering basis as an adjunct to full-time programmes. Students are charged fees to cover the cost of materials, tutorials and administrative services provided under each distance programme, while full-time students' fees at public universities are subsidised heavily by the government.

WHAT POLICIES ARE NEEDED?

Within the above scenario, the following recommendations are put forward to assist us to formulate relevant policies aimed at bringing distance and open learning to the forefront of national development.

- As most students in distance and open learning are working adults, they must be encouraged to participate in decision making that shapes their career and pursuit of knowledge. By their sheer number, they should be able to influence politicians, administrators of universities and the government as to the benefits of distance-education provision and lifelong learning. We should see students form associations and self-help groups such as those reported in SESAME of the UK Open University. Any national, regional and international body that promotes distance education should open its doors to student membership. In this regard, the Malaysian Association of Distance Education (MADE) which was established in May 2000 purposely provides a category of student membership. The association believes that students can form a strong voice and speak up for their rights and needs, while at the same time projecting a more positive image for distance learners as a whole.

- As already pointed out, most students have little or no idea about distance learning. It needs a change of mindset from on-campus learning to self-directed learning and that change is never simple. A well-planned and purposely designed programme to convince learners of their ability to become self-directed must be built in for all new students and potential students.
- Teachers and administrators of distance education also need to encourage positive thinking and to instil self-esteem among students from the start in order to prevent attrition and withdrawal from the programme. Even if we can convince policy makers to provide financial assistance to students, this may not be enough to keep them in the entire programme if the students' internal feelings are not nurtured. In the final analysis, the following principle still applies:

  'Students do not care how much you know,
  They only know how much you care',

  particularly among Asian students.
- Distance teaching institutions will benefit from a comprehensive study akin to tracer study, providing insights into success and failure factors of their students. Such studies will be useful in various ways. Success stories will become a model and inspire other students. They will also provide positive outcomes of the institution's performance and so help justify more financial investment from governments. At the same time a study of failure and attrition will enable us to find ways and means of better supporting and maintaining the learners. A good example is seen from the three-year research called the 'Student Retention Project' at the British Open University, which seeks to identify factors causing early withdrawals (*Open House* 1999b).
- The notion that the government can spend less on distance and open learning than on-campus conventional education needs to be revisited within the context of cost-effectiveness and performance measures of the distance-education system as a whole. Policy makers should not be carried away with spending less for more access without considering the results. The notion that students can be left alone (since most are working adults) to learn on their own, hence reducing expenditure on teaching staff, is misleading. As we have seen, there is evidence of attrition rates of about 50 per cent or more in the first year at open universities and among distance learners of dual-mode universities. In reality, the distance between learners and instruction calls for much more preparation and support on the part of administrators in order to keep the learners within the education system. In spite of the fact that there is abundant literature on student support (e.g. Tait and Mills 1996, Simpson 2000), there is equally abundant concern that distance-education administrators have not been able to meet the changing

needs of students (AAOU 1998). Such challenging tasks cannot be done cheaply. The outcome of the investment should be that, in the long run, we are able to reduce high attrition rates, produce graduates of high calibre and ultimately improve the prestige and image of distance and open learning.

REFERENCES

AAOU. See e.g. the proceedings of the Annual Conference of the Asian Association of Open Universities held in Hong Kong in 1993, Taipei 1995, Iran 1996, Kuala Lumpur 1997 and Hong Kong 1998.

Abdullah, S. (1998) 'Helping faculty to make the paradigm shift from on-campus teaching to distance education at the Institut Teknologi Mara, Malaysia', in C. Latchem and F. Lockwood (eds) *Staff Development in Open and Flexible Learning*, London: Routledge.

Abdullah, S. (2000) 'Changing the Way We Learn'. Workshop for Instructors of Distance Learners, Shah Alam, Universiti Teknologi MARA, 26 November (unpublished paper).

Abdullah, S., Zakaria, S., Rahman, H. A. and Dali, N. (1994) *A Survey of the Reading Habits and Reading Interests Among Students in Institutes of Higher Learning in Malaysia*, Shah Alam, Institut Teknologi MARA (a report of the IRPA project).

Alimohammadi, M. and Zohoor, H. (1998) 'The promotion of access to open and distance education in Iran', paper, twelfth AAOU Conference, *The Asian Distance Learner*, Open University of Hong Kong, 4–6 November, Part 1: 1–6.

Biggs, J. and Watkins, D. (1996) 'The Chinese learner in retrospect', in *The Chinese Learner: Cultural, Psychological and Contextual Influences*, Hong Kong: CERC and ACER, pp. 269–85.

Bijan-Zadeh, M. H. (1998) 'Counseling sessions as support for distance education students', paper, twelfth AAOU Conference, *The Asian Distance Learner*, Open University of Hong Kong, 4–6 November, Part 1: 17–23.

Boshier, R. and Pratt, D. D. (1997) 'A qualitative and postmodern perspective on open learning in Hong Kong', *Distance Education* 18 (1): 110–35.

Carr, R. (1997) 'Cultural relevance as a quality issue', Proceedings of eleventh AAOU Conference, *Quality Assurance in Distance and Open Learning*, Kuala Lumpur: Institut Teknologi MARA, 11–14 November.

Chunxin, Z. (1998) 'Catering for students' needs', paper, twelfth AAOU Conference, *The Asian Distance Learner*, Open University of Hong Kong, 4–6 November, Part 3: 449–52.

Daniel, J. S. (1996) *Mega-universities and Knowledge Media: Technology Strategies for Higher Education*, London: Kogan Page.

Delavar, A. (1994) 'Factors affecting dropout of students at Allameh Tabatahai University, Iran', unpublished report.

Dodds, T., Nonyongo, E. and Glennie, J. (1999) 'Cooperation, competition or dominance: a challenge in Southern Africa', in K. Harry (ed.) *Higher Education through Open and Distance Learning*, London: Routledge.

Douglas, G. (1996) 'Distance education at the University of South Carolina: Report of a case study', *Journal of the American Society for Information Science* 47 (11): 875–9.

Fung, Y. Y. H. and Carr, R. (1998) 'Tutorials in a distance education system: student expectations and preferred approaches', paper, twelfth AAOU Conference, *The Asian Distance Learner*, Open University of Hong Kong, 4–6 November, Part 1: 115–24.

Hills, K. (1998) 'Distance learning across the East-West divide: Asian learners' experience of Western distance learning', paper, twelfth AAOU Conference, *The Asian Distance Learner*, Open University of Hong Kong, 4–6 November, Part 2: 159–62.

Hormozi, M. (1998) 'The role of the academic self-concept in distance education students', paper, twelfth AAOU Conference, *The Asian Distance Learner*, Open University of Hong Kong, 4–6 November, Part 2: 164–72.

Hülsmann, T. (1999) 'The costs of distance education', in K. Harry (ed.) *Higher Education through Open and Distance Learning*, London: Routledge.

Ibrahim, D. Z. and Silong, A. D. (1998) 'The experience of managers in postgraduate studies through distance education', paper, twelfth AAOU Conference, *The Asian Distance Learner*, Open University of Hong Kong, 4–6 November, Part 2: 182–8.

Ismail, F. (1992) 'Relationship between self-concept and academic performance of Pakistani students', *Pakistan Journal of Psychology* 23: 29–37.

KEDI (1993) *Air and Correspondence High Korean Educational in Korea, Seoul*, Korean Education Development Institute.

Kumar, A. (1998) 'Academic self-concept, study habits, attitude towards distance education, and academic performance of distance learners', *Staff and Educational Development International* 2 (2): 167–73.

Lou, Yu Hai (1998) 'An analysis of the needs for distance education in Shanghai', paper, twelfth AAOU Conference, *The Asian Distance Learner*, Open University of Hong Kong, 4–6 November, Part 2: 293–8.

Moreira, C. (1998) 'The distance learning dilemma', *The Star* (Education section), 9 August, p. 2.

Morgan, A.R. (1995) 'Student learning and students' experiences: research theory and practice', in F. Lockwood (ed.) *Open and Distance Learning Today*, London: Routledge.

Murugan, K. and Savithri, S. (1998) 'Whose baby is a distance learner?', paper, twelfth AAOU Conference, *The Asian Distance Learner*, Open University of Hong Kong, 4–6 November, Part 3: 306–11.

Niu Jian, Wang, C. and Ding, X. (1998) 'The Open-entrance Trial Programme: establishing a learning support system at China RTVUs', paper, twelfth AAOU Conference, *The Asian Distance Learner*, Open University of Hong Kong, 4–6 November, Part 3: 327–36.

Open House (1999a) The Open University No. 360, May, p. 2.

Open House (1999b) The Open University, No. 362, October, p. 1.

Robinson, B. (1998) 'Asian learners, Western models', paper, twelfth AAOU Conference, Open University of Hong Kong, 4–6 November, Part 3: 70–5.

Rohani, F. (1980) 'Relationship between self-concept and its factors and educational achievement', unpublished master's thesis, Faculty of Education, Shiraz University, Iran.

Roy, J. (2000) 'Success in distance learning: a Malaysian study', paper, fourteenth AAOU Conference, University of the Philippines Open University, Manila.

Simpson, O. (2000) *Supporting Students in Open and Distance Learning*, London: Kogan Page, cited in J. Pennells, 'Review', *Open Praxis* 2: 20.

Stevenson, K. and Sander, P. (1998) 'How do Open University students expect to be taught at tutorials?', *Open Learning* 13 (2): 42–6.

Tait, A. and Mills, R. (eds) (1996) *Supporting the Learner in Open and Distance Learning*, London: Longman.

Yates, R. L. (2000) 'Mixing technology and tradition in teacher education', *Open Praxis* 2: 15–19.

Yoshimoto, K. (1998) 'Careers and activities of female graduates of University of the Air', paper, twelfth AAOU Conference, *The Asian Distance Learner*, Open University of Hong Kong, 4–6 November, Part 3: 306–11.

Chapter 5

People

Staffing, development and management

Santosh Panda

Editors' introduction

Open and distance learning makes different demands on students, and changes the way they learn, the theme of the previous two chapters. But it also makes new demands on staff. This chapter analyses the different demands it makes on staff, illustrating the argument mainly by reference to higher education. Santosh Panda looks at the way in which open and distance learning is changing the jobs of educational and administrative staff, examines the categories of staff that are needed in single-mode and dual-mode institutions, and looks at the variety of jobs they need to perform. This in turn leads to the need for an institutional emphasis on programmes of staff development.

   Much open and distance learning assumes a new division of labour with different staff undertaking the roles of, say, materials developer or individual tutor. This is not universally the case: specialised university programmes at master's level may be developed and taught by a small group of individuals as an extension of their regular teaching, while Agri-Service Ethiopia, when it began as a small project for teaching better farming practice to rural farmers, had a staff of two who were reported to do everything from designing teaching materials to working the duplicator to meeting the students. But in most cases, distance-teaching staff have different roles from those in conventional institutions; staff in dual-mode institutions may need to work differently in their on-campus and off-campus activity. In general, open and distance learning tends to blur the distinction between administrative and educational staff and to divide educational activities, which are concentrated in the head and hands of a single teacher in a conventional class, among different people.

   This in turn makes staff policy and staff development key activities. The changed roles, and sometimes unusual combinations of role, required for open and distance learning may not fit well with the traditions of conventional education. One of the editors recalls sadly how, from a lack of understanding of government schemes of service, he classified staff in a college in Africa as clerical when they would have done better if classified as technical, even while doing the same job. (In many bureaucracies it is more difficult to put things right later than to do them differently in the first place.) Dedicated distance-teaching institutions, and those moving from being single- to dual-mode, need to develop staff policies that are geared to the needs of their learners. Some aspects of these policies will be about good teaching, and about quality arrangements to ensure it, a theme picked up in Chapter 10. Some of them are about pay and rewards. The basis on which writers are rewarded for developing teaching material, or how it is built into their contracts, is likely to be critical to the timely development of teaching material. Experience suggests that the greatest difficulties are likely to arise with in-house, part-time writers in dual-mode institutions (see also Perraton and Creed 1999).

Programmes of staff development range from the one-off, in-house training seminar through short workshops on particular skills such as course development to full- and part-time college courses, some of them leading to diploma- and master's-level qualifications. (For a wide-ranging set of examples of staff development programmes see Latchem and Lockwood 1998.) They may use a variety of techniques, including those of distance education itself, and need to take account of the variety of different roles of staff and jobs to be done which Panda discusses. Inadequate staff development is likely to be a constraint on educational innovation. Effective use of new information and communication technologies in education, for example, is possible only where there are enough teachers who are themselves informed about and comfortable with the technologies.

Programmes of staff development demand attention to the needs of part-time as well as full-time staff as, for example, when district inspectors are to play a role in supervising the classroom practice of trainee teachers studying at a distance. When the British Open University decided to decentralise and subcontract the mentoring of students on its teacher-training course, it had in turn to devote resources to the training of the monitors. The complexities of that operation demonstrate how there is a necessary but added layer of difficulty in planning effective programmes when some of those who require new skills are employed not by the distance-teaching institution responsible for the programme but by one of its partners.

The development of e-learning makes new demands for staff development. Again, it is not quite like conventional teaching or the marking of correspondence assignments. We come back to this issue in looking at technological choices and their consequences in Chapter 8.

People are important to the creation, existence, success and progress of any organisation. Educational and distance-teaching institutions are no exception. In distance education, irrespective of technological advances facilitating delivery of educational and training programmes, 'responsibility for instructional quality and control, the improvement of learning, and the aggregate effectiveness of distance education still rest with the faculty' (Olcott and Wright 1995: 5). There are also a host of other people who together as a team make it happen. Their placement and working in the system is, to some extent, governed by the institutional mission, the broad goals and policies adopted, and the operational definition of distance education and the corresponding organisational structures developed for its practice.

With its gradual acceptability and growth, distance education is being viewed critically for its practices and potentiality. On the one hand, it is being pitted against traditional classroom education; on the other hand, the ongoing convergence has blurred the clear distinction between classroom, distance and technology-based learning. Both of these have far-reaching implications for people working in distance education. For the former, the view echoed, for instance, includes: 'On one hand the traditionalists often view distance education as the ultimate erosion of academic standards, whereas on the other hand distance education advocates see opposition to their cause as obstructionism and academic protectionism' (Kirby 1988: 115). For the latter, a few developments as reflected in the writings of leading scholars of distance education are in order. One concerns open and dual-mode universities: 'The idea, however, that the future lay mainly with the open universities is belied by the changes of the last decade. Open and dual-mode universities are now both major players' (Harry and Perraton 1999: 11). The other concerns the fusion of campus-based education, distance education and information technologies under the banner of 'flexible learning'. Citing examples from Australia and Sweden, Moran and Myringer suggest for such approaches 'comprehensive university-wide strategies, based on explicit integration of a well-articulated set of institutional values about learning, with a range of teaching strategies and technologies, plus a set of organisational systems and networks to support them' (1999: 60). Still another concerns the operation and organisational structure of distance education with a wide range of variations in the models, starting from correspondence education to virtual learning. Peters (2003) critically analyses these models which include: an examination preparation model, a correspondence education model, a group distance-education model, a learner-centred model, a multiple mass-media model, a network-based distance-education model, a technologically extended classroom-teaching model, and a virtual distance-teaching university; and concludes that 'distance education is by far the most open and flexible form of learning and teaching'.

Analyses of various organisational models, with their implications for those involved with distance education, are presented in Chapter 6. The varieties of forms, including convergence (Hall 1996), that distance education has evolved, have shaped the recruitment, placement, working, development, evaluation, tenure, promotion and management of people working within and outside it. It is within this framework that the discussion in this chapter has been built. That the roles of staff in distance education are different can be better appreciated when it is compared with traditional campus-based classroom teaching.

CLASSROOM VERSUS DISTANCE TEACHING

Three major areas of activity of a university include teaching, research and service/extension. In a conventional university, the distinction between teaching and non-teaching functions is very well defined, and a teacher may not need to be concerned with what happens in non-teaching and service activities. The single activity of teaching (and teaching-related activities) and scholarship is essentially judged from the research papers and other related publications. However, in a distance-teaching institution, the organisation of activities changes to team work and specialisation, and various tasks are lined up in a chain. This necessitates interdependence between teaching, supporting and service divisions. Although the teacher's major function remains teaching, its definition and organisation changes largely. The teacher loses 'control' over many things, and the equivalent of classroom teaching takes the shape of course planning, design and development (writing and editing), preparation of assignments and assessment mechanisms, scripting for audio and video programmes, coordination of design and development processes, tutoring and counselling of students (a task which part-time conventional teachers may carry out at local study centres), course maintenance, and training of people involved in the process of development and delivery (such as course writers and counsellors), apart from discipline-based and distance-education system-based research. So far, research has remained on the fringe due partly to course development workload and lack of time, and partly to lack of training in methods research. Those working in service divisions such as admission, materials distribution, evaluation, planning, regional services (or student-support services), computing, electronic media, training and research, and administration and finance, all facilitate the tasks of course design and development, and the delivery of courses.

The clarification has been exemplified by Paul (1987: 142–3) when he describes what difference an academic from a campus-based institution finds on reaching Athabasca University, a Canadian open university:

- No students on campus.

- Teaching is not an individual teacher's prerogative. One has to work in a team, comprising specialised people.
- Professional autonomy may be compromised to the demands of production process.
- Breaking down of traditional concepts of academic and support divisions, and emergence of new definitions of these concepts, and that material distribution is as important as academic planning.
- Unlike classroom's closed unrecorded lecture/discussion, the distance-learning materials are open to everyone to examine.
- The direct contact with students is largely by tutors/counsellors, who are outside the open university system.
- No beginning or end to the academic year; the whole system may operate throughout the year.
- Too much administration and management, and too little time for research.
- The campus atmosphere and socialisation is missing.
- Differing notions about disciplinary research, graduate work, university reputation – so important in a campus-based university.

Three features of distance education, not found in conventional education settings, are the use of instructional media by specialist staff, the adoption of quasi-industrial processes of production and distribution, and the use of means of communication for teaching and administrative purposes to bridge the gap between the institution and the students (Rumble 1986: 163–4). Discussion is complicated by the fact that distance education is practised and known by many other terms sometimes used synonymously but sometimes with drastic differences in meaning: open learning, flexible learning, distributed learning, independent and home study, external studies, off-campus studies, correspondence education, and so on. In the Americas, for instance, distance-education methodologies include independent study, telecourses, computer-mediated communications, teleconferencing, audio-conferencing, one-way video/two-way audio and audiographics (Purdy and Wright 1992). In these kinds of mediated teaching which may be synchronous or asynchronous, the core skills required of a teacher now include the ability to interface with the technology, the ability to understand the strengths and weaknesses of each medium for effective instructional design and the ability to communicate effectively with students using different media. In teaching through telecommunications, the basic requirement for a teacher is to be sensitive and to address the technical and communication problems that students experience, to have a contingency plan of activities for times of technical failure, and to make preparations for it well ahead of time (Gunawardena 1992: 59–60).

Within distance education, marked differences exist between the institutions which are more centralised and large in operation such as the

British Open University and the Fern Universität of Germany, and institutions which are more decentralised and small in operation such as those in Australian and Swedish universities (Willen 1988). In the case of the former, the students are fairly independent, and teaching is largely through printed materials and non-human media; while in the latter, the distance students are considered similar to on-campus students, and teaching is largely through print, telephone and strong face-to-face interaction with the teacher along with on-campus students. This apart, Daniel distinguished between large- and small-scale distance-teaching universities, and dual-mode universities and *ad hoc* application of technologies to teaching, which has implications for both the system and the people within it. While the former 'have first recognised the teaching-learning process and then used particular technologies and media within the context of the learning systems they have created', the latter 'start from the situation of the teachers instructing in a conventional manner and attempt to multiply their impact by using technology' (1999: 298).

Comparing campus-based and distance education with regard to utilisation of space, Evans and Nation (1996) point out that even distance teaching is campus-based in the sense that the teachers generally gather at a central site to develop materials and provide 'complementary teaching' to distance students, and that not even all campus-based learning takes place in the presence of teachers, since students largely study in libraries and undertake private study at home. What they point out is that not only the 'location of teaching and learning' but also 'the time frame within which they occur' are going to change in the context of globalisation, use of educational technology and pursuance of lifelong learning (1996: 162–76). As universities move to become learning organisations (Candy 1996), including distance-teaching and open universities, staffing issues gain new prominence. The shift towards open and distance learning for both the dual-mode and new players needs consideration of the following issues (Latchem and Lockwood 1998: xxiv–xxv) which have implications for staff roles within the organisation and for the dynamics of their development and management:

- environmental scanning and strategic planning;
- senior and middle managers' total commitment to institutional vision and plan;
- the institution becoming a learning community based on reflective practice;
- alignment of staff development to an institutional strategic plan and human-resource development system, and allocation of sufficient staff-release time, funding and facilities both at the centre and the periphery;
- course teams, support groups and schools, rather than individuals, to be the focus of change;

- systems of recognition and reward for new roles, risk and innovation.

All these issues demonstrate the need to have in place a strategic institutional plan and human resource policy.

HUMAN RESOURCE POLICY

Both autonomous institutions and distance-education departments or centres need to have a human-resource policy in place, showing the type and number of human resources required at different cadres or levels, their recruitment, placement, induction and continuing professional development, their workload, appraisal, benefits and incentives, tenure and promotion, transfer and termination and retirement, terms and conditions, and code of professional ethics. All these presuppose that there is a strong human-resource needs survey – both initial and continuing – and human-resource planning. The planning unit of the institution plays a crucial role here.

Generally, human resources may be categorised into: teaching–technical/professional–administrative, full-time (FT)–part-time (PT), headquarters–regional/study centres. A representative categorisation is depicted in Figure 5.1. At times, the faculty of the mainstream departments (including the staff at the educational-development units or flexible-learning centres) have the additional responsibility of distance teaching. This is often the case in Australia and the United States under the banner of flexible learning and telecourses respectively. The staff categorisation, placement and nature of work vary accordingly. The staff categorisation given in Figure 5.1 may be explained as follows.

Headquarters

Teaching: The full-time teaching staff may include teachers placed at various schools of studies/departments, staff development units and researchers. The other academic staff (who are not necessarily teachers) working in planning, accreditation, academic coordination, extension, international operation, student evaluation/examination, student support, quality assurance/audit units (and sometimes academic analysts and researchers) may be placed functionally within this category. The part-time staff working at or associated with headquarters may include consultants, course writers, editors and translators.

Technical/professional: These staff may be full-time or part-time, and include those working in information technology, electronic media units, material production, and library/learning resource centres.

Administrative/secretarial: This includes a range of functionaries – the

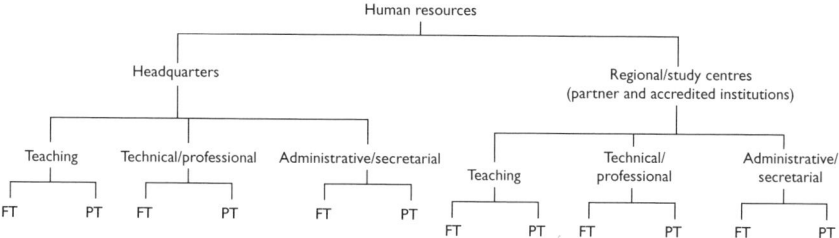

Figure 5.1 Some staff categories

pro-vice-chancellors and directors/heads of units (who may be termed as managerial), all official and secretarial staff working in administration, finance, material publication and distribution, maintenance, admission.

Regional/study centres

Teaching: The full-time staff includes teaching and other academic functionaries comprising regional director, assistant regional directors, staff tutors and researchers. The part-time staff include tutors and counsellors.

Technical/professional: People involved in information technology and electronic media operation and maintenance may be included in this category, and may be full-time or part-time.

Administrative/secretarial: The coordinators of study centres, learning resources centres, telelearning centres, secretarial staff dealing with administration, finance, admission and examination comprise this category. Sometimes, regional directors and assistant regional directors dealing with student support services are included in the administrative/secretarial category.

The categorisation will, of course, vary across institutions and the staffing pattern will depend on the job to be performed on role definitions. Any one individual might play either a singular specialised role or a variety of roles on different occasions (for which there may again be specialised people in some institutions). Rumble (1986: 122–3) provides a comprehensive list of staffing categories. The categorisation in terms of general management and management-related functions, materials development, materials production, materials storage and distribution, and student administration and teaching is based on 'assumptions about the location of particular functions within administrative and other areas' and 'the way in which work roles are defined' (1986: 121). The definition of staff roles, he suggests, depends on the educational model (such as institution-centred, person-centred and society-centred) that the distance education system adopts.

Staff structure and functions

The structure of staff – the types of staff, their number, the ratio of teaching to non-teaching staff, and so on – depends on a number of factors, usually within the decision-making of the institution. A few important factors are the following.

- Whether the institution is single-mode or dual-mode and/or adopts large-scale virtual distance teaching.
- Costing and cost considerations: for instance, course development involves fixed costs irrespective of the number of students to be admitted in its first and subsequent offers. Low course enrolments tend to increase the per capita cost of development of courses, and so may not justify full-time faculty involvement in course design and development. It may be cheaper to engage consultants along with a small core faculty, and adopt low-cost course production methods such as workshop-generated, personalised training, or wrap-around courses (Lockwood 1992). Of course, the methods adopted depend upon the exigencies of the institutions concerned and considerations of course quality.
- What kind of media mix the institution is opting for, and what mix is used for individual programmes or courses; and whether media production is outsourced or carried out through facilities owned permanently by the institution.
- The kind of learner-support network: whether a dedicated regional study-centre network for regular face-to-face contact, or contractual local support by trained tutors or mentors, or online synchronous or asynchronous support by the faculty, or through networking and consortia.
- The mode of delivery of courses – whether by post, on the internet, by courier or collection by learners personally from the institution or designated centres.
- The number and nature of courses to be offered with the option of adopting different models of materials development. Whether the concentration is on programmes for particular or minority interest audiences, liberal arts programmes, extension programmes, or vocational and professional programmes.
- The location of training and research in the institutional work structure; options for training include location in a separate training unit or on-the-job training. Research may be undertaken by all faculty members in their own discipline, while institutional or systemic research may be the responsibility of a designated unit.

The distinction between teaching–academic, technical–professional and managerial–administrative is possible when there is a defined role for each category and for all staff within that category. In this case the qualifications and skills required may be notified at the time of recruitment, and job roles defined at the time of placement. Usually, in large distance-teaching systems, the support or service divisions (e.g. admission, materials production and distribution, student support, evaluation, planning, training and research, media, information technology, library) facilitate the work of the faculty, and the managerial and administrative divisions (including finance) facilitate the work of the faculty and support divisions. Although it may sound unacceptable to be linear, in practice the roles played by divisions and individuals cut across specialised distinctions; divisions or units such as quality assurance and management information systems cut across divisions and schools, and become all-pervasive, penetrating almost everything visible and invisible. Further, transfers or promotions especially of administrative and technical staff, across administrative units, support divisions, schools of studies and regional/study centres, dismantle specialisation and rigid staff roles and result in more diversified managerial roles.

Of special concern to institutions is the ratio between teaching, technical and administrative staff, and those who provide learner-support services including counselling at study centres. This ratio depends on many factors including the number of students and courses offered, the financial position of the institution, and what is to be done in-house and what is to be outsourced. Experience suggests that it would be economical and contribute to quality if functions such as course design and development, course maintenance and revision, teleconferencing and computer conferencing, planning, evaluation, computer, quality assurance, training, research and programme evaluation, library, international operation, administration and finance are taken care of in-house; and some of the other functions such as admission, printing and publication, materials distribution, preparation of press-ready copy, audio-video materials production, student survey and feedback from the field (on learner-support services matters), computer data-feeding of student records, computerisation and development of LAN, hands-on and other lab experiments are outsourced with full institutional monitoring.

The different formulae for determining broadly the levels of staffing and quantum of staff given by Rumble (1986: 129–36) should be useful in arriving at staff requirements in a distance teaching institution. This though has to be considered in conjunction with the working style, work norms and processes adopted by the institution for various types of work. One concern has been the increasing number of non-teaching staff against teaching, and the role conflicts of various categories of staff. Evans and Nation note that 'It is perhaps ironic, that as the focus has become more on mass education in the world's universities, often the proportion of teachers has declined and the number of support staff has increased' (2000a: 3); and that instead of being a 'community of scholars', the universities are now becoming 'educational corporations', and that non-academic staff and non-academic operations are expanding over academic staff and academic operations (2000b: 162). In large distance-teaching institutions this is also a matter of growing concern, as are conflicts between teachers, professionals and administrators. Citing the example of the Indira Gandhi National Open University where in the initial years three groups of people were drawn from three different sectors of society (teachers from mainstream universities, professionals from established agencies, and administrators from government bureaucracy), Menon remarked:

> All these three agencies have had independent existence and identity and through their many years of operation have acquired certain unique and sometimes idiosyncratic characteristics and more important a certain amount of mutual mistrust and suspicion. An open university is a nascent phenomenon and as such it is quite amorphous in its character. Therefore, different categories of people who constitute it entertain diverse and sometimes mutually contradictory perceptions about its goals and functions and their respective roles in it. This makes it extremely difficult for them to readily gel into a cohesive team.
>
> (Menon 1989–90: 51)

Sometimes, non-traditional staff and academics drawn from mainstream universities working in distance-teaching institutions also may not gel well, and the former may not appreciate the latter's notions of disciplinary research and graduate work (so important in mainstream universities). Citing the example of Athabasca University, Paul comments: 'A healthy tension between these perspectives can be very stimulating and productive, but outright conflict can be debilitating for an institution if these different perspectives are not resolved over a period of time' (1990: 58).

Faculty role

In conventional universities, faculty recruitment is based on the concerns of high-quality disciplinary research, graduate work and high academic credibility. The autonomy granted to universities ensures the academic freedom and tenure that is essential for high-quality research and academic scholarship. Therefore, it is not surprising that managers of open-learning or distance-education institutions attempt to attract conventional academics to their institutions, with a commitment to traditional notions of academic freedom, autonomy and collegial modes of governance (Paul 1990). Such attributes, so crucial as a foundation to the ivory towers, may find it difficult to gel with the non-traditional teaching-learning culture of distance education, where there are always constraints of deadlines for writing and editing of course materials, their despatch, student assignments and projects, counselling, and the like, along with an unconventional workload which may be at the expense of scholarly research and publication, and professional development. Further, such traditional notions of and concern for academic credibility can result in overloaded courses which in turn increase the student workload much more than their defined credit value (Vijayshri *et al.* 1992) – a task which is balanced out by teaching-learning specialists and editors. On the other hand, the traditional faculty notions of research productivity and academic freedom *vis-à-vis* collegial modes of governance and management concern for control can lead to direct conflict with the requirements of the system and needs of the students (Paul 1990).

However, most distance-teaching institutions, adopting a policy of employing full-time staff with the major responsibility of course design and development, need to recruit faculty with high academic integrity and a commitment to research. Paul believes that 'maintaining high academic standards is essential to the success of an open-learning institution and that traditional norms of academic freedom and commitment to research are an integral part of this quest' (1990: 60). Whatever comparisons are drawn between distance-teaching institutions (especially open universities) and their traditional counterparts, one must not forget that it is the course packages with high academic merit, designed to promote effective student learning, that bring credibility to such institutions. Managerial, support and service operations are only there to facilitate this.

Faculty roles are likely to be different in systems of flexible learning or flexible delivery, as in the case of Australia, where the same faculty, in a dual-mode teaching system, uses a variety of development, delivery and teaching strategies to cater to the individual learning needs of both on-campus and off-campus students. In such situations, the universities usually do not have elaborate systems of materials production, or designated staff with defined course-development roles as exist in single-mode open universities; the trend has been towards non-industrialised and non-linear materials production systems with minimal support from specialised production personnel. In more technology-based and technology-supported teaching and learning, the faculty individually or in a small team carries the function of designing multimedia courseware with online learner support which is flexible and learner-oriented. The role of distance-education centres is confined to providing instructional design support, project management, learner support and quality control. A variation to this on- and off-campus flexible learning in Swedish university distance education is that the responsibility of design and production of learning materials lies with the individual academic (Moran and Myringer 1999: 64–5). The Swedish system resembles the system of materials development in the dual-mode university correspondence-course institutes in India.

With the increasing use of technology in teaching and learning, and adoption of virtual teaching-learning, the role of academics and academic support staff is changing. In technology-mediated teaching, the preparation time for the production of materials and formatting of a course is greater than for equivalent classroom teaching. In web-based teaching, video-conferencing, computer conferencing and so on, the role of the teacher changes to that of a facilitator of individual study, group interaction and activity-based learning, though the lead time for such preparation is much greater than teachers often anticipate. In the case of computer conferencing, 'teachers spend up to twice as long, overall, to give a course via computer conferencing as they do to give a course by traditional means' (Mason 1999: 43; also see Gunawardena 1992).

In such changing institutional priorities and policies, the role of the faculty *vis-à-vis* staff developers and staff development units needs special consideration. Latchem and Moran (1998) note that in Australia, the distance-education centres and academic-development units in universities have developed a tendency to act as 'one-stop academic and technological support' to all-mode flexible learning. People are always rare in areas combining teaching experiences in classroom, distance and technology-mediated learning.Therefore, the role of the centralised staff development support staff *vis-à-vis* departmental faculty needs to be redefined.

> One solution is to maximise the ability of centralised expertise to support academics by creating networks of departmental academics who become the local flexible learning guide and mentor to their colleagues. This solution has the added advantage of helping academics to construct their own knowledge and skills as teachers.
>
> (Moran and Myringer 1999: 63)

At the British Open University, the role of the educational technologists within the course team is well defined, and their placement at a central unit effectively establishes their credibility. In the early development of course materials their roles included helping faculty and the team on objectives, advance organisers and self-assessment questions; the university has since gone beyond the behaviourist model to more constructivist approaches. Subsequent criticisms of the earlier model appeared (Harris 1987), and the role of the educational technologist extended, beyond the earlier traditional role, to that of subject expert, executive manager, social analyst, and expert in any aspect of course design. Problems may arise when different roles are ascribed to such people in the distance-learning institutions. In Australia, for instance, which has also moved ahead of the approach of instructional industrialism, the designations have been classified (Inglis 1996) along organisational issues – distance-education developer, distance-education development facilitator – and teaching-learning issues – educational process consultant, staff developer, critical reviewer, instructional-process consultant, instructional editor, joint venturer, and transformer. Experience shows that it is more productive and facilitating if the school faculty is involved in initial curriculum and instructional design issues, as in the case of Indira Gandhi National Open University; and in that case, the specialist staff in training and research undertake research and try out alternative protocols for further development and application at various school faculties. While the teachers have learned the role through experience, in Australia most of the instructional designers who did not have formal qualifications in the field have developed themselves through experience on the job (Allen 1995).

With changing roles for instructional designers, and within institutional policy, the role of the academic faculty is also changing. However, the role of a distance teacher (equivalent to classroom teaching) involves both primary and secondary functions (Parakh 2000). The primary function, which should be compulsory, includes course writing, course editing, the preparation of assignments and question banks, and scripting for audio-video programmes. The secondary function encompasses curriculum or course design, programme or course maintenance, actual counselling and training of counsellors, and liaison with government and non-government functionaries for programme delivery (Panda and Jena 2000). The role of teachers in many distance-teaching institutions has shifted gradually from the primary functions to para-academic activities such as academic management, the printing, production and distribution of materials, establishment of student support and media networks, and training of non-teaching and counselling staff. While every teacher needs to undertake the primary functions, they should be involved gradually in secondary functions after gaining the required experience. For instance, a newly appointed teacher may be given course-writing work, to be followed up as his or her career grows by the development of assignments, question banks, audio-visual academic notes and scripts, and counsellors' training. Programme or course design and the coordination of its development should be handled when one has gained sufficient experience and confidence. A formula may be worked out, at each institution, on the role and workload of a teacher. A generic formula covering actual development of courses and coordination of course development is given as follows:

- *Lecturer*: 100 per cent development (after two to three years: 80 per cent development, 20 per cent coordination);
- *Reader/Associate Professor*: two-thirds development, one-third coordination;
- *Professor*: half of the time development, half of the time coordination.

Of course, in addition, there are other tasks to be undertaken: for instance, research (discipline-based and distance-education system-based) which at times may consume one-third of the workload of each faculty. Other tasks with potentially contentious roles include those of editor, media producer and translator. Where a course editor is a senior academic from the mainstream university, the working relationship between the editor and other faculty staff is crucial to the quality of courses. Similarly, problems may arise between media producers and translators about the language of distance education. While audio-visual programme production is recognised as a creative activity for the teacher and the producer, it has also been realised that transcreation from one language to another and fresh writing in regional languages are qualitatively richer than translation, and that development of the same course materials in different languages becomes more effective if the writers of all the media of instruction are oriented together for writing the same course units in different languages. This has been a major area of concern in India with sixteen recognised national languages, and as many as 1652 dialects and spoken languages.

From the point of view of management, the most contentious issue has often been faculty workload and faculty productivity. The faculty work includes course design and development, translation, transformation of materials, research and programme evaluation, and course revision. If the course design involves repetition of set methods of teaching, assessment strategies and support systems, the faculty time needed is less than if these are done afresh. If course development follows well-tried models, less faculty time is required than if new models or strategies are adopted. The question arises: Should each faculty need the same time to produce a course? Rumble (1997) quotes Sparkes' (1984) allotment of corresponding hours of academic effort needed to produce one hour of learning materials for students: lecturing: 2–10 hours; small-group teaching: 1–10 hours; telephone teaching: 2–10 hours; videotape lecture: 3–10 hours; audio-vision: 10–20 hours; teaching text: 50–100 hours; broadcast television: 100 hours; computer-aided learning: 200 hours; and interactive video: 300 hours. In the British Open University, the centralised academic staff spent about 120 days exclusively on course development. The exercise, carried out way back, showed that academic productivity (in terms of units of student study time per year, where one unit is equivalent to ten or twelve student study hours) varied across faculties: 1.4 units in technology and science, 1.6 units in mathematics and education, 2.4 units in social sciences, and 2.6 units in arts (Rumble 1997: 80). Further, it was assumed that a maintenance unit was equivalent to 0.1 new unit, and that development of a 450-student-hour course should take eighteen months. The central point is that in any distance-education institution the agreed faculty workload needs to be distributed across course design, course development, course translation, course transformation, course coordination, course revision, and research and self-professional development. Methodologies for arriving at production rates and productivity are described by Rumble (1997). With regard to staffing, he further remarks:

> Clearly, it is possible to change the level of staffing needed not only by changing the mix of media, but also by changing the processes involved in developing materials, or by making greater use of temporary staff paid on a piece-work basis.
>
> (Rumble 1997: 83)

The pressure of work at distance-teaching universities as also at dual-mode universities (where teachers teach both on-campus and distance students) leaves little time for research for the faculty. Paul contends: 'I have long been a strong advocate of engaging full-time academic faculty with commitments to research and scholarship in their respective fields to open-learning institutions' (1990: 59). In some instances, such as the British Open University, the faculty has conducted international-class research in both disciplines and the distance-education system, and has attracted larger research grants than some of its mainstream counterparts. The dispute between disciplinary and distance-education system research notwith-standing, it is contended that the distance-teaching institutions should contribute equally to the generation of new knowledge and reinterpretation of existing knowledge, and to the most effective ways of teaching-learning at a distance (Evans 2000). Besides the pressure of course workload, the constraint to systemic research has largely been the lack of training and mentoring support in this non-traditional teaching-learning method (Panda 2000). This brings into focus the need for human resource development for the people within and outside the system.

HUMAN RESOURCE DEVELOPMENT

In the context of the above, human resource development assumes greater significance as an investment in people both for individual professional development and institutional effectiveness, and that an institutional human resource development policy, within its strategic plans, needs to be put in place for teaching, technical and administrative staff, as well as for all part-time people associated with the institution's operation. Many institutions give low or no priority to the continuing professional development of non-academic staff. However, every staff member should have an induction, before placement, on areas of distance education, institutional strategic goals and operations, work culture and ethics, office automation, team work, and so on. This may be followed by appraisal at regular intervals, continuous training or updating on areas of information technology, and staff members' specific training needs. Every promotion should be preceded by attendance at refresher programmes and followed by induction to the new job. Similarly, incentives, rewards, promotion, welfare and other benefits (so also punishment) have to be viewed together as a package. Employees may be encouraged to undergo certificate or diploma programmes (which benefit them as well as the institution) with full fee compensation and with duty leave for short courses. As Olcott and Wright (1995) note, promotion and tenure, activities to be rewarded, and the degree of support (monetary compensation, release time, training, instructional and administrative resources) have to be seen in a continuum.

Staff development needs to be viewed as organisational change, and teaching and other professional staff are crucial to it. Robinson (1998) provides comprehensive strategic guidelines for staff development and steps in implementing a staff-development plan for open and distance learning, and stresses that staff development should be continuously evaluated, and that there should be transfer of training to real work situations. The faculties in many distance-teaching institutions gradually realise that, given the team-work situations, continuous professional development has a meaning to them as it does to the institution. The train-ing model, suggested by McWilliams and Mugridge (1998), of a variety of distance educators in different settings may form a base from which to consider such an initiative. Due to a new kind of role at distance-teaching institutions, changing roles across career promotions and (open) university as a learning organisation, continuing professional development (CPD) is crucial to faculty work and growth (Markowitz 1988). A CPD model for faculty may include:

- induction (at the time of joining the institution);
- orientation (during the first year of service);
- refresher (subsequently, in discipline areas and in areas of distance teaching-learning, before the next promotion, followed by orientation to the next job role);
- thematic/focused (relating to particular operational area such as new models of course development, new student assessment mechanisms, new formats of self-learning material, media mix and media integration, online teaching-learning);
- specialised (especially for technical and professional people).

Information-technology capacity building for all, including the faculty for handling course design, development, offer and evaluation, forms the core of such professional development in this constantly changing world. While in-house workshops, seminars or round tables may be used for the purpose, more benefit is derived when people are sent out to participate in conferences, workshops, seminars, and on attachment and sabbatical. Evans and Nation (1998: 51) remark, in the context of new educational technologies:

> staff development becomes less about offering workshops on 'how to' in relation to any particular pieces of equipment, and more about an holistic approach which encourages a critically reflective community in which new educational technologies are created to improve or enhance practice. Staff development under such conditions is more likely to occur as a form of action-oriented critical reflection and participatory enquiry and evaluation, or as a form of collaboration or dialogue between practitioners.

In regard to course writers, of which there is a shortage in many developing countries, Perraton and Creed (1999) suggest a broad-based training 'appropriate to the institutional and socio-cultural context', and staff developers and managers need to give consideration to the 'balance between generalist and more context-specific content areas, to the balance between initial and subsequent staff development, to complementary, further and appropriate type training' (1999: 13).

The Indira Gandhi National Open University which has the responsibility of coordinating and maintaining standards of distance-education systems in India, with ten open universities and sixty-two university distance-education institutes, extends one lifetime increment in the salary of both teaching and non-teaching staff of the university on successful completion of its long-term staff development programme, the postgraduate diploma in distance education. Any new teacher who joins the Open University has to complete the diploma, offered by the Staff Training and Research Institute of Distance Education, in order to fulfil probation successfully. Therefore, a CPD for staff needs to be viewed from a systems perspective for both faculty growth and development of the organisation (Dillon and Walsh 1992). The dilemma between faculty perception and management strategic plan though remains. Lentell (1994: 30) comments:

> However the central dilemma of the discourse and practice of staff development remains: training to perform a task versus learning and growth. Failure to address this contradiction will lead to a cynicism among staff and a sense that the language of staff development is merely empty rhetoric.

HUMAN RESOURCE MANAGEMENT

There is a crucial leadership role in human resource and performance management. Role clarification, coordination and networking all facilitate this; and an alert and continuously growing management information system helps the process. An acceptable, comprehensive and practicable performance appraisal and performance indicator system may provide additional instruments for quality work and quality assurance. It also requires continuous monitoring, evaluation and follow-up.

Different people may hold differing organisational values and attitudes, which are at times in conflict with each other. This may concern the mission of the university, the teaching-learning technologies designed to achieve it, or the support mechanisms for students, or the roles of various functionaries and their coordination and collaboration, or even matters of equity and cost considerations. Solutions are likely to depend on dialogue and the involvement of people at various stages of the development of policy and practice, and the display of leadership qualities showing that one not only preaches, but 'does'.

Faculty tenure, promotion and reward remain crucial issues to be addressed seriously. While in the United States the teaching of telecourses is neither highly regarded nor seriously considered for faculty tenure and promotion (Walcott 1997), and research productivity is valued more than teaching for tenure and promotion (and distance teaching figures much less prominently in this scheme of things), a study from Australia (Macpherson and Smith 1998) suggests that even if distance materials development does not help increase faculty status, career development and promotion, and even if the faculty is not released from regular teaching and takes up distance teaching as an additional task, it is willing to develop such materials because of the belief that the university should provide equity through distance education, that it helps in on-campus teaching, that teachers should have general skills in material development, and that these materials should be available to on-campus students. At the same time staff are aware of the usual constraints of lack of time, lack of recognition for promotion (since it consumes a greater chunk of research time), and less lead time for this activity.

Role of management

The heads of institutions and those involved in policy formulation and decision making within various authorities of any open university or distance-teaching institution are crucial within the organisation since they can influence the present and future of those institutions. In the context of tele-teaching and faculty participation in the United States, Olcott and Wright (1995: 7) remarked: 'Institutional support and leadership are critical if distance teaching is to be integrated into the mainstream academic culture.' On a comparative study of Athabasca University and the British Open University, Paul (1990) opined that while such Canadian universities tend to manage the institutions directly, in Britain, the OU is comparatively less open (than Oxford and Cambridge) to modern concepts of management. Things may have changed over the past decade, though the Asian open universities still follow a bureaucratic and directive model of governance and management (Zhang *et al.* 1999).

Within an authoritarian-hierarchical model of management, whimsical and high-handed tendencies of the management allow the adoption of policies and action plans which could be either imposing and correcting or detrimental and disastrous. The adoption of new educational technologies has been one such case. Managers need training about the technologies. In all their orientation and training they need to listen to various opinion groups and to become involved in the detail of how a policy is implemented (after its formulation) and its progress, as also in the formulation of innovations (such as, for instance, new ways of course design and development, flexible and viable learning support mechanisms, and so on) within those policies and their implementation guidelines. Further, and probably most importantly, they need to see to it that policies are formulated not for their own sake, nor even to show off to funding agencies and governments, but to be implemented to see the result and build further on these in order to take them forward. Successful, forward-looking and democratic institutional heads have involved researchers and critics of the system in an advisory role so as to enhance institutional performance reflected through transparent research data, critical reflection and public opinion.

A critical testing time for institutional heads is the introduction of technological changes for either academic solutions or extending equity in the face of stringent and vocal opposition from the faculty. Ignoring such concerns not only encourages academics to be unconcerned but also does not necessarily ensure successful implementation. Although a debate on technological solutions to educational problems and technology-led change is beyond the scope of this chapter (for critical discussion and case studies see Evans and Nation 2000c), what is important is the question of how the leadership manages such innovations and changes. This requires what Latchem and Lockwood (1998) have noted: a total and public commitment by them. Paul (2003: 6) remarks:

> the effective leader must encourage real debate on issues of change and capitalise on the positive energy that can be generated by an open and thorough consideration of alternatives. University faculty members are highly articulate and forceful in the presentation of their opinions and, while that doesn't make change easier, at its best, it can ensure that every major step has been well thought through and really does have significant support in the institution.

The situation in developing countries, and with single-mode institutions planning to move to dual-mode status, is more vulnerable. This transition should not be viewed from the perspective that distance education is cheaper (and at times generates surpluses), technology use within it is a solution to mass education, and that it is time to shift since every other institution is doing so; rather such a transition needs careful planning, proper investment and consideration of models appropriate to one's own context. All these issues have implications for a variety of people (within and outside the institution) who would be affected by this shift. In this context, Perraton and Creed (1999: 19) emphasise that:

> Managers and policy-makers need new opportunities to consider how different modes of ODL – organisational, technological and pedagogical – fit in with national/institutional strategies and infrastructure. The difficulties involved in a transition to dual-mode status, for example, can only be addressed if they are appreciated. Broader-based and case-study approaches would help these managers to frame models and practices that are appropriate (and therefore durable) in the context in which they are working.

CONCLUSION

We need to think again about people – who may be in sympathy with a system of teaching-learning, which greatly enhances equity and enforces lifelong learning, in spite of many constraints on their developing status including tenure and promotion. Distance education has come much closer to the mainstream, and convergence has seen the light, though it needs further articulation and research. Research and scholarship are crucial foundations to distance education too, and their relevance to the open and flexible goal of distance education needs to be emphasised in any institutional strategic plan in dual-mode institutions, and to be reflected upon critically in the single-mode distance-teaching institutions. Visionary and committed leadership is the foremost need. What Stein (1961, quoted in Black 1992) held about home study in the United States forty years ago holds good even today: that distance educators have to be more active professionally, and should do quality research and always be concerned with high standards of (distance) education.

ACKNOWLEDGEMENT

The author sincerely acknowledges the critical comments on the draft of this chapter by Professor Suresh Garg, Director, School of Sciences, IGNOU.

REFERENCES

Allen, M. (1995) 'The activities and qualifications of instructional designers in Australia', *Crossing Frontiers*, papers for the 12th Biennial Forum of ODLAA, Central Queensland University, Rockhampton.

Black, E. J. (1992) 'Faculty support for university distance education', *Journal of Distance Education* 7 (2): 5–29.

Candy, P. C. (1996) 'Promoting lifelong learning: academic developers and the university as a learning organisation', *The International Journal for Academic Development* 1 (1): 7–18.

Daniel, J. (1999) 'Open learning and/or distance education: which one for what purpose?', in K. Harry (ed.) *Higher Education through Open and Distance Learning*, London and Vancouver: Routledge and The Commonwealth of Learning.

Dillon, C. L. and Walsh, S. M. (1992) 'Faculty: the neglected resource in distance education', *The American Journal of Distance Education* 6 (3): 5–21.

Evans, T. (2000) 'The stragegic importance of institutional research in open universities: building on reflective practitioner', *Indian Journal of Open Learning* 9 (1): 1–12.

Evans, T. and Nation, D. (1996) 'Educational futures: globalisation, educational technology and lifelong learning', in T. Evans and D. Nation (eds) *Opening Education: Policies and Practices from Open and Distance Education*, London: Routledge.

Evans, T. and Nation, D. (1998) 'Research and staff development in open and distance education', in C. Latchem and F. Lockwood (eds) *Staff Development in Open and Flexible Learning*, London and New York: Routledge.

Evans, T. and Nation, D. (2000a) 'Introduction', in T. Evans and D. Nation (eds) *Changing University Teaching*, London: Kogan Page.

Evans, T. and Nation, D. (2000b) 'Understanding changes to university teaching', in T. Evans and D. Nation (eds) *Changing University Teaching*, London: Kogan Page.

Evans, T. and Nation, D. (eds) (2000c) *Changing University Teaching: Reflections on Creating Educational Technologies*, London: Kogan Page.

Gunawardena, C. N. (1992) 'Changing faculty roles for audiographics and on-line teaching', *The American Journal of Distance Education* 6 (3): 58–71.

Hall, J. (1996) 'The revolution in electronic technology and the modern university: the convergence of means', in T. Evans and D. Nation (eds) *Opening Education: Policies and Practices from Open and Distance Education*, London: Routledge.

Harris, D. (1987) *Openness and Closure in Distance Education*, London: Falmer.

Harry, K. and Perraton, H. (1999) 'Open and distance learning for the new society', in K. Harry (ed.) *Higher Education through Open and Distance Learning*, London: Routledge.

Inglis, A. (1996) 'Teaching-learning specialists' conceptions of their role in the design of distance learning packages', *Distance Education* 17 (2): 267–88.

Kirby, D. M. (1988) 'The next frontier: graduate education at a distance', *Journal of Distance Education* 3 (2): 115–21.

Latchem, C. and Lockwood, F. (1998) 'Preface', in C. Latchem and F. Lockwood (eds) *Staff Development in Open and Flexible Learning*, London: Routledge.

Latchem, C. and Moran, L. (1998) 'Staff development issues in dual mode institutions: the Australian experience', in C. Latchem and F. Lockwood (eds) *Staff Development in Open and Flexible Learning*, London: Routledge.

Lentell, H. (1994) 'Staff development in distance education. Who says it is a good thing?', *Open Praxis* 1: 29–30.

Lockwood, F. (1992) 'Alternative methods of materials production', *Media and Technology for Human Resource Development* 4 (4): 233–8.

Macpherson, C. and Smith, A. (1998) 'Academic authors' perceptions of the instructional design and development process for distance education: a case study', *Distance Education* 19 (1): 124–41.

McWilliams, P. and Mugridge, I. (1998) 'Staff development for open and distance education: the case of the Commonwealth of Learning', in C. Latchem and F. Lockwood (eds) *Staff Development in Open and Flexible Learning*, London: Routledge.

Markowitz, H. Jr. (1988) 'Continuing professional development in distance education', *The American Journal of Distance Education* 2 (3): 64–73.

Mason, R. (1999) 'The impact of telecommunications', in K. Harry (ed.) *Higher Education through Open and Distance Learning*, London: Routledge.

Menon, S. (1989–90) 'A nation-wide distance education system', *Journal of Higher Education* 15: 41–53.

Moran, L. and Myringer, B. (1999) 'Flexible learning and university change', in K. Harry (ed.) *Higher Education through Open and Distance Learning*, London: Routledge.

Olcott, D. Jr. and Wright, S. J. (1995) 'An institutional support framework for increasing faculty participation in post-secondary distance education', *The American Journal of Distance Education* 9 (3): 5–17.

Panda, S. (2000) 'Mentoring, rewards and incentives in research as professional development', a keynote presentation at the International Conference on Research in Distance and Adult Learning in Asia, Open University of Hong Kong, 21–24 June.

Panda, S. and Jena, T. (2000) 'Changing the pattern: towards flexible learning, learner support and mentoring', in F. Lockwood and A. Gooley (eds) *Innovations in Open and Distance Learning*, London: Kogan Page.

Parakh, J. M. (2000) *Personal Communication*, New Delhi: Indira Gandhi National Open University.

Paul, R. (1987) 'Staff development needs for universities: mainstream and distance education', in P. Smith and M. Kelly (eds) *Distance Education and the Mainstream*, London: Croom Helm.

Paul, R. (1990) *Open Learning and Open Management*, London and New York: Kogan Page and Nichols Publishing.

Paul, R. (2003) 'Institutional leadership and management of change', in S. Panda (ed.) *Planning and Management in Distance Education*, London: Kogan Page.

Perraton, H. and Creed, C. (1999) *Distance Education Practice: Training and Rewarding Authors*, London: Department for International Development.

Peters, O. (2003) 'Models of open and flexible learning in distance education', in S. Panda (ed.) *Planning and Management in Distance Education*, London: Kogan Page.

Purdy, L. N. and Wright, S. J. (1992) 'Guest editorial – Teaching in distance education: a faculty perspective', *The American Journal of Distance Education* 6 (3): 2–4.

Robinson, B. (1998) 'A strategic perspective on staff development for open and distance learning', in C. Latchem and F. Lockwood (eds) *Staff Development in Open and Flexible Learning*, London and New York: Routledge.

Rumble, G. (1986) *The Planning and Management of Distance Education*, London and Sydney: Croom Helm.

Rumble, G. (1997) *The Costs and Economics of Open and Distance Learning*, London: Kogan Page.

Sewart, D. (1987) 'Staff development needs in distance education and campus-based education: are they so different?', in P. Smith and M. Kelly (eds) *Distance Education and the Mainstream*, London: Croom Helm.

Sparkes, J. J. (1984) 'Pedagogic differences in course design', in A. W. Bates (ed.) *The Role of Technology in Distance Education*, London: Croom Helm.

Stein, L.S. (1961) 'Is home study a step child?', *Home Study Review* 2: 29–40.

Vijayshri, Garg, S. and Panda, S. (1992) 'A preliminary study of student workload for IGNOU physics elective courses', *Indian Journal of Open Learning* 1 (2): 19–26.

Walcott, L. L. (1997) 'Tenure, promotion, and distance education: examining the culture of faculty rewards', *The American Journal of Distance Education* 11 (2): 3–18.

Willen, B. (1988) 'What happened to the Open University: briefly', *Distance Education* 9 (1): 71–83.

Zhang, W., Jegede, O., Ng, F., Kwok, L. and Tsui, C. (1999) 'A comparative study of the administrative styles, educational processes, and outcomes of selected Asian open universities', *Conference Proceedings*, 13th Annual Conference of Asian Association of Open Universities, Beijing.

Chapter 6

Resources

Hilary Perraton

In this part of the book we have put people first and money last but we neglect it at our peril. In analysing open and distance learning we look at a special case of a general question: who pays for education and who benefits from it?

Assumptions about this have shifted over the years. In the pre-industrial north education and training were funded by religion, the economy and the family. The church provided clerks who could read and other kinds of learning were done through apprenticeship, funded partly through paying to be articled, partly through the surplus generated by the apprentices' own production. The industrialised economy, and notions of a right to education, grew together, and by 1948 the Universal Declaration on Human Rights established that:

> Everyone has the right to education. Education shall be free, at least in the elementary and fundamental stages. Elementary education shall be compulsory. Technical and professional education shall be made generally available and higher education shall be equally accessible to all on the basis of merit.
>
> (Universal Declaration of Human Rights, article 26,1)

The Declaration enshrines both the notion of a right – which the world now hopes to achieve in 2015 nearly seventy years after the Declaration, without in reality expecting to do so – and a different, meritocratic principle that above the basic level education should be based on capacity and desert. The Declaration implies that free and universal education is to be funded by the state but might be treated as more equivocal about funding higher levels of education. More recently, shifts in ideology have brought into public currency two other ideas about funding: that, at least at tertiary and possibly at secondary levels, some of the cost should be met by the learners who will derive long-term personal benefits from their education and that the market has a role to play in making education available. The market is now more sophisticated, and a national, regional or global, rather than local market which determined the supply and price of apprenticeships, and plays a role both in employing the products of the educational system and in moulding the policies of its providers. Human rights, the dictates of the economy, meritocracy and the market all shape the funding of open and distance learning as of other forms of education.

SOURCES OF FUNDING

Most education and training is funded from one or more of five sources: from government funds; from the learners themselves or their families, either through the payment of fees or by their meeting some of the indirect costs; from community support; from the private and nongovernment sector, and from funding agencies and donors. For the planner, government funding is likely to be a preferred option and one that can probably be expected to have a bias towards equity. There is a strong case for seeking public funding where open and distance learning is being used to extend the basic cycle of education to groups who cannot get to school, or where, as for teacher education, its use is to support the system generally. Where students are working as well as studying, or it is possible to assume they can do so even if there are no jobs, fees may appear to be an attractive option to the planner. Community resources are an important resource in many programmes of nonformal education, especially where student support rests on these. The Latin American radio schools, for example, have relied heavily on community resources, often provided through Roman Catholic church organisations. The private sector is involved in funding open and distance learning in various ways: for example, through corporate training programmes and by making broadcasting facilities available as a public-service activity. In Brazil, for example, private and public sector involvement in education has led to programmes for secondary equivalence and for teacher education (Oliveira and Orivel 1982, Oliveira forthcoming). External funding agencies have played an important role in the development and expansion of open universities: British support, for example, flowed for more than ten years to Allama Iqbal Open University in Pakistan.

State funding could almost be regarded as the default option: for many programmes public educators are likely to start by asking about the limits of what government can provide before thinking about other sources. But government funding often comes with constraints; within pluralist countries, some nongovernment organisations see a distancing of themselves from government as a positive advantage. Box 6.1 illustrates how the National Extension College in Britain, an educational nongovernment organisation, is funded, keeping itself by choice at arm's length from government. Student fees are often a staple source of funding.

Box 6.1   Funding the National Extension College

The National Extension College is a distance-teaching organisation, set up in 1963 to act as a pilot for the Open University and registered as a charity under English law. It was founded in the expectation that it would become self-financing by offering distance education courses of a quality that was not available from the commercial correspondence colleges which dominated distance education in Britain at the time. However, to start it off, its founding fathers sought and gained a grant and a loan from the Calouste Gulbenkian Foundation. It has once received general government funding. A postal strike in 1971 threatened to cripple it. Its chairman and director appealed to the Secretary of State for Education for a one-off rescue grant. Mrs Thatcher approved the grant and is reported to have said: 'How can I refuse you a few thousand when Harold Wilson gave millions to the Open University?'

Today its income is from three main sources. First, it still runs distance-education courses, for which students pay fees that have to be set at an economic price. Since one of its founding principles was the widening of access to education there is an inbuilt tension between economic pressure to put up fees and political desire to keep them down. The continuing demand for secondary equivalence courses, and for a range of professional courses, provides one source of income. Second, its learning materials are multi-purpose so that these are also sold to schools, colleges, companies and individuals who want materials without signing up for a course. Third, it runs a variety of educational projects under contract with other agencies in the private or public sector. It has, for example, run a degree programme for young employees of Coca-Cola Schweppes (described in Box 2.2), and projects for small business managers and prison officers among others.

This is not, however, the total picture of its funding. It works closely with publicly funded colleges of further education so that some of its courses are made available through them. From the college student's point of view the cost of these courses is shared between government (through the college) and the student (where a fee is paid). From time to time, too, government initiatives mean that state funding flows indirectly into the college where, for example, public agencies commission material from colleges or where students can themselves obtain grants for their study.

From time to time, as government attitudes to distance education have shifted from total suspicion to the launching of national initiatives, the college's trustees have asked themselves whether life would be better inside government rather than outside but decided not to pursue a move inside, even if that were possible, ultimately valuing flexibility over stability. Their judgement is heavily influenced by their reliance on three different income sources and by the fact that they can tap some government funding indirectly without coming under government control.

Funding is often mixed: Table 6.1 shows how funding from each of the five sources flowed to ten different projects of teacher education, itself an area that is generally funded with state finance. Even here, the sources of funding are more varied than might be expected; Chinese students pay fees and programmes funded from a single source are the exception rather then the rule. Funding may be mixed in a different sense, too, with different parts of a programme funded in different ways. If, for example, a programme can get access to state broadcasting facilities then these costs will fall on a different part of government from the Ministry of Education.

Trade-offs between different sources of funding in relation to the same set of teacher-education programmes were analysed in the following terms:

> In some jurisdictions there may be an expectation that government should meet the full costs of teacher education because of its impor-tance for the quality of the education service as a whole. Total funding from a ministry of education may hold down available funds and will give the ministry – and its finance section – strong direct control over the programme. There may therefore be pressure on the part of the institutions concerned to seek funds outside the ministry or to pass on some of the costs to the learners. On the other hand, the imposition of student fees may hold down enrolment, discourage students, and is likely to be socially regressive. There is little reported experience of the use of community resources in teacher education of this kind. The nature of private-sector and nongovernment involvement is culturally determined: this sector is involved in the projects in Brazil [providing inservice education for serving teachers with television and local face-to-face support] and at OLSET in South Africa [offering radio education to schools and teachers] but there are significant differences between the two. The provision in Brazil is through funds generated within the country by an established consortium, while OLSET is dependent on external, donor funding and despite its successes, seems unable to attract government funding. The freedom of action and non-bureaucratic structure that marks effective non-government organisations has to be balanced against difficulties they may face in integrating their work with regular state activity and ensuring its sustainability.
>
> External finance from funding agencies may also present problems of sustainability. Many funding agencies have been willing to meet capital costs, and to fund pilot projects, but expect governments to meet recurrent and continuing costs. Course development has some-times, but not always, been treated as capital expenditure even though its major cost element is likely to be for staff time.
>
> (Perraton *et al.* 2002: 49)

Table 6.1 Sources of funding of ten teacher-training projects

	Sources of funding				
	Government	*Fees*	*Community*	*Private sector and NGO*	*Funding agency*
Brazil: Television based inservice programme			✓		✓
Burkina Faso: Specialist project for headteachers				✓	✓
Chile: Inservice programme on computer education	✓	✓			
China: Television Teachers Training College	✓	✓	✓		
India: Open University Programme on Guidance	✓	✓			
Mongolia: Reorienting primary teachers to new approaches	✓				✓
Nigeria: National Teachers' Institute Initial Training Programme	✓	✓			
South Africa: OLSET Radio Project for schools and teachers					✓
South Africa: University degree programme	✓	✓			
Britain: Open University postgraduate certificate in education	✓				

Source: Perraton *et al.* 2001: 36–7

Different sectors of education have tended to be funded in different ways. Since basic education is almost universally accepted as the responsibility of government, one might expect that equivalence programmes of basic education should be state funded. Some, such as the long-established correspondence schools of Australia and New Zealand, are indeed funded in parallel with the funding of regular schools, but there are other patterns of funding. Many nonformal programmes, especially in Latin America and Africa, have been funded by charities and nongovernment organisations with students paying at most a nominal fee. Funding agencies, too, have helped to pay for some distance-education approaches used in school: interactive radio programmes have been established because there is external funding to meet those costs which are additional to the regular costs of schools. Students of the National Open School in India, in contrast, have to pay a fee which is in principle intended to cover the full cost as the organisation moves towards self-sufficiency. Much vocational education and training is funded by employers although sometimes with part of the cost being paid by the learner.

As already noted in Table 6.1, the funding of teacher education tends to be complex with funds flowing from all five types of source. In higher education, once institutions have been established, the costs of both dual-mode and open university institutions tend to be met in part by government and in part by student fees. A study of five open universities found, for example, that government funding met from 27 per cent of the cost (Israel) to 95 per cent in Germany while figures from Asian open universities tend to show a higher proportion of the cost falling on students with figures for government grant falling as low as 28 per cent in India and an expectation that the institution would become self-financing at the Bangladesh Open University. Some reported figures are given in Table 6.2.

The planner may want to consider not only the balance of funding between different sources but also the changing balance over time and the possibility of using different sources of income for different purposes. Many new institutions and projects have external funding in place at their foundation, either from a government grant, or a charitable foundation as in the case of the National Extension College already referred to, or from an international funding agency, as in the case of the Open Learning Systems Educational Trust in South Africa. Funding agencies, too, have often provided funds for initial planning activities. The Ford Foundation, for example, funded the initial planning that led to the establishment of the Botswana Extension College and the Mauritius College of the Air while international funds make it possible for the African National Congress to draw up a review of experience and blueprint for the future at the time of transition in South Africa. Continued reliance on external funding is more unusual though it has been a feature of nongovernment, development-oriented organisations such as AMREF – the African Flying doctor service

Table 6.2 Funding of some open universities

Institution and date	Percentage of income from			Comment
	Government	Student fee	Other	
Bangladesh: Open University 1995	n/a	75–114	n/a	Aims to be self-financing
Britain: Open University 1995	60			Bulk of other non-research funding is from student fees
Canada: Athabasca University 1995	57			
China: RTVUs 1988–89	52	5	43	Employers and other agencies separate from central government meet high proportion of costs
Germany: Fernuniversität 1995	95			By convention student fees are nominal in much of western Europe
India: IGNOU 1991–92	71	26	3	Government funding of IGNOU thought to have fallen since 1991–92
India: BRAOU 1995	28	60	3	
India: YCMOU 1995	30–45	65–70	n/a	Conventional students receive more state subsidy
Indonesia: University Terbuka 1992–93	41	38	21	
Israel: Open University 1995	27			
South Korea: Air Correspondence University 1993	62	38		
Spain: UNED 1995	40			
Sri Lanka: Open University 1991–93	67			
Thailand: STOU 1993	23	49	28	

Source: based on Guri-Rosenblit (1999: 174), Perraton (2000: 186–7)

which provides health education at a distance – and INADES-formation with forty years' experience of raising funds in Europe for rural education in Africa. For the most part, however, once programmes are established, they generally need to look to students and to government for the bulk of their expenditure, even while seeking other funds for new and experimental developments.

In that search for funds it may be useful to consider separately the range of activities to be provided; these are likely to vary in their demands for capital or recurrent expenditure and may lend themselves to funding from different sources. (Traditions of pluralism help: the Brazilian project already referred to in Table 6.1 benefited from being able to call on a group of private- and public-sector agencies (Oliveira forthcoming).) In this search, too, it is necessary to ask where the costs will fall. If teaching materials are delivered physically to students, for example, then the costs of doing so will fall on the institution which may or may not then decide to recover them. But if students have to collect materials, or they are provided electronically so that they have to download and print them, then the costs are passed entirely to the students. The choice of technology may call for decisions about the location of costs; in many cases it will be reasonable to assume that a learner has a radio and, in more and more parts of the world, access to television. Using computer-based approaches forces the institution either into requiring students to have a computer or into providing one: often threatening to limit access in one case and the budget in the other. Decisions here will vary from case to case. Some of those required for teacher education are set out in Table 6.3.

An analysis of these costs argued that:

> The development of teaching materials, as already noted, requires expenditure before students are enrolled. A variety of strategies have been used for funding this, depending on the organisational structure chosen for the programme. . . . Strategies need to be put in place that allow for the effective development and editing of material that is fair to staff and ensures materials are delivered on time (see Perraton and Creed 1999). Funds for writers are not enough: editing of materials, to ensure their educational effectiveness and get them to camera-ready state or undertake desktop publishing is likely to cost as much as their initial writing.
>
> The costs for reproducing and distributing teaching materials may fall in various places. If material is broadcast, transmission costs may be met by the broadcasting agency. . . .
>
> Costs for reception of materials for an individual learner will often fall on the learner. . . . Where the distance-teaching system brings learners together there may be costs for the development or supply of specialist centres or equipment or negotiations for their use by learners

Table 6.3 Activities and resources

Activity to be funded	Type of funding required	Comments on possible sources
Planning and initiation	One-off	May be from MOE funds but often also from funding and international agencies
Materials development	Funding mainly for staff time but may be treated as capital where materials are used over several years	Upfront funding usually from MOE, NGO or funding agency grants. Funds for revision and updating also required
Materials reproduction and distribution	Recurrent	Regular expenditure that may be recovered from operating grant or from student fees Where distribution is through public broadcasting, government mail, or by internet, costs may be borne on other budgets
Reception costs	May be some capital (e.g. supply of radios, development of video-conference facilities) but recurrent costs then arise	Initial funding may be from one-off grant (e.g. funding agency) Individual recurrent costs (e.g. maintenance of radios, computers) likely to fall on individual learner/centre
Student support and classroom practice	Recurrent	Regular expenditure that may be recovered from operating grant or from student fees It may be possible for some costs (e.g. for deployment of school or college staff to support students) to be met from other institutional budgets
Training and capacity building	Recurrent	Heavy initial expenditure needed, especially where project is unfamiliar to those working on it, but continuing expenditure then required
Maintenance	Recurrent	Continuing expenditure that is often neglected (especially for materials updating) and needs to be built into budgets for previous areas

Source: Perraton et al. 2002

(e.g. the supply of radios, development of videoconference facilities, the use of telecentres).

There will always be costs for the continuing support of students and arrangements for supervision of their teaching practice (where it is likely to be possible to use existing resources within the educational system, providing that their costs, including the opportunity costs, of this are acceptable). . . .

Funding will be needed for training and capacity building, especially as an unfamiliar project is being set up. . . . Finally, funding is not a once-off activity: maintenance of the whole system, of any equipment, and of teaching materials all incur costs. The costs of maintaining teaching materials, in particular, are often under-estimated at the outset: the effort to get them created the first time diverts attention from setting up a programme of continuing revision, improvement and updating.

(Perraton *et al.* 2002: 51)

Slightly different questions will need to be answered for other areas of education; these are included not so much as a guide to the answers, but as an illustration of the kind of questions that the planner will ask.

CONCLUSION

In choosing between possible sources of funding, the planner is engaged in politics as well as economics and forced to make several different kinds of trade-off.

The first set of political questions are about the use of public funds. Many distance educators argue that their students deserve public expenditure on the same basis as those attending conventional institutions. In rare cases, this is accepted as a principle. Historically, for example, Australian part-time university students have been funded in the same way, whether studying on the campus or at a distance. In England, the recently established Learning and Skills Council, in trying to formulate a policy for funding different styles of education, has argued that the mode of study should not influence the level of public subsidy which it provides. Where completion rates are lower for distance education than for conventional education, this policy means that the cost per successful student for distance education is higher than the cost for conventional education. Much more often it is argued that, as distance education is done part-time, students may be expected to meet a significant proportion of the costs. Distance-education students are also scattered, which makes it more difficult for them to organise and protest at disproportionate fees even if they are seen as such.

The political standing of open and distance learning affects its capacity to gain funding from anything other than student fees. So does the shortage of data about its outcomes, discussed in Chapter 11. Institutions seeking generous public funding need to document and make their case. The economic choices are likely to require trade-offs between access and quality, between variety and cost, and between enterprise and sustainability.

Where students are required to meet some or all of the costs of their course there is likely to be pressure from them to keep costs down while educational planners, seeking quality and often wanting to use a range of different media, will feel the need to keep expenditure up. The poorest students will not be able to afford the best courses, or to finance their development. The nature of open and distance learning gives an extra twist to the argument. Many practitioners will argue that student support, and face-to-face meetings with students, are a necessary part of high-quality distance education and that they are likely to increase completion rates. (Surprisingly, we lack good research data to establish that this is the case.) In their absence, e-learning systems demand interaction through computer communication, probably at even higher cost (Rumble 2001). But these are the elements of open and distance learning in which there are no economies of scale. It follows that the administratively attractive option of ensuring that student fees cover all the variable costs of open and distance learning may either result in fees that are socially regressive or hold down the quality of educational service.

The trade-off between variety and cost is similar. If large numbers of students can be enrolled on a small handful of courses, then the fixed cost per student falls. The pressures towards variety, whether from student demand, or a sense of market need, or from the interest of academic staff who want to develop courses in their own specialism, are all likely to increase the cost per student. They will not do so if new courses attract new students in as big measure as old but, in practice, pressures for more variety for a fixed number of students are common and difficult for the planner to resist. Henry Ford had it easy selling black cars.

The trade-off between enterprise and sustainability may be as difficult as the others. In many jurisdictions it is not too difficult to raise one-off funding for enterprising new projects: charities and international funding agencies are looking for new solutions to long-standing problems. But funding to maintain new approaches beyond a pilot is more demand-ing and has resulted in the demise of – even promising – ventures in open and distance learning. The government of Côte d'Ivoire, for example, closed down its educational television service, into which the World Bank, UNESCO and the government of France had poured millions, once it had to meet the recurrent costs itself. Enterprise should not be stifled, and some of the best projects have been started in the exciting hope that something will turn up. The pessimistic and cautious planner will, however, have thought about long-term recurrent funding if only to have an answer to the sceptical agency's questions about sustainability.

REFERENCES

Guri-Rosenblit, S. (1999) *Distance and Campus Universities: Tensions and Interactions*, Oxford: Pergamon.

Oliveira, J. B. (forthcoming) 'Brazil: Television-plus – journalism in the service of teacher education', in H. Perraton *et al.* (eds) *International Case Studies of Teacher Education Through Distance Learning*, Paris: UNESCO.

Oliveira, J. B. and Orivel, F. (1982) 'The Minerva project in Brazil', in H. Perraton (ed.) *Alternative Routes to Formal Education: Distance Teaching for School Equivalency*, Baltimore, MD: Johns Hopkins University Press.

Perraton, H. (2000) *Open and Distance Learning in the Developing World*, London: Routledge.

Perraton, H. and Creed, C. (1999) *Distance Education Practice: Training and Rewarding Authors*, London: Department for International Development.

Perraton, H., Robinson, B. and Creed, C. (2001) *Teacher Education Through Distance Learning: Technology, Curriculum, Cost, Evaluation*, Paris: UNESCO.

Perraton, H., Creed, C. and Robinson, B. (2002) *Teacher Education Guidelines: Using Open and Distance Learning*, Paris: UNESCO.

Rumble, G. (2001) 'The costs and costing of networked learning', *Journal of Asynchronous Learning Networks* 5, 2: 75–96 (available at http://www.aln.org).

Part III

Process

The weakness of the input–output model of education, first discussed on p. 4, is that it concentrates on resources and results rather than the all-important process. And yet it is the process that matters; for many educators process is of the essence, while for many children and adults we remember and mind about what happened in the classroom or playground more than the marks we got, or the wages our teachers got.

As in conventional education, the process of managing open and distance learning shapes the quality of learners' experience. Questions about management take us back to resources and on to outcomes; choices about the deployment of resources will in turn influence and to some extent determine those outcomes. This section therefore sets out to ask how we can best manage the resources needed for open and distance learning in order to provide a good education, as well as one that scores adequately on outcomes that can be readily measured. Key decisions on the process of management are needed about organisational structure, the choices of technology, the changes brought by globalisation, and the arrangements for governance, quality control and accreditation.

In examining how to manage the process of open and distance learning we begin by looking, in Chapter 7, at organisational options, since these provide the framework within which all the other management choices will be made. The options here are necessarily different from those for conventional education and less familiar to many educators. Rumble and Latchem look at the structural options that will meet the needs of the various audiences and educational purposes examined in Part II above. They look in particular at the merits of free-standing or dual-mode institutions, either limited to open and distance learning or combining distance and conventional approaches under one administration. Structural decisions here will also affect the way materials are developed and students are tutored and supported; these topics are not examined in detail here, partly because many of the decisions are at a management rather than a policy level but as much because they are covered extensively in the literature (e.g. Lewis 1984, Lockwood 1998, Mills and Tait 1996, Rowntree 1994, Simpson 2002).

In Chapter 8 we move on to questions about the choice of technology or teaching media, examining the options available to policy makers and their consequences for learners, for tutors and for costs. The policy maker has to find a balance here between convenience for the learner, teaching effectiveness and variety, and cost. New technologies are bringing new issues; computer-based learning allows new kinds of interaction between students and tutors, and provokes new questions about the need for synchronous and asynchronous communication under differing circumstances.

Policy choices about both organisation and the deployment of technologies have begun to be reshaped by globalisation, examined in Chapter 9. Given the appropriate technology, educational resources can now be carried across borders almost as easily as they can be taken outside the walls of a conventional school or college to the community just outside. Institutions, in both the public and the private sector, have seen this as an opportunity to spread their influence, or widen their market. Globalisation is forcing on to the policy-maker's agenda questions about new kinds of collaboration and competition and about the changing role of a teaching institution now that educational materials, once part of its stock in trade, are marketed internationally or available free at the click of a mouse.

Judicious responses to questions about organisation, technology, and the new global context, should in turn ensure the quality of the educational process. At the same time, measures to ensure good governance and to safeguard quality are usually needed and in some jurisdictions required. In Chapter 10 we look at the variety of measures put in place to govern and accredit distance-teaching institutions and the policy questions that need to be addressed at an institutional, national or international level. The discussion here takes as a starting point the shifting focus of responsibility for quality, seen increasingly as something for a number of stakeholders rather than solely the concern of government. It goes on to look at questions about the location and mechanism of structures to govern institutions and assure quality for learners.

Three themes run through all four chapters. First, in each area authors examine the contrasts, similarities and differences between open and distance learning and conventional education. At one level, open and distance learning necessitates a new set of policy decisions for educators whether about organisation or technology or quality control among other themes. But at the same time there is evidence, already touched on in Chapter 2, of the convergence between conventional and distance approaches so that some of those policy decisions also demand the attention of conventional institutions. Convergence, and comparison between alternatives, inevitably provoke questions about parity of esteem between different approaches to education; the authors of Chapter 7 warn against the possible marginalisation of open and distance learning while Chapter 10 notes that open and distance learning still lacks a measure of credibility in countries as different as New Zealand and Malaysia. In Part IV below we look at the evidence needed to determine the legitimacy of open and distance learning, as compared with conventional education, but in this context we need also to examine how, and how well, it is managed.

Second, open and distance learning almost always requires partnerships. As technologies change and global relations develop, so the opportunities for partnerships become more varied, and questions about management and about governance and quality more complex. Chapter 8 looks at a variety of models for partnerships while Chapter 9 examines the new role of brokers. Partnerships necessarily distribute the responsibility for quality assurance and are likely to make its management more difficult. And, in any form of partnership, decisions are needed about the location and nature of student support, usually critical to quality for the individual learner.

Third, while Chapter 10 concentrates on issues of governance and quality control, this theme runs strongly through the other three chapters. The form in which quality is assessed and managed is a function of the management structure adopted. Questions of the quality of the educational experience need to be addressed in choosing technologies while accountability and governance become more complex where technologies diffuse responsibility among partners. Globalisation forces us to take a new look at quality, and at ways of ensuring it within new and changing organisational forms.

REFERENCES

Lewis, R. (1984) *How to Tutor and Support Learners*, London: Council for Educational Technology.

Lockwood, F. (1998) *The Design and Production of Self-instructional Materials*, London: Kogan Page.

Mills, R. and Tait, A. (1996) *Supporting the Learner in Open and Distance Learning*, London: Pitman.

Rowntree, D. (1994) *Preparing Materials for Open, Distance and Flexible Learning: An Action Guide for Teachers and Trainers*, London: Kogan Page.

Simpson, O. (2002) *Supporting Students in Online, Open and Distance Learning*, London: Kogan Page.

Chapter 7

Organisational models for open and distance learning

Greville Rumble and Colin Latchem

This chapter examines the strengths and weaknesses of various organisational models used to provide distance and open learning and why these have emerged. It concludes by looking into the future and at the emergent structures for e-distance education.

ALL ON ITS OWN – THE SINGLE-MODE OPTION

In 1987, Perry and Rumble wrote *A Short Guide to Distance Education* and one of its chapters dealt with the question, 'Which organisational model to choose'. Life was simpler then, and only three possibilities were considered:

- single-mode institutions, founded to provide either face-to-face education or distance education;
- dual-mode institutions, designed to teach both on- and off-campus;
- distance-education consortia of educational, publishing, broadcasting and other organisations.

The authors concluded that:

- single-mode distance education systems 'have a first loyalty to distance education', battle against scepticism to achieve real standards and professionalism in distance education, are expensive to develop and therefore need to be big to achieve economies of scale;
- dual-mode institutions in theory offer courses of exactly the same standards on- and off-campus, but in practice have to overcome many difficulties to do this (not least the lower level of interest that academics often demonstrated towards the demands of their off-campus students, and the lower status accorded the distance operation within a traditional institution);
- consortia 'are a splendid idea which all too seldom work in practice'.

The arguments for single-mode distance education institutions stem partly from the history of distance education, partly from beliefs in their inherent superiority, and partly from arguments about economies of scale.

The first distance-teaching organisations – the commercial corre-spondence schools dating from about 1840 when Pitman's correspondence school for the teaching of shorthand was established – were single-mode institutions, created to provide training for those entering the expanding commercial and business world of nineteenth-century Europe and America. The correspondence schools were run essentially as businesses and many pursued profit at the expense of quality. Students paid all or most of their fees up front, tutors were paid on a piecework basis, and high drop-out rates coupled with up-front payments maximised profits from what the industry called 'drop-out money' (Noble 2000: 15). Poor-quality 'correspondence education' gave the business a bad name and as a consequence, when the British Open University was first proposed, it met with considerable scepticism (Perry 1976: 18–19, 32–3) as did the start-up of, for example, the Bangladesh Open University (Shamsher Ali 1997: 153) and the Open University of Hong Kong (Boshier and Pratt 1997).

Concern for the quality of single-mode institutions leads some to suggest that standards are better maintained within a dual-mode setting, as dis-cussed below. However, in a number of jurisdictions across the globe, as, for example, Perry (1976: 5) noted of the United Kingdom, and Leibbrandt (1997: 102) of the Netherlands, traditional institutions were originally extremely reluctant to teach adults (one of the main markets for distance education), or engage with distance education. Setting up new institutions thus proved to be an effective strategy for bypassing intransigent tradi-tional institutions, although their success was always dependent upon strong political backing (Dodd and Rumble 1984). As Hanna and Associates (2000: 134) observe, most of the open universities were established by national governments to serve goals that were more immediately political and overtly developmental than the other models of open and distance education. For example, establishing a single-mode open university:

- does away with the need to push change through traditional institu-tions which, as Lewis (1994), Bashir (1998), Lueddeke (1998) and Ellis (2000) show, requires institutions to rethink their priorities and change their cultures;
- means that there is no 'wasteful duplication of effort and resources through co-operation and collaboration', which was the concern of the British Columbia Minister of Education when setting up the Open Learning Institute of BC (Ellis 1997: 87);
- means that there is no need to 'bring together institutions differing in so many ways in their traditions, regional interests and political experiences under a national umbrella organisation which still has to

be tried and tested' – a course of action that the Minister of Higher Education and Research, in the government of North-Rhine-Westphalia that set up the FernUniversität, did not believe could work (Peters 1997: 57).

Throughout the 1970s and early 1980s, writers such as Peters (1973: 310, 1983), Perry (1976: 55), Daniel and Smith (1979: 64), and Snowden and Daniel (1980), argued that the administrative structures of conventional institutions were not best suited to the development and management of distance education. The view was that distance-education systems involved a number of quasi-industrial processes and that the best results would be obtained where the corporate culture encouraged adherence to production schedules, and where academics and managers understood the very different cost structures and hence budgetary needs of distance-teaching methods. Strong arguments were also advanced that the needs of part-time, adult students were served better through institutions teaching wholly at a distance. The marginalisation of distance-education students in dual-mode institutions lent support to this view, as evidenced by, for example, the Indian Correspondence Directorates (Singh 1979: 87), the University of Zambia (Siaciwena 1988: 201), and the US experience (Hall 1991: 31). These arguments were also bolstered by the success of the British Open University, whose much evaluated system showed that a dedicated distance-education system could deliver high-quality teaching materials, responsive and effective student support, and excellent administration and logistics.

The case for separatism was strengthened further by arguments based upon the distinctive technology of distance education. In the 1970s and 1980s, the argument that distance education was a technologically based form of education with a distinct pedagogy was easier to make than today with the mix of on- and off-campus resource-based independent and collaborative learning. Since then the expansion of higher education, the failure of governments to provide commensurate resources, and the consequent scramble to compete for new fee-for-service and national and international markets, have led 'traditional' institutions to adopt approaches that lessen the amount of direct contact between teacher and student and erode the difference between the 'on-campus' and 'off-campus' learning experience.

Single-mode institutions have one distinct advantage, and that is their capacity to be very large indeed. All the large-scale dedicated distance-education systems, from India's National Open School to the 'mega-universities'– single-mode distance-teaching universities with more than 100,000 enrolees (Daniel 1996) such as China's TV University System, the University of South Africa, Turkey's Anadolu University, the Centre National d'Enseignement à Distance in France and the British Open

University – aim for economies of scale. However, such economies can be achieved only by restricting the scope of the curriculum. Single-mode distance-education systems cannot offer the variety of courses provided by traditional institutions without:

- incurring heavy investment costs in courseware production and spreading their student bodies more thinly so that course populations come down; and/or
- adopting course-design strategies that reduce the amount of in-house production of materials and require students to buy textbooks or other generic resources unsuited to remote learners.

Daniel (1996: 32, 1998) makes the case for the long-term future of the 'mega-universities'. He points out that the eleven mega-universities, as a group, enrol 2.8 million students at an average institutional cost per student that is at most half that of the combined 182 higher education institutions in the United Kingdom (about $10,000 per student with 1.6 million students) or the 3,500 institutions in the US higher education system (about $12,500 with some 14 million students). However, this argument applies only to first-generation (correspondence-based) and second-generation (multimedia-based) distance-teaching institutions which depend heavily upon materials-based learning, reduce the amount of direct contact between students and teachers, and enrol large numbers of students. Such institutions can achieve economies of scale because they replace traditional teaching methods, which are labour intensive (and have low fixed costs but high variable cost structure), with a capital-intensive form of teaching based on high up-front investment in materials production but low teaching costs (giving high fixed and low variable cost structure).

In the small-scale 'cottage industry' distance education found in both the public and private sectors, a few people can create the materials, tutor the students and manage the administration. However, distance-teaching institutions with significant curricula and large enrolments have to resort to specialisation and division of labour. Generally, administration is hived off to become a separate and powerful function that regulates what academics do – with the aim of achieving economies of process – while the traditional academic task of designing *and* teaching the course is divided between those who design and write the materials and those who tutor and assess the students. These differences are then reflected in the employment patterns with administrative staff almost invariably on permanent full-time contracts; the academics who create the material on full-time contracts (as at the British Open University) or short-term authorial contracts (as at the National Extension College in Britain); and the tutors on hourly contracts (for conducting tutorials), or piecework rates (for scripts marked). This reliance on part-time staff on the periphery is one of the key structural features of single-mode distance education, and a key factor in its cost-efficiency. It may also be its Achilles' heel because such staff may receive inadequate induction and training in the institutional values and practices, have no control over the course content and assessment criteria, and may not perceive themselves as stakeholders, all of which factors impact on the quality of their work.

Until a few years ago, all single-mode distance-teaching institutions were 'correspondence' or 'multimedia' based. The advent of third-generation systems, based on interactive technologies offering the possibility of much enhanced teacher–student contact at a distance, has changed the cost structure of distance education, moving it from high-fixed, low-variable cost to a (potentially) high-fixed, high-variable cost. Institutions adopting the new interactive online technologies are likely to see their unit costs increase sharply once their teachers demand wages in line with the amount of time they put into supporting the students. The rise in unit costs pushes up the costs to the students, and/or of the governmental subsidies. The former will run into elasticities of demand, the latter into pressures to curb subsidies – and the only way this can be done will be to reduce the size of the institutions, or to find some very different structural solutions, some of which are discussed below.

The second problem with Daniel's thesis is that he compares the 'mega-universities' with systems that are still highly traditional in their teaching methods. If the traditional system were to become fully re-engineered, adopting open and flexible learning methods to teach both off-campus and on-campus students, the comparison might be somewhat different. In the absence of proper research to inform decision makers, the better option is scepticism, not least because the studies that we do have suggest that the adoption of flexible learning and independent study within traditional institutions has brought unit costs down sharply. Scott (1997: 38), for example, points out that:

> the massification of British higher education is demonstrated [by] the sharp reduction in unit costs. Overall productivity gains of more than 25 per cent have been achieved since 1990. . . . This pattern, which exactly matches the expansion of student numbers, closely follows the cost curves in other countries where mass higher education systems developed earlier than in Britain. *It supports the claim that mass systems have a quite different economy from that of élite systems* [italics added].

One of the reasons why first- and second-generation single-mode distance-education systems have been so successful in reaching large audiences and reducing unit costs has been their adoption of industrialised approaches to education. The thesis that distance education is an industrial-ised form of education was advanced first by Otto Peters who, drawing on

Weber's concept of bureaucracy, argued that it was a highly rationalised form of education involving mechanisation, standardisation, the use of capital-intensive technologies, centralised planning and control, division of labour, reduction in the autonomy of the academic producers, and an objectivisation of the production process leading to increased alienation (see e.g. Peters 1973, 1983).

The bureaucratisation of education is, however, by no means restricted to distance education: it is now endemic in traditional campus-based systems (cf. Ritzer 1993, 1998). Ritzer holds that in the United States, education, including higher education, has been marked by 'the culmination of a series of rationalisation processes that have been occurring throughout the twentieth century' that are best exemplified in the practices of the McDonald's fast food chain (Ritzer 1993: 31–2). He points to:

- the pressures for efficiency (larger classes, reliance on resource-based learning and particularly customised textbooks, and the use of machine-graded multiple-choice questions for assessment);
- calculability (use of Grade Point Averages to summarise in one figure a student's achievement, quantified examinations to filter applicants, and student rating forms to evaluate professors);
- predictability (imposed by the format and grading of multiple-choice questions, thus eliminating subjective judgement on the part of professors);
- control (training students to accept highly rationalised procedures such as objective testing, timed lesson plans, and the definition of what is to be taught in particular lessons); and, as an outcome,
- the growth of irrationality, with many staff and students put off by 'the huge factory-like atmosphere of these universities' where education can be 'a de-humanising experience', and in which it is difficult for students to get to know other students, and virtually impossible for them to know their professors.

(Ritzer 1993: 55–7, 73–7, 115–16, 141–2)

Thus education – including distance education – is perceived to have succumbed to a characteristically twentieth-century form of administration based upon large-scale hierarchies and large-scale mass production, both of which are encompassed within the concept of Fordism (Campion 1995). Some distance educators have been deeply critical of the implications of Fordism for distance education, namely, the increased administrative control and disempowerment and deskilling of academic staff (see e.g. Campion 1991, Campion and Renner 1992). Fordist structures are also seen as resulting in low levels of product variety and process innovation (Campion and Renner 1992: 9).

Given such criticism, it is not surprising that post-Fordist models involving product innovation, process variability and labour responsibility have proved attractive to academics, both as a means of retaining autonomous control over their courses (ibid.: 11), and providing a rapid response to the demands of the consumer. Third-generation distance education, giving power to the academic to control and change course content and pace, and providing a more constructivist learning environment, approaches a post-Fordist ideal by reducing 'the need for reliance upon bureaucratic structures and practices' (Campion 1995: 211). These ideas will be explored further below.

LOCATING DISTANCE EDUCATION WITHIN THE EXISTING INSTITUTION – THE DUAL-MODE OPTION

There are basically two ways in which dual-mode institutions can teach both on-campus and off-campus students: through asynchronous 'correspondence' methodologies using print, correspondence, multimedia and the internet/web (which can encourage autonomous and constructivist learning), and by extending the traditional classroom by using face-to-face instruction via satellite television and other connective technologies (which tends to reinforce teacher-centred approaches).

If some jurisdictions have found the single-mode approach more appropriate, others – for example, Australia and Sweden (see Dodd and Rumble 1984) – believe that the dual-mode approach provides a more satisfactory outcome. The first American university to widen access through an extension service using correspondence methods was the Illinois Wesleyan University which in 1874 introduced undergraduate and graduate courses at a distance. The University of Chicago followed along with others so that by 1919, seventy-three colleges and universities were offering distance-education courses (Noble 2000: 15). Similar developments occurred in Australian, Canadian and Soviet higher education. At the school level, correspondence education was also introduced in Europe, Australia, Canada and the Soviet Union to support home-based learners or learners in small disadvantaged schools, typically in remote and rural areas.

The quality of these programmes was again a matter for concern. In the USA, although the universities were not-for-profit organisations, they were caught in the same economic web as the commercial colleges, so that:

> Before long, with a degraded product and a dropout rate as bad as the commercial firms, they had come to depend on dropout money. At the end of the 1920s . . . Abraham Flexner, a distinguished and influential observer of higher education, excoriated the universities for commercial preoccupations, for compromising their independence and integrity, and abandoning their unique and essential function of disinterested critical and creative enquiry.
>
> (Noble 2000: 15, reporting Flexner 1930)

This reads like a critique of the university of the late twentieth century (see e.g. Halsey 1995, Smyth 1995, Barnett and Griffin 1997, Readings 1997, Barnett 2000). However, it was essentially a criticism of the values of the departments set up within the universities in the earlier decades of the twentieth century to extend the teaching and learning beyond the physical boundaries of the institutions, and this view has never been totally countered. According to Noble (2000: 15), some thirty years after Flexner's criticism, 'the General Accounting Office was warning Vietnam veterans not to waste their federal funds on such [distance-education] courses'. More recently, Perraton (2000: 199) reminds us that while distance education has had a measure of success, a harsher view is of an approach to education that is 'regarded as a second-rate system used to offer a shadow of education while withholding its substance'. Perraton ends his survey of distance education in the developing world: 'Paraphrasing Gandhi, my answer to the question "can we make open and distance learning as good as conventional education?" will be "I think it would be a good idea"' (Perraton 2000: 200).

The different approaches to the organisation of dual-mode systems have been exactly this – attempts to make distance education as good as conventional education. Distance-education programmes could be set up by individual departments (as happened at the University of Waterloo in Canada) or by the institution as a whole. In the latter case, a central administrative unit might be set up to coordinate the distance-teaching activities of a number of departments – as at the University of Zambia and the University of New England – while in other cases, a separate unit was established to teach and administer the distance programme, as occurred at the University of Queensland, Deakin University (until 1982), and in the Indian Correspondence Directorate system. This second model, isolating the distance system from the mainstream university, tended to reinforce the second-class status of distance education; in India, for example, the Correspondence Directorates were accorded low status (Singh 1979: 87). Integration along the lines of the 'New England model' was seen as the solution to this problem (Smith 1979: 200). However, this model has also been criticised because it 'tends to transfer an internal teaching model to the external teaching situation' (Ortmeier 1982). Certainly, integration has not always worked well. Siaciwena (1983: 70), reporting on problems encountered at the University of Zambia where the New England structure was adopted, said that 'the system of assigning the same lecturers to both internal and external students has, in fact, been disadvantageous to the correspondence programme' because overworked staff tended to use the available time for internal teaching and ignore external teaching, which they found exacting and difficult. Such negative attitudes, he concluded, 'undermine both the status of correspondence education and the very concept of parity of standards' (ibid.: 71).

The integrated model developed at New England nevertheless retained a degree of separation, inasmuch as the external students were administered through a separate unit. However, when in 1982 Deakin University adopted the integrated model it absorbed the administrative as well as the academic services into the mainstream structures of the university. Although this change was criticised by those who thought 'that off-campus students need a special unit of their own because "out of sight, out of mind" can all too easily become true' (Jevons 1984: 27), the fully integrated approach worked well. Nevertheless, it is worth interjecting a note of caution here: what works well in one setting may not do so elsewhere, particularly where there is no shared vision and support from senior management, and distance learning is still perceived as a marginal activity diverting scarce resources, embraced by a few and threatening time-honoured roles and practices.

These different approaches – once deeply contentious – are ceasing to have relevance in a number of countries. In Australia, for example, as in many other countries, higher education has been confronted with changes in student demographics, the need to provide for nontraditional students and demands for expansion while experiencing severe cuts in government funding and staffing. The universities have had to search for cheaper ways to teach these greater numbers of more diverse students and new ways of generating income, and with the mainstreaming of technology into teaching and learning. The answer has been seen to lie in flexible resource-based learning. Thus on-campus teaching has become more distant – not in geographical terms, but in transactional terms, which is a function of two variables: dialogue and structure (Moore 1983:157). Dialogue involves interaction between the learner and the teacher. First- and second-generation distance-education systems, and dehumanised forms of 'traditional' higher education such as Ritzer's McUniversity, permit little dialogue. Structure is a measure of the programme's responsiveness to individual needs – what is sometimes referred to in Britain as 'openness' (Lewis 1990). Fordist distance-education systems – rationalised, predictable and formalised – are highly structured. These features, combined as they are in first- and second-generation distance-education systems, make for highly distant systems.

The distance in these systems can be mitigated to a degree by increasing the amount of dialogue and loosening the regulatory tightness of the systems – but both of these strategies cost money. The current tendency, as Scott (1997: 38) reminds us, is to drive down costs. Australian universities have realised that they can reduce the costs of their on-campus provision by using the same methods and materials to teach their on-campus and off-campus students, replacing the labour-intensive lecture with the videotape, self-instructional text or internet/web material, and generally reducing the amount of contact time between students and teachers (see

Taylor and White 1991). Moreover, they can do this without cutting back on the curriculum. Rumble (1992) argued that this ability to deliver a wide curriculum cheaply gave dual-mode institutions a distinct competitive advantage over their single-mode counterparts. Renwick (1996: 59–60) suggests that traditional universities adopting dual-mode approaches may have an edge on single-mode providers because 'they already offer a wide range of degrees and qualifications that rival open universities, could diversify at less cost, would not necessarily have to rely on large numbers of enrolments to be viable as providers of distance programmes, and could offer a wider range of options to potential students'. In the process, the distinction between distance and traditional education, on-campus and off-campus, is blurred and replaced by flexible learning.

COLLABORATION – THE NETWORKED ALTERNATIVE

As mentioned above, Perry and Rumble (1987) suggested that consortia 'are a splendid idea which all too seldom work in practice'. This judgement derived from such ill-fated consortia as the University of Mid-America and the Università a Distanza in Italy, both of which demonstrated the inherent instability of collaborative ventures in distance and open education. On the other hand, the National Technological University (NTU) in the USA provided an early example of the potential benefits of collaboration, even though it ultimately failed to achieve the graduate enrolments originally envisaged (Cunningham *et al.* 2000). The NTU was established as an independent university with its own accreditation and degree programme authorisations, and functions as an administrative and coordinating unit for the engineering departments of over thirty participating universities that provide graduate and non-credit distance-education programmes for such major corporations as IBM and Motorola, by means of live, satellite video courses uplinked from the originating universities.

Today, the imperatives of global competition, the opportunities provided by telecommunications, and the need to leverage complementary strengths for greater market share and geographic coverage are leading to an increasing number of interinstitutional, intersector and international consortia. These include, for example, the Scottish Knowledge global higher education consortium, comprising Scotland's fourteen universities, Australia's Edith Cowan University and other providers, together with News International plc, which is targeting the international corporate sector with postgraduate distance-education courses; a number of multinational university consortia such as Universitas 21, which aims to establish itself as a major force in international distance education by a partnership of elite universities; and the American Education Consortium (ADEC) with sixty institutional and affiliate members providing specialised courses from their members and using satellite time to make them available (Poley 2001).

What we are witnessing here is the internationalisation, competitiveness and commercialisation of distance education leading to a plethora of mating calls and courtship rituals between public and private organisations as they reposition themselves in a volatile market and adapt to the realities of what Alvin Tofler (1980) calls the third wave economy. Tofler (ibid.: 263) characterises the second wave organisations as: large; hierarchical; permanent; top-down; mechanistic; and designed to deliver repetitive products and decisions in a relatively stable environment. In the third wave economy, dominated by service organisations and transformed by new technology, he suggests that there is a need for organisational systems rather than physical entities and that these new systems cut across traditional managements, departments and functions and operate through a variety of networks, partnerships and alliances which are interactive, interorganisational and international. These systems are 'messily open' rather than 'neatly closed', comprising temporary configurations of organisations that share common interests and which members join and leave as opportunities arise and wane.

Such network configurations are not restricted to postsecondary education. India's National Open School (NOS), a system developed to serve educational drop-outs and provide alternative foundation, secondary and vocational education, operates through its headquarters in New Delhi, regional centres in Kolkata for the eastern region, Pune for the western region, Hyderabad for the southern region, Agra for the northern region, and Guwahati for the north-eastern region, and 1000 centres, comprising a mix of:

- institutions committed to the poor and educational drop-outs;
- commercial or nongovernment agency centres;
- institutions lacking the minimum necessary infrastructure and qualified teachers;
- institutions with good buildings, laboratories, libraries, workshops and qualified teachers to teach the relevant subjects;
- private schools running a parallel fee-for-service 'open school stream' for regular day scholars who find difficulty with science and mathematics.

Only through such networking and partnership can the NOS reach out to serve the huge numbers of pupils who drop out from India's 112,000 secondary schools. In 1998 to 1999, the NOU had more than 500,000 students on its rolls and an annual enrolment of over 130,000, of which 35 per cent was female.

Consortia, partnerships, strategic alliances and so on are formed by educational, training and corporate providers for a variety of reasons, but principally to:

- share costs or spread these over a larger number of students;
- share courses, resources and academic and commercial experience and expertise;
- share risk;
- form alliances with potential competitors and interlopers;
- attract funding opportunities (particularly in the European Union which makes interinstitutional collaboration a condition of funding);
- form public–private partnerships to provide online courses, as with Colorado's community college system contracting with e-College (Bates 2000: 173) and the global consortium using online education company NextEd's technology to deliver programmes into international markets;
- achieve a competitive edge and greater market share;
- be fast to market or cope with major market demand through joint course development and optimising complementary strengths, as shown by Open Learning Australia in its earlier years of operation (Latchem and Pritchard 1994), and the joint Master's in Social Work developed by Cleveland State University and Akron University (Bates 2000: 166);
- promote and operate credit transfer/recognition of prior learning systems, as with the three research universities and Open Learning Agency in British Columbia (Bates 2000: 168), and the Australian universities involved with Open Learning Australia;
- jointly market and broker programmes, as with Open Learning Australia, California Virtual University (Bates 2000: 171–2) and Western Governors' University (Cunningham *et al.* 2000: 46);
- capitalise on partners' knowledge of, and reputations in, local markets;
- accommodate other countries' governmental requirements for local institution involvement as a condition of entry;
- ensure adequate provision of local services such as marketing, counselling, admissions, registration and examination invigilation;
- de-bundle learning materials, tutorial support and course assessment to provide expanded market opportunities, as with Athabasca University's partnership with TAC, a private Japanese company whose adult learners sit the American CPA exams and use Athabasca University's courseware and summative assessment while TAC provides on-site learner support and tutoring (Abrioux 2001);
- achieve a franchise arrangement, as between the University of British Columbia and Monterrey Institute of Technology in Mexico with its twenty-six campuses in Mexico and Latin America (Bates 2000: 164).

Establishing consortia, partnerships and other such interdependent systems can be difficult and time-consuming for institutions, subgroups and individuals accustomed to more autonomous ways of working, and many consortia and alliances fail or fall short of achieving their potential. Neil (1981: 172–6) and Moran and Mugridge (1993: xiii, 5, 9–10, 152–7) identify a range of factors which may inhibit collaboration. These include: the existence of cultural differences between institutions; traditions of institutional autonomy; the 'not invented here' syndrome; poorly constituted collaborative objectives; failure to articulate mutual benefits; lack of clarity in specifying the terms of an agreement; incompatible organisational structures and administrative procedures; inadequate funds to implement agreements; poor interpersonal relations; weak leadership; lack of real commitment on the part of one or more of the parties; and lack of trust.

Bates (2000: 176–9) suggests that there are many potential advantages in collaboration and partnerships but that these depend upon: defining the strategic benefits; picking the right and best partners; gaining general support for the partnerships throughout the organisations; putting in the time and up-front investment; planning for both the short term and the long term; determining the relative roles of the institutions and their suborganisations; sound project management with clearly defined tasks and agreed-on budgets; and formal agreements signed off by the CEOs. For institutions that can face up to these challenges, there may well be exciting opportunities for collaboration and paradigmatic change within the context of e-distance education.

CORPORATE UNIVERSITIES AND CORPORATE TRAINING

Some US corporations (e.g. Aetna, American Express, Apple, Arthur Anderson, Cisco Systems, Dow Chemicals, Ford, General Electric, General Motors, IBM, McDonald's, Merrill Lynch, Motorola, Sears, Sun Microsystems Inc, Xerox) have centralised their training under one umbrella and renamed these departments or divisions 'corporate universities'. Despite their adopting such a nomenclature, few of these institutions have ever offered accredited degree programmes, and of those that have, several have either withdrawn from offering them or have merged them with the academic programmes of more conventional universities.

Many academics scoff at the idea of courses provided by the Disney University or McDonald's Hamburger University and question whether these institutions meet the standards required to call themselves universities. However, the message from these corporate providers is loud and clear. Learning is important, needs to be given greater prestige and demands major investment. The corporate sector is in the market for programmes that are relevant to business efficiency and employee performance, that acculturate the employees into the changing environment, that develop the necessary skills and knowledge about the companies' products and services, that help to recruit, retain and advance the best employees, and that are customised, flexible and appropriate to today's fast-moving, knowledge-based economy.

Cunningham *et al.* (2000: 15) conclude that while it is easy to dismiss the more extreme examples of corporate universities, 'organisations which seriously invest in their corporate programs have much to offer the traditional education sector in the professionalism with which they approach their teaching and learning programs, and the funds expended on these activities'. Worldwide, major investments are being made in the corporate education market and flexible learning is increasingly seen as an integral part of HRD or training policy. Another emerging model is the sector-based online university such as the US Real Estate University (Cunningham *et al.* 2000: 40).

Many smaller companies also provide internet, intranet or other forms of flexible training, targeting priority areas of need and relating learning to the job. However, as Rowntree (1992: 23) notes, most in-company programmes may be 'flexible' in terms of time, place and pace, but are 'open' only to those who are eligible for such training within their organisations, and typically offer little choice in objectives, content, teaching and learning methods and assessment.

Some private-sector organisations offering their own courses seek credit from public-sector institutions. For example, Microsoft and Novell have contracted with Tucson's Pima County Community College, an arrangement which also enables the students to have their fees paid for by their employers or receive a tax break on their fees (Bates 1995: 173). The alternative model is for corporations to contract with universities and colleges to provide courses matched to their needs. Thompson (1998) identifies three reasons for this sea change:

1 A growing tendency of corporations to focus their attention and resources upon their core business and to outsource corporate education.
2 The demands of the accreditation process.
3 A growing willingness of colleges and universities to assist corporations in meeting their educational needs.

Thus, British management consultants Ernst and Young partner with Henley Management College to offer their staff worldwide MBA and PhD programmes in business and leadership, an arrangement which both parties regard as mutually beneficial. Ernst and Young see it as a means of accumulating intellectual capital, retaining staff and maintaining competitive advantage. Henley Management College staff look upon it as an opportunity to gain firsthand knowledge of the issues currently confronting the corporate sector (White 1999). And at the national level, through its Green Paper, *The Learning Age*, the British government has established a major public–private partnership, the University for Industry (UfI). UfI has not been conceived as a single, self-contained institution such as the British Open University, but again as a system, drawing upon a wide range of educational and training providers to offer courses and programmes which stimulate and meet demand for lifelong learning among businesses and individuals through online delivery into homes, workplaces and 400 'learndirect centres'.

Such developments are also being transacted through separate for-profit entities attached to existing universities and colleges, an arrangement which again may give rise to conflict within the academic culture of the more traditional institutions.

THE NEW KIDS ON THE BLOCK – FOR-PROFIT INSTITUTIONS

For-profit distance-teaching institutions are again largely an American phenomenon although this model seems likely to be replicated elsewhere across the globe. The prime US examples are the University of Phoenix (UoP), DeVry Inc, Strayer Education Inc and Sylvan Learning Systems Inc, all of which are dual-mode. The UoP now has the largest enrolment of any US private nonprofit or for-profit university (Sperling and Tucker 1997: 36). Its undergraduate and graduate enrolments in the USA, Puerto Rico and elsewhere have reached 65,000. The UoP operates primarily through a network of learning centres but about 10 per cent of its students are enrolled in UoP Online Division programmes which generate US$12.8 million a quarter. DeVry, through its undergraduate DeVry Institutes and postgraduate division, Keller Graduate School of Management, also remains committed to teaching through local outlets but is positioning itself in the asynchronous online market. Strayer has an aggressive strategy of programme and campus replication across the USA, but in 1999 opened an online division called Strayer Online. Sylvan Learning Systems Inc provides personalised instructional services to students of all ages and skill levels through a network of over 640 Sylvan Learning Centers and adult professional education and training through its Caliber Learning Network.

For-profit institutions arise through a combination of:

- dissatisfaction with the responsiveness of traditional institutions to the professional and vocational needs of working adults who require convenience, year-round compressed courses, and individually tailored and individually satisfying flexible learning;

- recognition of the enormous potential of the education market (US$772 billion per year in the USA or 10 per cent of the country's gross domestic product, and the fifth largest service sector export in Australia);
- e-commerce entrepreneurism.

The major US for-profits are listed on the New York Stock Exchange and Cunningham *et al.* (2000: 16) observe that such institutions have as their primary goal profit from selling education and training as a service, are run strictly according to rigid business principles, offering niche client groups a limited range of educational 'products', and in Meister's (1998: 231) terms, focus on 'convenience, self-service and uniformity'.

Hanna and Associates (2000: 139–40) suggest that these for-profit universities are important in the mix of higher education models because they:

- have access to private capital and funds needed for start-up and expansion;
- can purchase, lease or modify facilities quickly;
- focus upon a specific niche of the adult marketplace for education, namely those knowledge workers who require high levels of education and whose employees can afford to pay their tuition fees in many cases;
- stay close to their customer base, thereby producing a high-quality educational product;
- are managed as well as governed; are focused upon making necessary changes as needed rather than as mandated;
- operate all year round;
- are experiencing significant enrolment growth overall.

Such institutions are borderless and have the potential to present formidable competition to the traditional universities. Cunningham *et al.* (2000: xvii–xviii) suggest that these new providers are not bound by the norms and ideals of traditional higher education such as collegial governance, linked research and teaching, or academic autonomy and control, and adopt a strategic and systematic approach to the professionalism of education and training that does more than pay lip-service to the rhetoric of being a 'learning organisation'. White (1999) suggests that these institutions 'have the advantage of being able to hire and fire managers and teachers and offer them a share of the profits', and notes that Wall Street analysts eye the multi-billion education sector as ripe for investment because 'it is seen as a low-tech industry managed by amateurs'. However, the for-profits have fared poorly on the New York Stock Exchange over the past few years and there are still serious questions about their quality, governance and treatment of staff (see e.g. Cunningham *et al.* 2000).

IS THERE ANYONE OUT THERE? VIRTUAL INSTITUTIONS

The 'virtual institution' has become the metaphor for online enrolment, distribution, tuition and administration. Cunningham *et al.* (2000: 16) suggest that the virtual institution may be conceived of in two ways:

1   As an institution which offers all of the conventional university services via information and communications technology (e.g. New York University Online or Jones International University, America's only accredited private online university).
2   As a 'hollow' organisation which unbundles services convention-ally provided in-house and subcontracts these to other organisations (e.g. Western Governors University, brokering competency-based programmes).

In a third model, the institution acts on behalf of a number of different providers (e.g. the Californian Virtual University providing online catalogues and courses on behalf of its partners, and Britain's emerging e-university which is envisaged as doing something similar for the entire British higher education sector, while retaining the right to refuse to accept courses on quality grounds; see O'Shea 2000: 10).

Cunningham *et al.* (2000), however, found that despite all the rhetoric and hype, virtual institutions remain embryonic. Farrell (1999: 2–3) observed that the term 'virtual' is used broadly and indiscriminately, that there are few examples of virtual institutions or campuses in the purest sense, that development is still experimental, unfocused, not necessarily matched to clientele learning needs, and that those using the web, do so as a publishing medium rather than as an interactive tool. However, he records a great deal of interest and activity in this area from four different sources:

1   Institutions that have historically been involved with single-mode or dual-mode provision.
2   From within traditional institutions ranging from schools to universities, on a programme-specific basis and in order to add quality, increase productivity, reduce costs, increase revenue and attract new students.
3   The corporate sector developing internal programmes based upon information and communications technology and marketing these under a virtual label.
4   Individuals, who for reasons ranging from altruism to profit have created online learning opportunities for anyone who is interested.

Farrell (1999: 8) suggests that there is also evidence through SchoolNet initiatives in Canada, South Africa and India and similar developments elsewhere across the globe that virtual education models will start to pervade primary and secondary education. However, here the technology may be used either to support the teacher, enable the teacher to teach across distances or networked schools, or deliver information, knowledge and learning opportunities directly to the learner.

GAZING INTO THE CRYSTAL BALL

The development of third-generation distance education opens up new prospects for structuring distance-education systems. The models described above are fluid, transmuting and converging. The question is: Can new structures be established that will enable distance educators to make use of the new technologies to provide cheap, mass-educational access or, on the other hand, profitable global enterprises? Like it or not, higher education has now been thoroughly 'corporatised' and is perceived as a mass business, with private investment only likely to increase. Oblinger (2001) foresees even more change in the wake of mergers and acquisitions among existing e-distance businesses, and by media, publishing and communications businesses currently outside distance education. Such consolidation will, she believes, 'provide scale, and in education, scale matters . . . [enabling] leverage for research and development, curriculum development, sales efforts and overall operating expenses' (Oblinger 2001: x).

The costs of online education are currently being investigated but it is already clear that the costs of putting suitable materials online may be very high, while the costs of supporting students online look as if they are going to cause the unit costs of distance education to increase substantially (Rumble 1999). Against this, e-commerce practices such as online registration are likely to bring some costs down. Nevertheless, the extensive adoption of online learning by single-mode distance-education systems is likely to push their unit (and total) costs up, thus undermining their efficiency relative to traditional educational systems. Dual-mode systems may, however, be able to use online teaching as a substitute for face-to-face contact without affecting their overall cost structures too much – particularly if they also eschew the development of materials in favour of using pre-existing textbooks, and if they keep course numbers down. The initial thrust within e-distance education may well be, therefore, to find less expensive ways of undertaking routine operating transactions, while the greatest overall success may come within dual-mode systems. If the latter is true, then single-mode institutions are going to face greatly increased and very cost-effective competition.

Technology and e-business approaches make it possible for integrated processes of open and distance education to be disaggregated into their constituent parts: curriculum development; content development; learner acquisition and support; learning delivery; assessment and advising; articulation; and credentialing. These processes can then be managed by different organisations.

Conversely, e-distance education may enable academics to regain control over the teaching-learning process, provided that:

- course modules are small enough and so designed as to enable a single academic to develop them;
- the number of students following the course is no greater than one person can handle in terms of marking assignments, responding to students and so on;
- control over administrative processes is devolved to the academic, who reports the outcomes only to a central record-keeping administration (Rumble 1998: 136).

The emergence of such 'reaggregated' jobs could parallel the twelfth-century emergence of the intellectual – one 'whose profession it was to think and share their thoughts' (Le Goff 1993: 1) and who taught in schools that 'were workshops out of which ideas, like merchandise, were exported' (ibid.: 62). During the twelfth century these intellectual artisans began to organise themselves within corporations or colleges of masters and students, out of which emerged the universities in the thirteenth century. The salaries of these masters derived from two sources: the students, and stipends or scholarships from private benefactors, and civil and public organisations. Masters who could live off what their students paid them were free of temporal and ecclesiastical powers and private patrons.

It is perhaps too fanciful to predict that the internet/web will enable the twenty-first century 'master' to sell his or her wares in the e-marketplace, and be paid directly by the learner. With the possible exception of a few international gurus, most teachers will need to operate within a framework which advertises their availability, assures potential students of their worth, and provides acceptable and transferable certification and accreditation. Once accepted into such a framework, it will be in the interests of these teachers to ensure that the organisation succeeds as a whole. Systems 'in which everyone takes responsibility for the success of the whole' are the key characteristic of what Hechscher (1994: 24) refers to as post-bureaucratic organisations. Applied to third-generation e-distance education, this would mark a significant departure from the way in which first- and second-generation systems have been organised. The function of the institution would be to provide learner acquisition, quality assurance, articulation and credentialing. The academics' function would be to develop and deliver the courses and support and assess the learners via the internet. Global alliances, and globalised credit accumulation and transfer schemes between organisations of a similar standard, would allow for the emergence of multi-cultural partnerships of globally distributed teachers serving students across a borderless world. Such organisations might be so re-engineered as to allow academics to be paid directly by their students, the university to be reimbursed for the registration and recognition of their learning (and possibly levy a charge on the academics for their continued recognition as accredited teachers) and grant academics the freedom to regulate their student load to suit their needs and combine this with work in other fields or for other organisations.

Having opened up these possibilities, Rumble (1998: 142) asks whether such models could happen. There is no one answer to this – but what is clear is that the field of distance education is changing and will change even more as new players enter the field, exploiting the possibilities of e-commerce, and that time-honoured structures and systems may wither or be swept away.

CONCLUSIONS

All the organisational structures described above have worked in particular cases; and all have been shown to have advantages and disadvantages. There can be no absolute policy guidelines, although it seems inevitable that most traditional institutions will become involved with mixed-mode provision, and that there will be an increase in alliances and partnerships, some of which will be transient. The international agency offering community-based open learning programmes in HIV/AIDS awareness in developing countries will almost inevitably need to work in collaboration with various health, education, government, community and telecommunications organisations. The national government setting up an open schooling system will need to involve a range of partners, including the existing schools, to maximise scarce resources. College and university educators and trainers, telecommunications and media providers, publishers and the corporate sector will endeavour to capture each other's primary strengths. However, each of these structures has economic consequences which will in turn determine what works best in given circumstances. It seems likely that the development of e-distance education will significantly affect the way in which distance education is structured. The one certainty facing policy makers is that the environment is changing, and that this will impact fundamentally on the structures through which distance education is delivered.

The knowledge economy demands lifelong learning and the private sector is assuming a growing responsibility for this. There are calls for significant educational reform and greater accountability, and an increasing number of institutions are now reinventing or realigning themselves to expand and enhance their education and training operations. Some will opt to maintain a local or national focus; others will aim to become global and multinational; most, if not all, will seek commercial benefit from their operations. The internationalisation of education is really only at what Davis and Botkin (1995) define as stage one: export, or stage two: setting up partnerships and in-country development and delivery. The greater vision will be realised when institutions achieve stage three: truly two-way exchange and development of programmes and services through borderless education.

All organisations have life cycles which proceed from start-up and experimentation to maturity and ageing, during which process they become increasingly rigid and entrenched in their organisation and operation. It is yet to be seen whether the institutions emerging from the second wave or Fordist economy will recognise and respond to the need for risk-taking, responsiveness, results-oriented programmes and services, reciprocity and relationships and transform their organisational, administrative and academic systems, or whether new providers will prove quicker, more flexible and more effective in responding to the need for a working-learning culture and infrastructure. Hanna and Associates (2000: 134), and Cunningham *et al.* (2000: xviii), caution that great care will be needed to prevent unproved or disreputable operators from exploiting this industry and individuals' educational aspirations. It will be equally important to ensure that, with so many in the world still denied educational opportunity, open and distance education still upholds the principles of access and equity and is not subjugated totally to the politics of economic liberalism.

REFERENCES

Abrioux, D. (2001) 'Athabasca University: change management in a non-traditional university setting', in C. Latchem and D. Hanna (eds) *Leadership for 21st Century Learning*, London: Kogan Page.

Barnett, R. (2000) *Realizing the University in an Age of Supercomplexity*, Buckingham: Society for Research into Higher Education and Open University Press.

Barnett, R. and Griffin, A. (eds) (1997) *The End of Knowledge in Higher Education*, London: Cassell.

Bashir, T. H. (1998) 'Dangerous liaison: academics' attitude towards open learning in higher education', *Open Learning* 13 (1): 43–5.

Bates, A. W. (1995) *Technology, Open Learning and Distance Education*, London: Routledge.

Bates, A. W. (2000) *Managing Technological Change: Strategies for College and University Leaders*, San Francisco, CA: Jossey-Bass.

Boshier, R. W. and Pratt, D. (1997) 'A qualitative and postmodern perspective on open learning in Hong Kong', *Distance Education* 18 (1): 110–35.

Campion, M. G. (1991) 'Critical essay on educational technology in distance education', in T. Evans and B. King (eds) *Beyond the Text: Contemporary Writing on Distance Education*, Geelong: Deakin University Press.

Campion, M. (1995) 'The supposed demise of bureaucracy: implications for distance education and open learning – more on the post-Fordism debate', *Distance Education* 16 (2): 192–216.

Campion, M. and Renner, W. (1992) 'The supposed demise of Fordism: implications for distance education and higher education', *Distance Education* 13 (1): 7–28.

Cunningham, S., Ryan, Y., *et al.* (2000) *The Business of Borderless Education: The Impact of Corporate and Virtual Providers on Higher Education Provision*, Department of Employment, Education, Training and Youth Affairs, Evaluations and Investigations Program, Higher Education Division, Canberra: AGPS. http://www.detya.gov.au/highered/eippubs.htm#00_3.

Daniel, J. S. (1996) *Mega-universities and Knowledge Media: Technology Strategies for Higher Education*, London: Kogan Page.

Daniel, J. S. (1998) 'Virtually all you'll need to know', *Guardian Higher Education Supplement*, 7 April, pp. ii–iii.

Daniel, J. S. and Smith, W. A. S. (1979) 'The management of small open universities', in M. Neil (ed.) *Education of Adults at a Distance*, London: Kogan Page.

Davis, S. and Botkin, J. (1995) *The Monster Under the Bed*, New York and London: Simon & Schuster.

Dodd, J. and Rumble, G. (1984) 'Planning new distance teaching universities', *Higher Education* 13: 231–54.

Ellis, E. M. (2000) 'Faculty participation in the Pennsylvania State University World Campus: identifying barriers to success', *Open Learning* 15 (3): 233–42.

Ellis, J. F. (1997) 'The Open Learning Institute of British Columbia', in I. Mugridge (ed.) *Founding the Open Universities*, New Delhi: Sterling Publishers Private Ltd.

Farrell, G. (ed.) (1999) *The Development of Virtual Education: A Global Perspective*, Commonwealth of Learning, http://www.col.org/virtualed.

Flexner, A. (1930) *Universities: American, British, German*, New York: Oxford University Press.

Giegerich, A. (2000) 'Corporate strategies: the benefit of education', *Business Journal of Portland Online*, 27 March 2000, http://www.bizjournals.com/portland.

Hall, J. W. (1991) *Access through Innovation: New Colleges for New Students*, New York: American Council for Education and Macmillan Publishing.

Halsey, A. H. (1995) *Decline of Donnish Dominion: The British Academic Professions in the Twentieth Century*, Oxford: Clarendon Press.

Hanna, D. and Associates (2000) *Higher Education in an Era of Digital Competition: Choices and Challenges*, Madison: Attwood Publishing.

Hechscher, C. (1994) 'Defining the post-bureaucratic type', in C. Hechscher and A. Donnellon (eds) *The Post-bureaucratic Organization: New Perspectives on Organizational Change*, Thousand Oaks, CA: Sage.

Jevons, F. (1984) 'Distance education in a mixed institution: working towards parity', *Distance Education* 5 (1): 24–37.

Latchem, C. and Pritchard, T. (1994) 'Open Learning: the unique Australian option', *Open Learning*, 9 (3): 18–26.

Le Goff, J. (1993) *Intellectuals in the Middle Ages*, Oxford: Blackwell.

Leibbrandt, G. (1997) 'The Open Universiteit of the Netherlands', in I. Mugridge (ed.) *Founding the Open Universities*, New Delhi: Sterling Publishers Private Ltd.

Lewis, R. (1990) 'Open learning and the misuse of language: a response to Greville Rumble', *Open Learning* 5 (1): 3–8.

Lewis, R. (1994) 'Embedding open learning in higher education', in M. Thorpe and D. Grugeon (eds) *Open Learning in the Mainstream*, London: Longman.

Lueddeke, G. (1998) 'The management of change towards an open learning framework: an higher education inquiry', *Open Learning* 13 (3): 3–17.

Meister, J. (1998) *Corporate Universities: Lessons in Building a World-Class Workforce*, New York: McGraw Hill.

Moore, M. (1983) 'The individual adult learner', in M. Tight (ed.) *Adult Learning and Education*, London: Croom Helm.

Moran, L. and Mugridge, I. (1993) *Collaboration in Distance Education: International Case Studies*, London: Routledge.

Neil, M. (1981) *Education of Adults at a Distance: A Report of the Open University's Tenth Anniversary Conference*, London: Kogan Page.

Noble, D. F. (2000) 'Comeback of an education racket', *Le Monde Diplomatique*, April, p. 15.

Oblinger, D. (2001) 'Will e-business shape the future of open and distance learning?', *Open Learning* 16 (1): x–xx.

Ortmeier, A. (1982) *External Studies in Australia*, Armidale: Institute for Higher Education.

O'Shea, T. (2000) 'e-asy does it', *Guardian Higher Education Supplement*, 10 October, pp. 10–11.

Perraton, H. (2000) *Open and Distance Learning in the Developing World*, London: Routledge.

Perry, W. (1976) *Open University. A Personal Account by the First Vice-Chancellor*, Milton Keynes: Open University Press.

Perry, W. and Rumble, G. (1987) *A Short Guide to Distance Education*, Cambridge: International Extension College.

Peters, O. (1973) *Die Didaktische Struktur des Fernunterrichts Untersuchungen zu einer industrialisierten Form des Lehrens und Lernens*, Weinheim: Beltz.

Peters, O. (1983) 'Distance teaching and industrial production: a comparative interpretation in outline', in D. Sewart, D. Keegan and B. Holmberg (eds) *Distance Education: International Perspectives*, London: Croom Helm.

Peters, O. (1997) 'The Fern Universität', in I. Mugridge (ed.) *Founding the Open Universities*, New Delhi: Sterling Publishers Private Ltd.

Peterson, R. W., Marostica, M. A. and Callahan, L. M. (1999) *E-Learning: Helping Investors Climb the e-Learning Curve*, Minneapolis, MT: US Bancorp Piper Jaffray.

Poley, J. (2001) 'The American Distance Education Consortium: from rural provision to virtual organization', in C. Latchem and D. Hanna (eds) *Leadership for 21st Century Learning*, London: Kogan Page.

Readings, B. (1997) *The University in Ruins*, Cambridge, MA: Harvard University Press.

Renwick, W. (1996) 'The future of face-to-face and distance teaching in post-secondary education', in OECD *Information Technology and the Future of Post-secondary Education*, Paris: OECD.

Ritzer, G. (1993) *The McDonaldization of Society*, Thousand Oaks, CA: Pine Forge Press.

Ritzer, G. (1998) *The McDonaldization Thesis*, Thousand Oaks, CA: Sage.

Rowntree, D. (1992) *Exploring Open and Distance Learning*, London: Kogan Page.

Rumble, G. (1992) 'The competitive vulnerability of distance teaching universities', *Open Learning* 7 (2): 31–49.

Rumble, G. (1998) 'Academic work in the Information Age: a speculative essay', *Journal of Information Technology for Teacher Education* 7 (1): 129–45.

Rumble, G. (1999) 'The costs of networked learning: what have we learnt?' Paper presented to the FLISH99 Flexible Learning on the Information Superhighway Conference, Sheffield Hallam University, Sheffield, UK, 25–27 May; available at http://www.shu.ac.uk'flsh/rumblep.htm.

Scott, P. (1997) 'The postmodern university?', in A. Smith and F. Webster (eds) *The Postmodern University? Contested Visions of Higher Education in Society*, Buckingham: Open University Press.

Shamsher Ali, M. (1997) 'Bangladesh Open University', in I. Mugridge (ed.) *Founding the Open Universities*, New Delhi: Sterling Publishers Private Ltd.

Siaciwena, R. M. C. (1983) 'Problems of managing an external degree programme at the University of Zambia', *Journal of Adult Education* [University of Zambia] 2 (1): 67–77.

Siaciwena, R. M. C. (1988) 'The external degree programme at the University of Zambia', *Prospects* 18 (2): 199–206.

Singh, B. (1979) 'Distance education in developing countries – with special reference to India', in J. R. Hakemulder (ed.) *Distance Education for Development*, Bonn: German Foundation for International Development.

Smith, K. C. (1979) 'External Studies at New England – a silver jubilee review, 1955–79', reprinted in D. Sewart, D. Keegan and B. Holmberg (eds) *Distance Education: International Perspectives*, London: Croom Helm.

Smyth, J. (ed.) (1995) *Academic Work*, Buckingham: Society for Research into Higher Education and Open University Press.

Snowden, B. L. and Daniel, J. S. (1980) 'The economics and management of small post-secondary distance education systems', *Distance Education* 1 (1): 68–91.

Sperling, J. G. and Tucker, R. W. (1997) *For-profit Higher Education: Developing a World-class Workforce*, New Brunswick, NJ: Transaction Publishers.

Taylor, J. C. and White, V. J. (1991) *The Evaluation of the Cost-effectiveness of Multi-media Mixed-mode Teaching and Learning*, Canberra: Australian Government Publishing Service.

Thompson, G. (1998) *Unfulfilled Prophecy: The Evolution of Corporate Colleges*, University of Saskatchewan.

Tofler, A. (1980) *The Third Wave*, London: Pan Books.

White, D. (1999) 'A studied approach to "virtual" learning', *Daily Telegraph, Business File*, 9 December, p. A9.

Chapter 8

Technology

Hilary Perraton and Kurt Moses

Editors' introduction

The policy maker is faced with two levels of question about the use of technology in open and distance learning. The higher level questions belong mainly in the domain of national policy. They include issues about the regulation of telecommunications, about educational access to communications media and about national policies in relation to the digital divide. At the second level are questions about the most appropriate ways of using technologies within education, about choices between them for a specific educational purpose, about staff development in relation to them, and about their costs. Some issues bridge the two levels; a planner's choice between, say, using satellite communication or digital radio will be affected by national policy but will also need to be shaped by micro- or meso-educational needs.

Some of the higher level issues are discussed in Chapter 2 in relation to the new agenda of e-learning, in Chapter 7 where they bear on organisation, and in Chapter 9 on globalisation in the context of cross-border enrolment. Many of them are beyond the scope of this book. Perhaps the most important are about the relationship between the new technologies, globalisation and economic development. There is wide concern about the digital divide, and about measures that may be taken to bridge it, or weaken its negative effects, a major theme, for example, of the British government White Paper on development of 2000 (Secretary of State for International Development 2000). Some of the direct effects, already touched on in previous chapters, are about the political environment in which decisions about the technologies are made. Where telecommunications are deregulated, for example, access to them for an educational agency may in principle become easier, but in practice more costly.

Within this chapter we bring together two contributions to the debate about the sound use of technology. Both confront the starting question:

How does the planner choose between technologies? Perraton proposes a set of criteria by which choices may be made between educational technologies. These raise questions of education and of economics. The second part of the chapter, by Moses, examines the theme of costs, looking at the costs of computer-based education. His study is valuable not only in summarising our understanding of costs in this area, but also in suggesting an approach that will help the planner in making sound decisions on costs, once educational priorities have been set.

CHOOSING TECHNOLOGIES FOR EDUCATION

Hilary Perraton

Communication technologies have been used for three purposes: to widen access to education, to raise its quality, and to reform it. The last two tend to shade into each other as qualitative change can be seen as a way of reforming, even transforming, education. We could illustrate this from a range of technologies. Hindsight makes it easy to draw illustrations from television. It was used by universities, starting with the British Open University, to widen access to education and make it available to people outside university and college walls. By bringing resources into the classroom, it was seen as a way of raising the quality of classroom teaching. In addition, in a handful of cases, it was set up with the intention of transforming education. Today we have a much wider range of technological options than, say, the choice between conventional teaching, radio and television, but we can probably ask the same questions about a number of them. Experience of using the older and the newer technologies makes it possible to propose four questions – about convenience, constraints, curriculum and cost – which need to be answered in developing a national policy for the use of communication technologies in education. An educational policy of this kind probably needs to be framed within the context of a national policy for communications. The nature of that policy will vary from one jurisdiction to another. It will also present particular challenges to small states; today they have improved access, through the technologies, to the world's intellectual resources but at the same time confront ever greater dangers of cultural hegemony by the large countries and large international companies who control the production of hardware and software.

Availability and convenience

First, we need to ask what technology is available for a particular audience and acceptable to that audience. Globalisation means that we can have internet access, at a price, almost anywhere in the world. It does not mean that computer-based education will be suitable for any particular audience. Convenience and acceptability may be more significant than the desire to be at the cutting edge of technology. Television, for example, has proved to be a potent way of widening access to education where it is available in learners' own homes. Its record where people have to go somewhere else in order to watch it is more chequered. An early experiment in Uganda, for example, found that the only place where people could watch television was in bars, where the atmosphere did not lend itself to serious study. More recently, teachers offered inservice programmes of continuing education in India, who had to attend at centres away from home in order to take part in video-conferences, voted with their feet by staying away.

The need to relate technologies to our audience forces us also to ask about the prerequisites that need to be in place for any particular technology to be useful for education. Education seems to have been most successful in its use of technology where it has followed the commercial and entertainment sector rather than attempting to lead it. If costs are brought down, and a technology is made widely available, by a demand that is greater than that of education, then it may be more realistic to use that technology for educational purposes.

Local and national constraints

Second – and this point is closely related – we need to look at international variations in the ways in which technologies may be used. Issues here may be geographical, regulatory or economic. In Thailand or India, for example, it is possible to consider the use of a dedicated satellite or dedicated satellite transponders for education because of the scale of the country. In Latin America, outside Brazil, it looks as if satellite use may make sense only if there can be agreement between countries about educational programmes that cross frontiers. A World Bank attempt to get agreement on this in the late 1990s yielded little success. Small states are likely to be much more constrained in the access they have to various forms of communication. Regulatory issues will limit the access to international communication highways. If Cable and Wireless has a monopoly of external communication within a territory, then this will limit the extent to which users can gain cheap and easy access to things outside the territory. Economic constraints always restrict us. Schools, in many parts of the world, have started to use computers as a means of gaining access to resources on the internet, or of communicating with other schools, but in many cases are inhibited by the cost of an internet service provider (ISP) and the line charges. The costs of computer communication in southern Africa, for example, are absolutely higher than they are in North America and relatively much higher.

Curriculum

Third, once we have considered the availability of a particular technology, and related it to the national situation, it is possible to move on and consider what makes sense educationally. Our starting point here is a series of research findings, yielding consistent results, showing that there are unlikely to be significant differences in the educational effects of different media. (Chu and Schramm (1968) and Clark (1983) are among the many overviews that have demonstrated this important finding.) The fact that, by and large, one may use any medium to teach anything, is a liberating one: the educator can consider the needs of the audience and the appropriate combination of media that make most sense for a particular purpose. For there may be good practical reasons for some choices – an aural medium for teaching a language with tones, for example, or a visual medium such as television for demonstrating a simulation. But the important thing is to start with the curriculum rather than with preconceptions about a particular medium. We may also want to use a particular medium for broad social as well as narrower educational reasons. Television in the past, a website today, may be a significant part of the public image of an educational institution.

In making educational choices we need to distinguish between the use of technologies to distribute learning material to students and their use to allow interaction. We may, for example, use a computer network to distribute teaching material to distance-education students or to allow schools to print materials, available through the internet, for their students. The main consequence here is likely to be a shift of costs from the centre to the periphery, or from the teaching institution to the individual student. Alternatively, we can use computer links to facilitate dialogue with students, perhaps replacing the slowness of correspondence education through the post with the near-immediacy of e-mail and computer conferencing. This second type of use is educationally and economically quite different from the first. It is about two-way, not one-way communication, and, by easing contact between student and tutor, is likely to increase the demands on tutors and therefore increase costs (see Chapter 7 for a discussion of this point).

Above all, in seeking appropriate educational use of technology, we need to start with the curriculum. In thinking about this, we can try to relate educational content to the appropriate technology at the same time as we relate the technologies to learners' own circumstances. Many different typologies have been produced, seeking to match technologies and curriculum, and looking at the particular needs for synchronous and asynchronous communication (e.g. Moore and Kearsley 1996, Hülsmann 2000, Laurillard 2000). Table 8.1 sets out one summary of the strengths of various technologies.

The choice of technologies is often a function of these three factors of student convenience, local constraints and curricular purpose. Computer-based teaching provides an illustration with a hierarchy of possible uses. If students have access to computers, but not to the internet, then it may be possible to distribute teaching materials on CD-Rom and, in principle, they may contain simulations and illustrations that go beyond what can be done just in print. Once students have some access to the internet other possibilities are opened up. At the lower end of the hierarchy, the internet may be used to distribute materials to students even if they have only intermittent access to it, perhaps by occasional attendance at a tuition centre. Next, it is possible to provide tutoring by e-mail, with e-mail links replacing post or fax. While there are advantages if students have daily access to e-mail, this will work with more spasmodic access, again perhaps when students visit a tutorial centre. At the same time it places demands on institutions which need to train the tutors who will be working with students. Moving up the hierarchy, some e-learning programmes have created virtual learning environments so that there are online seminars in which students take part. These may be provided as an optional part of a programme, providing enrichment, in which case students can still, while at a disadvantage, follow the programme with only intermittent access. Educational institutions and private-sector companies have developed a variety of software packages so that it is becoming relatively simple for individual teaching institutions to set up environments of this kind. But if they are an integral part of the programme, then students need regular, easy access to the internet. Similarly, and also at the top of the hierarchy, where learners are expected to undertake extensive web searches for materials they will use in their course, or to take part in virtual seminars as an integral part of their course, then easy, regular and cheap access to the internet is necessary. As a result, while this kind of approach is being used increasingly by universities in industrialised countries, it remains a constraint on institutions in many developing countries and on cross-border enrolment on to programmes launched in the north and offered in the south. The hierarchy of uses is set out in Table 8.2

Costs

Costs come next and are the theme of the second section of this chapter. We have two difficulties in calculating the cost of the technologies. First, the behaviour of the costs of technology differs from that of conventional education. Second, we are short of data on the costs of various technologies from developing-country evidence.

In order to make sense of the cost data, we need to distinguish between the use of technology to provide an alternative type of education, thus reducing the cost of teaching staff, and its use to raise quality without

Table 8.1 Technologies for open and distance learning

Medium	Educational strength or weakness	Type of communication	Implications for access	Cost implications
Face-to-face study	Adaptable; may allow immediate individual response to learner; can be highly motivating	Simultaneous, two-way communication is possible	Requires attendance at fixed time and place	Costs generally rise in relation to student numbers
Print	Provides convenient permanent record; limited in its effectiveness to motivate students; may be of restricted value for some practical subjects	One-way communication; two-way communication possible where correspondence assignments are designed and returned through mail, fax or e-mail	Generally no problems of access	Significant fixed costs in developing printed materials; reproduction costs used to show economies for large print runs but with digital, just-in-time, printing may no longer do so
Broadcasting (radio and television)	Can motivate, excite, dramatise, illustrate; ephemeral unless students record off-air	One-way communication	No problem of access, with universal access to radio and TV, but timing of broadcasts may be inconvenient	Production costs generally higher than for print; television generally up to ten times as expensive as radio; transmission costs may be met by broadcasting authority

Cassettes	Similar educational qualities to broadcasts but not ephemeral	Generally one-way communication; audio-cassettes used occasionally for delayed response to tutors	Problems of access if students do not have audio- or videocassette player	Production costs in principle as for broadcasting; costs in practice lower as lower quality is often acceptable; distribution cost falls on teaching institution
Video-conferencing	Allows up-to-date, live, two-way communication, giving a sense of immediacy; ephemeral	Can be two-way synchronous communication, generally between two sites, or with many sites if one-way video and two-way audio	Access open only to those who can reach location with equipment	Significant investment needed in video-conferencing equipment; high bandwidth line charges; cost a function of number of sites involved
Computer-related learning	Allows simulations and activities that depend on computer capacity; can be used as communication medium	Allows two-way asynchronous communication	Major, but reducing, problems of access; e.g. 25 per cent of UK households had PC (1995) but smaller proportion had internet access	Heavy initial cost to develop computer-based learning material; significant personal investment needed for computer; cost of communication through internet dependent on line charges and local practice of ISP services

Source: Perraton and Hülsmann 1998: 6

Table 8.2 Hierarchies of computer use for communication with students

Use of technology	Demands on institution	Demands on students
Distribution of printed material on CD-Rom	Basic computer facilities	Occasional access to computer with CD-Rom drive and printer
Distribution of material including simulations and illustration or interactive software	Basic computer facilities with capacity to develop more sophisticated software	Access to computer as often as needed to benefit from software
Tutoring by e-mail	Modest. Needs to provide staff training for tutors	At minimum, intermittent use of computer with internet access. Regular use desirable
Optional participation in virtual learning environment	Needs appropriate software package and licence. Staff training	At minimum, intermittent use of computer with internet access
Use of web searches as source of necessary material for course	Modest. May reduce need to reproduce material	Regular use of computer with good internet access
Participation in virtual learning environment as integral part of course	Needs appropriate software package and licence. Staff training	Regular use of computer with good internet access

affecting staff numbers. There are various examples referred to in Chapters 11 and 12, where distance education, using a range of technologies, can achieve costs per student lower than those of conventional education. In contrast, where technologies are used to raise quality, generally within the classroom, they are likely to increase costs as no staff salaries are saved. To illustrate: interactive radio instruction has been used widely to raise the quality of teaching in schools. The cost per student per annum is estimated at between US$3.26 and US$8.12 (in 1997 US$) but these costs are over and above those of ordinary schooling (Adkins 1999: 40–1). Similarly, the reported costs of using computers in school are add-on costs amounting to between 10 and 37 per cent of existing costs per student in Chile and 13 per cent in Costa Rica (Potashnik 1996: 19–21, Wolff 1999: 29–30). (In England it appears that we are prepared to spend 0.6 per cent of the primary school budget and 1.6 per cent of the secondary school budget on computer-based education; some agencies in the north do seem to be urging the south to spend proportionately more on technology than the north is willing to (Perraton and Creed 2000: 72, Audit Commission 1999, DfEE 1999).) The second part of this chapter warns against making quick judgements based on a partial analysis of the costs.

Table 8.3 Comparative costs of some technologies

Medium	Cost per student learning hour ££	Cost in 1998 US$	Ratio to print cost
Print	500	825	1
Radio	15,000 to 27,000	24,750 to 44,550	x 50
Television	90,000 to 125,000	148,500 to 206,250	x 150 to x 180
Audio	17,000	280,050	x 36
Video	18,000 to 84,000	29,700 to 138,600	x 36 to x 170
CD-ROM	20,000	33,000	x 40

Source: based on Hülsmann 2000: 17–19

While there is a shortage of cost data, work for the European Commission identified a range of costs for a variety of technologies for open and distance learning in higher education within Europe. While the costs would obviously be different in other continents and at other levels of education, the relationship between the costs for different technologies may well hold fairly constant.

The analysis began by establishing the cost of developing and producing material in print, assuming that one always starts with a text and finding that distance teaching based on print was the least-cost option in developing materials. Costs of student support were not included in the calculation. The development costs were calculated in terms of student learning hours. This then gave us the costs shown in Table 8.3. Two conclusions follow: first, we need to find solid social and educational arguments for moving away from the simpler technologies. There will often be such arguments, but they need to be clearly worked out and openly stated. Second, the data are limited and more research is needed on the costs, benefits and outcomes of different technology choices in developing countries.

To make sense of the costs, within a communication policy, we need therefore to ask whether we are trying to strengthen education, which is likely to increase costs, or to extend to new audiences using new approaches, which may – only may – be possible at lower unit costs; then we need to seek out hard evidence on what the costs really are.

Conclusions

There are three conclusions. First, if these four questions are asked and answered, they should lead to a hard-headed choice between technologies: tough thinking is better than following fashion in choosing technologies.

Second, we are underinformed. We need to know much more about the actual benefits of technology use in developing-country situations and the actual costs achieved.

Third, the educational questions come first. Large sums have been wasted, of government and international agency funding, through ill-considered investments in the technologies. A good slogan would be: 'Consider the curriculum and count the costs.'

EDUCATIONAL COMPUTER SYSTEM MAINTENANCE AND SUPPORT: THEY COST MORE THAN YOU THINK!

Kurt D. Moses

Editors' note

We move from the broad issues of changing approaches to teaching, and of retraining educators for new approaches, to specific questions of cost, looking, as an example, at the costs of technologies in schools. It is possible to draw general conclusions from this example about some of the cost constraints on the technologies in any level and type of education, including open and distance learning.

Computer system maintenance and support, along with professional development (of teachers and administrators), are probably the most important factors in how well computers support educational activities. Computers, connections, or services that do not work cannot support educational purposes.

Over the past twenty-five years, both in developing and so-called developed countries, we have learned some things about maintenance and support in an educational setting:

- Maintenance and support are much more costly than originally thought. Keeping computers, connections, and the necessary supplies in place can amount to between 30 and 50 per cent of the total initial investment in computer hardware and software.
- Most schools, be they primary, secondary or tertiary, will trade off service level and convenience for cost. Schools will often tolerate computers not working for weeks and months because they have no money to fix them, in contrast with businesses that will not tolerate lack of computer functioning for more than hours or a few days at most.
- Some gifts to schools will actually be more costly to accept than to reject – because older or used equipment and software may require too much time, adaptation and cost for upgrades to be useful. Most schools are

not used to turning down 'gifts' even when they are too expensive to accept.

- The rise of the internet for educational purposes adds a further source of ongoing cost. Many early installations for computer laboratories or computer access in classrooms have not easily accommodated these costs.
- Even in countries with low labour costs, the cost of trained, available personnel to service computers and networks, and of training of staff to make good use of computers, is really the largest single cost item of owning computers. Hardware continues to fall as a percentage of total cost of a computer system.

Categories of cost

As more computers appear in schools throughout the world, new computer configurations and more comprehensive approaches to making them useful have been developed. One of the most important approaches, long used for assessing large computer installations, is Total Cost of Ownership (TCO). This approach looks at computer-related investments not only in terms of initial purchase, but all the costs associated with keeping the investment running and supported over the five- to seven-year life of a computer system investment. The basic elements of computer system costs are:

1 *Professional development*: These are all costs associated with training and retraining people to use a computer investment.
2 *Support*: All costs associated with actually keeping the computers, software and connections operating, as well as spare parts and other items for the computers.
3 *Connectivity*: Costs for internet or e-mail connections.
4 *Software*: All costs associated with initially obtaining software and then upgrading it to stay current.
5 *Replacement costs*: Costs to replace computers and software – which have a working life – for most schools it is five to seven years, for businesses eighteen months to three years.
6 *Retrofitting*: The cost of modifying buildings, space, electrical wiring and network connections to make a computer useful.

In simpler terms, when one purchases a car, the cost of using an automobile is not only the purchase price, but petrol, insurance, repairs, maintenance, and in some cases a driver. Similar operating costs are important elements of the cost of having computer systems. Typically, the more features a computer system has, the more maintenance and support will cost. Most school systems, anywhere in the world, are always struggling to meet their costs. Most school systems underbudget for these costs, thereby reducing the educational effectiveness of their computer system investment.

Costs for support – level of use and cost

We can distinguish between costs for maintenance, supplies, utilities, training and connectivity.

Computer software and hardware maintenance

These are costs, largely tied to personnel, to 'fix' a computer that does not work, or to repair software that may have become 'corrupted' or does not operate. In many US schools, where an ideal ratio would be one trained technician for every 150 users, the schools tolerate ratios of one technician to every 500 to 700 users. About 40 per cent of recently surveyed schools in the USA frequently used teachers to provide the majority of their support. In many developing countries there are no support personnel at all. Effective computer software and hardware maintenance in these countries hovers around 3 to 5 per cent of the initial investment amount – even if the investment was donated.

For most situations, schools and administrators need to budget at least 15 per cent of the original purchase price (even if donated) for software and hardware maintenance – and preferably 20 per cent if they can afford it. This amount needs to cover a technician at a minimum ratio of 150 users per technician (as opposed to 50:1 that many businesses use) plus costs of spare parts (keyboards, hard disks, mouse devices, computer monitors) and reasonable costs for getting around if the computer sites are separated. In addition, depending upon the level of training, a portion of these funds can support a 'Help Line' function – people located nearby who can answer computer-related questions and possibly avoid a visit from the more expensive computer technician. This level of support will mean that when 'broken' a computer or network system will be inoperative for only days, rather than weeks or months. For administrative support within schools, it means that computers and systems will be inoperative for only hours and perhaps two days, rather than weeks.

Some schools and school systems outsource this function to a private company or nonprofit group. At times, if the schools cooperate well, money can be saved by this method. Using a so-called 'thin client' solution, where students and teachers are at terminals (not PCs) and all the computing power is centralised, can reduce maintenance costs. Similarly, standardising equipment and software can reduce maintenance and support costs – because fewer different things will go wrong and people will become more adept at fixing routine problems.

Supplies

Computer supplies can be extremely costly. They include items that might be called consumables such as paper (for printers), ink and toner cartridges for printers, diskettes or ZIP disks for transfer of data, and new virus software (either downloaded from the internet or supplied via diskette to allow monthly or weekly updates of virus protection). The cost of supplies can be greatly affected by the exact equipment and software chosen and level of use. For example, laser printers costing about $1,200 use toner cartridges that cost on average $120 per cartridge to replace and generally provide 10,000 pages or $.012 per page. Inkjet printers costing $100 use cartridges that cost $24–30 per cartridge for 1,000 pages or about $.024 per page. When one adds colour printing, the cost per page for cartridges increases about three to fourfold.

Paper costs vary dramatically, from $.005 to $.02 per page, and higher quality printers require higher quality paper. Therefore, the produced cost of a single piece of paper from a computer laboratory might be over $.06 per page. In many developing countries, even if money were available, just getting the supplies is a crucial issue. Hence there is often the need to stockpile supplies (therefore requiring secure cabinets, lockable space and administration). Storage media such as 'floppy disks', ZIP disks, CDs or cartridges vary in price from $0.20 per floppy to $1.00 per CD.

Generally, schools need to budget at least 8 to 10 per cent of original purchase prices for supplies to keep the systems going, at the high end if heavy use is expected, the lower end if very little use is being made. Budgeting funds at this level means that computers and peripherals can be used for their intended purpose. In the case of using printers, it means that students can in fact make use of the equipment for instructional purposes. Upper levels of schooling, such as secondary schools and instructional programs in the sciences, can make extensive demands on supplies budgets. Costs at this level can easily approach the cost of thirty textbooks, so a school will definitely want to consider trade-offs.

Many school systems charge students separately for supplies (thereby shifting costs to the student and the parent) but this has serious consequences when students are disadvantaged – which is the case in much of the world. Educational equity is strongly affected by these various 'user fees' which are applied to defray the cost of operation.

Electricity and utilities

All computer systems run on electricity. Often the actual increase in use of electricity is not considered when gifts of computers are made. Typically, in many developing countries, there is insufficient electrical service to even support many new demands. Assuming that electricity is available, and reasonably reliable, the average modern desktop computer requires between 200 and 400 watts of power (the amount of power consumed by three to seven sixty-watt light bulbs). Laser printers require 800 to 1000 watts, with inkjet printers using 70 to 150 watts on average. Electricity costs around the world vary considerably: $.06/kilowatt hour in some places, up to $.22/kilowatt hour on certain Indian Ocean islands. At 10 cents per kilowatt hour, and using about 400 watts per computer, just one computer used eight hours a day for 200 days a year will cost an additional $64 per year in electricity. A laboratory of twenty computers without a network server will cost the school an additional $1280 per year in electricity. If there is any cooling done for the computer laboratory (air-conditioning or high-capacity fans) electricity costs could be double or triple these values.

Depending upon the relative cost of electricity, schools need to budget between 4 per cent and 8 per cent of initial purchase price for annual electricity costs for each computer system.

Primarily this level of budgeting for costs will support the actual use of computers. If electricity planning is not done, then schools will be in for very unpleasant surprises, usually cutting back on other purchases or supplies just to pay the electricity bill.

So-called 'green' or environmentally friendly computers and peripherals have been rapidly introduced. These computers and printers require lower total levels of electricity (less than half of older models) and also go into 'sleep' mode where power consumption is reduced further. This can have a major effect on electricity costs, particularly for large groups of computers.

Computer training

These are the costs associated with basic computer literacy and ability to use the core programs available on a computer. These training components are directed at students, teachers and administrators – and are separate from professional development costs (in order to learn how to make full use of the computer tools for their professional task). Computer training includes keyboarding skills (learning and practising to type), operation of the computer (use of the devices and peripherals, navigating the operating system – such as Windows), and first-level use of the computer in instructional settings – use of word-processing and spreadsheet programs.

Studies completed with various teachers have indicated that teachers need between twenty and thirty-two hours of computer training to feel comfortable with a new computer system. If teachers do not have any keyboarding skills this amount of time could double. In many developing countries this training is not given, and it is expected that teachers and administrators will simply learn from others. Often, if no or poor computer training takes place, more expensive technicians need to become involved to fix simple problems.

To help estimate costs, in parts of southern Africa, training costs of this type in medium-sized groups are about $1.50 to $3.00 per hour, excluding means and transport. For thirty-two hours this means a cost of $48 to $96 per teacher or administrator for this most basic training. Student training costs could be even lower if done in larger groups and by less senior personnel from the teaching staff. In schools with high turnover of teachers, this training needs to be repeated at least annually.

In general, a range of 5 to 10 per cent of original investment cost needs to be set aside each year for computer training. This is particularly true in the first few years of investment if no prior computer use has occurred, and it will be necessary to repeat training and provide some ongoing refresher training due to staff and student turnover.

A level of basic computer knowledge is required so that teachers and certainly students may begin to make effective use of the tool. It will also ensure that the school gains full benefit from expensive technical resources by avoiding needless service calls or time-wasting trips.

Typing or keyboarding instruction can now be supported by simple software programs (e.g. Mavis Beacon) as well as CD-Rom-based programs. The same is true for introduction to basic computing and introductory courses for word processing and spreadsheets as well as the internet. If teachers and administrators can use these instructional techniques, costs can be halved and they have the advantage of being used over and over again for no additional cost. Most of these self-instructional approaches do not require internet connection, since the techniques change so little.

Connectivity

These are costs associated with linking one or many computers to a local area network or to a wide area network such as the internet. Connectivity costs depend dramatically on the amount of 'bandwidth' (how much capacity is purchased), and the local, regional and national infrastructure. Adding internet capacity to a school computer laboratory or into a classroom in the USA can add 14 to 20 per cent to overall support costs. Connections into rural areas will generally be much more expensive than connections within urban areas. Connectivity costs will also vary dramatically depending upon how much connection is being used for the instructional program. Fairly constant connection, for example, for internet searches, will raise costs considerably. Infrequent access for support of specific parts of the curriculum will often be much less costly (using 'dial-up' connections, for instance). These costs will be measured, for example, at $3 to $12 per hour for connection for a teacher.

Because of the wide variation in level of use and infrastructure costs, it is difficult to set a reasonable value. This portion of the estimated operating costs needs to be worked out carefully, often on a trial basis, within the specific setting. What is clear is that for any school, but particularly those at secondary and university level, reasonable access to the internet is absolutely essential for a modern education, and will become increasingly so with each passing year.

Internet access is becoming cheaper every year in virtually every country. Bandwidth available is rising geometrically, and more and more countries understand how to make it a part of their basic communications infrastructure. With proper planning, schools will benefit from all these commercial and public improvements. Technological improvements that are increasing capacity and lowering cost include: more use of satellite accessed internet (traditional and low earth orbiting satellites), wireless terrestrial networks, more fibre optic cable in urban areas, and deregulation of internet service providers.

Summary

Considering only ongoing support and maintenance costs, the needed annual expenditure (without a network) for a healthy education computer system can range from 30 to 50 per cent of the initial investment in computer hardware and software. Even if these items are donated, an educational institution needs to consider carefully what it will require to keep this investment productive. Educational institutions all over the world have used computer systems successfully and creatively to enrich, revitalise and reform their educational activity. The best ones have done it with good planning and the rapid inclusion of these very real additional costs into the annual budgeting. The majority of schools are getting less than they need for this support function, and many 'corners are being cut' because the advantages of computers and the internet in instruction appear so obvious in the modern age . . . worth making the sacrifice. All too frequently, the sacrifice is being made by teachers – who are already being asked to do a great deal more.

The issue for education systems is not whether to integrate computers and connectivity into their educational programmes, but how to do it effectively and at levels that yield a true educational benefit.

REFERENCES

Adkins, D. (1999) 'Cost and finance', in A. Dock and J. Helwig (eds) *Interactive Radio Instruction: Impact, Sustainability and Future Directions*, Washington, DC: Education and Technology Team, World Bank.

Audit Commission (1999) *Local Performance Indicators: Education Services*, London.

Chu, G. C. and Schramm, W. (1968) *Learning from Television: What the Research Says*, Stanford: ERIC.

Clark, R. E. (1983) 'Reconsidering research on learning from media', *Review of Educational Research* 53 (4): 445–59.

Department for Education and Employment (DfEE) (1999) *Survey of ICS in Schools, 1998*, London: HMSO.

Hülsmann, T. (2000) *The Costs of Open Learning: A Handbook*, Oldenburg: BIS, University of Oldenburg.

Laurillard, D. (2000) *Rethinking University Teaching: A Conversational Framework for the Effective Use of Learning Technologies*, London: Routledge.

Moore, M. G. and Kearsley, G. (1996) *Distance Education: A Systems View*, Belmont: Wadsworth.

Perraton, H. and Creed, C. (2000) *Applying New Technologies and Cost-effective Delivery Systems in Basic Education* (mimeo) (Thematic study for Education for All 2000 Assessment), Paris: UNESCO.

Perraton, H. and Hülsmann, T. (1998) *Planning and Evaluating Systems of Open and Distance Learning*, Sheffield: Department for Education and Employment.

Potashnik, M. (1996) 'Chile's learning network', *Education and Technology Technical Notes Series* 1 (2).

Secretary of State for International Development (2000) *Eliminating World Poverty: Making Globalisation Work for the Poor* (Cm 5006), Norwich: HMSO.

Wolff, L. (1999) 'Costa Rica: are computers in school cost-effective?', *TechKnowlogia*, November/December (www,TechKnowLogia.org).

Chapter 9

Globalisation

Glen Farrell, Yoni Ryan and Andrea Hope

Editors' introduction

> Globalization is in danger of becoming, if it has not already become,
> the cliché of our times: the big idea which encompasses everything
> from global financial markets to the Internet but which delivers little
> substantive insight into the contemporary human condition. Clichés,
> nevertheless, often capture the lived experience of an epoch. In this
> respect, globalization reflects a widespread perception that the world
> is rapidly being moulded into a shared social space by economic and
> technological forces and that developments in one region of the world
> can have profound consequences for the life chances of individuals or
> communities on the other side of the globe.
>
> (Held *et al.* 1999: 1)

Those economic and technological forces have borne on education as
on other human activities. Educational institutions have to respond to
demands from the workforce and from employers. These demands in turn
are shaped by the staffing needs of global employers and of enterprises
that are global in their activities and expectations: you need some of the
same skills to repair a car in the south as in the north and probably all
the same skills to repair a computer. Globalisation is likely to be making
curricula more homogeneous. At the same time changes in technology
and in particular in information technology have been seen as reflecting

> a new international division of labour. The division is based less on
> the location of natural resources, cheap and abundant labour or even
> capital stock, and more on the capacity to create new knowledge and
> apply it rapidly through information and telecommunications to a wide
> range of human activities in ever-broadening space and time.
>
> (Carnoy 1995: 212)

Globalisation can therefore move jobs across frontiers, with a migration of employment that operates alongside physical mobility, and which reinforces the trends towards a global curriculum. At the same time the same changes in information and communication technology that help global financial flows are influencing employment and in its turn education. Data processing, followed by software development, followed by real-time communication systems such as the work of call centres, have moved across frontiers, generally from the north to the south. As Chapter 2 argued, education is also moving across borders. Homogenised curricula, and the technology to carry teaching across borders, offer new opportunities to education at the same time as globalisation is making new demands upon it.

The increasing integration of the world's economies in the 1980s and 1990s was accompanied politically by the rise of neo-liberalism with its new respect for market forces and values. 'International economic integration, on the liberal view, is what happens when technology allows people to pursue their own goals and they are given the liberty to do so. If technology advances to the point where it supports trade across borders, and if people then choose to trade across borders, you have integration, and . . . you would expect there to be economic benefits as well' (Craig 2001: 4). The neo-liberal agenda has affected the public as well as the private sector so that educational institutions are seen increasingly as being in competition with each other and expected to respond to market forces and seek out new sources of income. The combination of educational demand, technological possibility and restricted funding has encouraged educational institutions to seek overseas as well as home markets. At the most extreme, or in the eyes of their critics, they have treated education as a commodity to be traded across frontiers like any other.

Globalisation thus places new issues on the educational agenda, whether this is defined in terms of conventional or of distance-teaching institutions, and does so within a political context that is sympathetic to the global operation of market forces. All sectors of education are influenced by these processes in terms of what they teach and how they teach it. But globalisation has a particular significance for policy development in open and distance learning whose methods easily cross national frontiers. Distance-teaching institutions are influenced both in terms of the content of what they teach and by the possibility of widening their student body by teaching internationally in an unprecedented way. While student mobility has been a feature of university education since it began, virtual mobility is a new phenomenon presenting new issues to policy makers.

Both open and dual-mode institutions have seized the opportunities presented by globalisation, and there are the beginnings of international virtual mobility at secondary and tertiary level. Universities such as the Indira Gandhi National Open University now teach students on specialist courses all around the world. At the same time, as conventional universities have begun to use communications technologies in their teaching, so they too have seen opportunities to internationalise some of their work. The consequences for educational policy are such that major reviews of experience have recently been undertaken – in Australia, Britain and Canada – on which this chapter is largely based. We look in turn at what has been happening, examining the drivers of activity, and at the issues this raises for policy makers. As many of these require an institutional response we then look in detail at the new agenda from that perspective, asking questions about the key issues – different since globalisation – of student support and quality assurance before examining the organisational structures they demand. This makes it possible to conclude by identifying in more detail the policy agenda at three levels: institutional, national and international.

The following four sections of this chapter are adapted from the Commonwealth of Learning's overview of *The Changing Faces of Virtual Education* (Farrell 2001).

DRIVING THE POLICY AGENDA

Glen Farrell

We can distinguish between forces driving and constraining global activity in education.

Driving forces

- The perception that the application of ICT to the delivery of educational opportunities will reduce costs, and lead to an increase in market share.
- The need to respond to criticisms about the quality of the traditional 'distance education' learning experience by using ICT in ways that enable more access to learning resources and enhance interactivity and collaboration between and among learners and teachers.
- The escalating demands for access to lifelong learning opportunities, particularly those related to upgrading and staff training, are causing both institutions and corporations to adopt ICT applications to reduce the cost of travel.

- The ability to 'unbundle' or 'disaggregate' functions that have traditionally been provided solely by a single institution through its administrative systems and its individual classroom-based teachers.
- The adoption of ICT by educational organisations allows them to proclaim their involvement in virtual education. Such involvement allows them to be seen to be 'with it' and to overcome their fear that if they are unable to find a way to be involved in some virtual education venture, they may face a doubtful future.
- The increasing capacity of ICT to facilitate educational processes makes the application more appealing to educators, and the reducing costs of both hardware and bandwidth make adoption more affordable.

Constraining forces

- The lack of access to ICT appliances and connectivity, what has come to be called the 'digital divide', remains a severe constraint, particularly in developing countries.
- The front-end costs associated with the development of ICT infrastructure and ICT-based instructional materials are difficult for organisations to finance without a substantial reallocation of current resources. Within most institutions that is a difficult decision to get support for!
- Teachers and faculty remain concerned about the quality of education that is delivered through the use of virtual models. They are also finding that it adds to their workload without commensurate rewards or clarity about intellectual property issues.
- Experience with virtual education to date is proving the necessity for extensive training and support both for faculty as well as learners. This too is costly.
- Learner support systems are still not providing the level of service that is available to the 'on-campus' learner.
- The lack of agreed-upon standards . . . for initiatives such as the development of learning objects databases restricts the ability of institutions to collaborate in terms of sharing costs and resources. The lack of shared standards is manifest in other areas as well. For example, the lack of measurable, shared standards for academic quality restricts the portability of skills and knowledge from one institution to another.

There is mounting evidence that the size and profitability of the international market for online learning and e-education is more limited, and much more competitive, than originally perceived.

(Farrell 2001: 144–5)

ISSUES FOR POLICY MAKERS AND MANAGERS

Yoni Ryan

Many of the issues faced by policy makers and managers, especially those in developing countries, may be inferred from the above discussion. To reiterate those that have been canvassed:

- Virtual education is no silver bullet that can solve all educational problems, notwithstanding its undoubted promise. This is due partly to the immense costs involved, even if wireless applications and satellite links can replace land links in remote and rural areas, and where physical infrastructure is commercially unfeasible. It is also because of entrenched beliefs about education as a social and socialising experience which can never be satisfactorily replicated in a virtual environment.
- Although distance education is perceived generally as less costly than classroom-based education, and organisations such as the UKOU have demonstrated that with volume they can educate an adult for substantially less than an on-campus student costs and at significantly less cost to the student as a result of savings in travel and living expenses and the opportunity costs of full-time study, these savings are based on print and post-delivery modalities. Development costs of online materials and the systems to support them are considerable; ongoing institutional costs increase with the necessity of help desks for technical and academic learner support. Learner costs increase as download volumes increase, and the student bears the costs of printing.
- The digital divide in current computer ownership and connection rates, even in developed economies, means that internet-based education denies one of the underlying principles of distance education: to cater for those disadvantaged by income and circumstance. We cannot exclude students because they lack the means and the skills to benefit from education at any level. Equally, we cannot exclude those whose circumstances include computer ownership and connectivity, but who lack the time or ability to learn on campus. Balancing the opportunities provided by ICTs while striving to overcome the divide is crucial.

A further issue relates to the retention of cultural and national identity in a borderless education market. While there has been an encouraging increase in the number of general and education websites emanating from non-Western sources, the high cost of creating original resources continues to reinforce the dominance of US web browsers and sites (Wilson *et al.* 1998). This is not to denigrate the quality and usefulness of materials on the simplistic grounds of source or ideological opposition. However, most national governments are concerned about providing for their citizenry materials which reflect their cultural, social and economic contexts, and which contribute to national interests.

Policy makers must also confront the inevitable plethora of programmes, courses and opportunities offered to their citizens in an emerging globalised learning environment, including the implications of such movements for credit banking and transfer of prior learning. Under the combined pressures of vocationally oriented education and training, web-based short courses, the promises of individually customised and modularised topics of study and the interests of educational institutions and commercial vendors in the continuing professional education and lifelong learning market, it would appear inevitable that evaluation and assessment of learning activities will become a significant component of the education sector.

Many US companies such as Sylvan/Caliber have already established a niche in evaluation of certification programmes, such as those in the ICT industry (Adelman 2000). Certification in the ICT industry has therefore become a globally recognised form of accreditation. No similar global accreditation programme applies in formal education, and no agency exists with the authority to validate educational attainment at the individual subject/course level, although the Association of Commonwealth Universities acts to verify at the institutional level. It is left to individual departmental authorities to gauge subject credit transfers towards a formal degree programme. At the school level, no agency verifies distance programmes.

There would appear to be an urgent need to establish a low-cost, independent agency which could validate distance-delivered subjects and courses for all institutions and sectors, similar to the University of Phoenix's database, and which could also act as an authoritative database of accredited distance providers and courses. The Commonwealth of Learning and the World Bank's Global Learning Network might provide a credible base for such an agency.

While the promise of ICTs in learner support is improved access to the rich resources of on-campus education, as well as access to education itself for those disadvantaged by distance or circumstance, the digital divide (measured as economic, social and dispositional factors) may actually exclude many students if ICTs are the sole form of learner support.

Further, while the potential of ICTs to enhance the quality of learning and the learning process itself is exciting, as has been demonstrated in many projects, there has been no systematic research into the efficacy of online support services in improving retention, progression, attainment and satisfaction rates. Common sense would suggest a positive correlation between improvement in these rates and extension of learner support services, but the very newness of these services, and their patchy implementation, has prevented the definitive research needed.

The jury is out on cost efficiencies via learner support. Thus far, cost savings in quality programmes have proved ephemeral. Learner support in both on- and off-campus situations is labour intensive, as with any quality customer service. Yet the costs of not providing such services are even greater in terms of student frustration and failure, wastage of institutional resources and the immeasurable loss to any society of a citizenry lacking the education it desires.

(adapted from Ryan 2001a: 90–2)

STUDENT SUPPORT

Yoni Ryan

Editors' note

Conventional institutions support their own students. Open universities and open schools usually do the same, though sometimes in cooperation with other local agencies. But where a distance-teaching institution is operating across frontiers or teaching predominantly through e-learning, it may need a new approach to student support and to work with partners in providing that support. While much of the following analysis concerns support for students on e-learning courses within a single country, the conclusions apply all the more strongly to international enrolments.

Pre-enrolment

For the potential student, there are any number of commercial and agency websites that extol the virtues of e-learning and provide a database of distance and online courses and programmes. However, not all their links are to accredited providers, and it is often unclear if subject enrolments in commercial programmes attract credits to fully accredited providers. The activities of unscrupulous operators (see www.virtualuniversities.net) demonstrate the need for an authoritative listing of accredited online providers, and the nature of the qualifications gained, including their acceptance in other jurisdictions.

At the next level, students want information about the range of courses available. This would suggest not merely the usual brief description of a course and its potential benefits in terms of career opportunities, but all subject requirements, their sequence, any limitations in their offering, the nature of their delivery and the support mechanisms students might expect. Most institutions are weak at providing such details in on-campus study, where informal communication between students, and between students and staff, substitutes for 'hard information'. For the prospective online student, these tacit knowledge sources are unavailable, so they have to be made explicit online via telephone support.

For most prospective students in distance education, the next questions are 'Can I do it?' and 'What will it entail?' Since distance education requires strong self-motivation and independent learning skills, pre-enrolment support ideally would include a checklist to help students decide whether this is an appropriate modality for their circumstances and learning style. Several providers have rudimentary self-assessment tests that are designed to help students realistically appraise their capacity to undertake an online course.

Learning style preference checklists are useful to the prospective distance student: the student who prefers to learn through reading and reflection is likely to prefer print-based modes, even if they are delivered online, over a video-based course, for example. At this stage it is also crucial to provide details of equipment requirements, indicate the costs of purchase and ongoing connection, clarify the technical skills levels required and indicate the level of technical support provided. Students should also know whether the institution provides subsidised ISP services, and whether internet access attracts a long-distance or local call charge.

Students also want ease of textbook purchase, and there is strong evidence that in this requirement at least many institutions excel, since online book orders reduce provider costs and are therefore an attractive proposition. However, information about library resources and costs appears to be less well handled.

Since distance education by its nature is an out-of-hours activity, telephone and e-mail help desks with restricted hours are not helpful. Several institutions have developed imaginative solutions to the budget blow-out that is likely to result from a twenty-four-hour service, the ideal if online provision is to fulfil its promise of 'anytime, anywhere, anyplace' learning. For example, Macquarie University in Australia and the London School of Economics have partnered to provide a twenty-hour help desk, without adding to institutional cost, by using the different time zones between the two institutions to provide coverage of each other's students.

Tuition fees and any available financial aid are also crucial information, although distance part-time studies do not qualify for aid in most countries.

Most institutions have invested heavily over the past three years in the infrastructure of their online systems with varying degrees of success in integrating student management systems, instructional support systems such as library databases and course content and communication systems. Network platforms that support student–teacher communication and student–student collaboration, chat rooms, bulletin boards and the library have generally taken priority, as the Computer Supported Intentional

Learning Environment (CSILE) network project at the Ontario Institute for Studies in Education demonstrates. But the urgent need is for an electronic 'one-stop shop' for the individual student which provides transparent links to the many servers carrying different systems. Distance-education providers must embrace e-commerce solutions to payment and admission procedures. Indeed, many vendors which began as application service providers providing optional institutional service levels (from basic server space and a teaching template through to professional development for faculty, student record systems and individualised design and development services) have seen the advantage of adding an e-commerce strand.

What is clear from examining institutional websites is that pre-enrolment support is patchy at all levels. While most institutions have designed graphically attractive home pages, navigation to important information for pre-enrolment is often difficult, since it is rarely designed from the user's perspective. On some sites, even the most fundamental design principles are ignored: back buttons do not work; pages of text are displayed with no exit or back-to-menu option; and vital information is buried several layers down, almost guaranteeing that prospective students will abandon their search.

Post-enrolment

After enrolment there also appear to be wide variations in the support services necessary to increase student satisfaction with the learning experience. Online enrolment should be possible and should immediately generate further information on subject content guides, suggested study schedule, learning resources required and recommended, contact names of teachers and tutors and their qualifications, and details of who developed the materials if the developers differ from the teacher.

Orientation to the particular systems of the provider are essential at this point, and many institutions are now finding that at least one face-to-face session in information literacy skills and basic computer access is necessary for online learning. UCLA's for-profit continuing professional education arm, OnlineLearning.net (OLN), has a mandatory online orientation programme for new students to ensure basic competence with course software. Gunawardena and Duphorne (2000) also argue the importance of practice with listservs and e-mail before the subject proper starts. Alternatively, for relatively confident users, a self-paced module to assist in accessing online resources should be provided, along with a module in independent learning skills and time management. Although most research in this area (e.g. Rossiter and Watters 2000) suggests that such skills are best learned in a subject-specific context, and hence integrated into the subject materials, there are information retrieval skills which can be taught independent of particular knowledge domains. Library services are crucial to external students, and the mere provision of access to databases and catalogues often represents only a tantalising glimpse of what might be available – if it were online. A reference librarian available in real time as a distance student is searching would constitute an excellent support service.

Constructive and timely feedback from the teacher appears to be a fundamental support service (though it should be a routine teaching method). Continuous communication and contact between students, and between students and staff, is critical in all cultural contexts. This suggests that the commercial vendors who tout the cost-effectiveness of virtual education for thousands at little marginal cost are deluded, at least until automated response systems are routine and affordable. Certainly the more serious online providers, such as the University of Phoenix and OLN, work on ratios of 9/10:1 to enable close attention to individual students and constant encouragement and feedback. The University of Phoenix's pedagogical philosophy is predicated on collaborative learning and a Vygotskian principle of social group motivation, even in its on-campus courses. Hence classmates will progress through a programme together, and students are expected to 'meet' (virtually or physically) once a week outside their online times to provide their own group learner support. Frequently asked question pages, non-curricular and curricular chat rooms and class conferences provide essential support. Yet it is apparent that the teacher plays a critical role in explaining and demonstrating, and that a virtual environment requires a different mindset for learning, one that does not always demand an 'expert' teacher answer to every question, in the same way that on-campus students explore concepts and clarify mis-understandings together.

Obtaining texts and other resources is an issue of concern to all distance students. Current copyright laws limit access to many texts online, although many institutions (such as Queensland University of Technology) are developing limited digitised collections in some areas under licensing regulations. Other agencies have developed fee-based regimes to assist distance learners, such as UnCover, the Colorado Alliance which has a document delivery service.

Online support for lifelong learning

It is widely accepted that the greatest potential for online education is in the realm of lifelong or continuing education, most particularly workplace-based education. Certainly this is the sector targeted by commercial providers and the training units of corporations, where the drive is as much budgetary as it is the competitive drive for speed of distribution. Predictions of savings in the order of 15 to 50 per cent are expected because travel and per diem costs can be slashed. Yet many companies are reporting strong resistance to losing face-to-face training, for the same reason that online education has been resisted within school-leaver populations at university: that the *social* process of company training is as important as the technical or performative knowledge gained (Cunningham *et al.* 2000).

Nevertheless, a company intranet for education and training has become a standard feature of large professional consultancies, such as Arthur Andersen Performance and Learning, and PricewaterhouseCoopers. Policies and procedures are quickly shared across the globe; a query posted to a bulletin board elicits answers or suggestions or examples from a dozen different offices. This, of course, is informal learning in the main and may be termed 'distributed expertise'. It reveals the power of the medium to stimulate collaborative social learning within a group: in this case a group ethic has already been developed, albeit one based on company and individual performance. But the learning process could well be applied in an educational situation if a community of learners has been formed. It is significant also because it has spawned a fruitful area for further exploitation of the technical power of networks through knowledge management systems.

(adapted from Ryan 2001a: 78–88)

QUALITY ASSURANCE

Andrea Hope

Editors' note

The structures that protect quality within frontiers do not necessarily work beyond them. And approaches to the maintenance and monitoring of quality that are appropriate for a conventional institution, teaching face-to-face, will always need some adaptation if they are to be appropriate for a new style of teaching and learning.

Protecting local providers in a global marketplace

The application of new technologies in the learning environment is not only removing the distinction between conventional and distance education, it is also eroding political and geographical barriers to the movement of knowledge. Whereas within frontiers either at the state (e.g. USA, Canada), national (e.g. South Africa, New Zealand) or regional (e.g. EU) level, structures exist for the regulation or self-regulation of educational activities, there has traditionally been less regulation across frontiers and there is certainly less still in cyberspace. The growth of the export trade in educational products during the past ten to fifteen years has alerted countries which are net recipients of such products that there is a need to erect barriers in order to safeguard their citizens and institutions against the worst excesses of some entrepreneurial providers, whose major concern is the financial bottom line rather than the educational experience of the students on the course. Butcher and Welch (1996) describe the problem in Nigeria in graphic terms: 'Adventurous entrepreneurs see a juicy field of operation because of the imbalance of demand and supply with a ready market for ever-increasing applicants who are desperate for educational qualification through correspondence measures.'

While limited access to the appropriate technology may continue to provide a barrier to web-cowboys in Nigeria, the same is not true of Hong Kong. As one of the traditional net importers of higher education, Hong Kong's response has been to pass the Non-local Higher and Professional Education (Regulation) Ordinance (1996) which requires all overseas providers, not operating through accredited Hong Kong institutions, to register with the government and to meet the stringent quality criteria required for registration (www.hkcaa.edu.hk). Nevertheless, these mechanisms cannot be applied to institutions which operate globally online and have no physical or legal presence in Hong Kong.

Australian universities have been among the most aggressive exporters of educational products to the Asian market in the 1990s. In her paper 'Higher education as a business: lessons from the corporate world' (2001b), Yoni Ryan describes how Australia has acted to protect the 'brand' of Australian universities against incursions from cyberspace by publishing National Protocols for Higher Education Approval Processes (www.detya. gov.au/highered/mceetya_cop.htm). The protocols provide for virtual universities to be prosecuted in the jurisdiction in which their operations have an adverse effect as well as in their home jurisdiction and make it illegal to use the term 'university' in Australia without formal accreditation by state government agencies. As Ryan points out, 'it is apparent that, in Australia at least, government has asserted its right to regulate borderless education'.

While protecting local institutions from the threat posed by the global ambitions of entrepreneurial offshore institutions, such legislation may, paradoxically, increase the risk to the unwary individual student that the credentials earned through participation in an online course may not be recognised for further study or employment in the participant's country, even though the institution which offers the course may be accredited in its own home jurisdiction. The increasingly global nature of educational provision therefore brings with it a need and a market for consumer advice about what to avoid and what to choose in terms of technology-mediated learning opportunities to make sure that they live up to the claims of convenience, relevance and interactivity that are often made for them.

Protecting local consumers and promoting local values

In response to the need for guidance on how to select reputable and appropriately accredited online courses, a number of distance-learning hub sites have been developed which offer advice on how to avoid falling victim to diploma mills and fly-by-night 'institutions' offering cheap degrees. Sites offering this service include Degree-net (www.degree.net), AboutEducation (www.about.com/education) and WorldwideLearn (www.worldwidelearn.com).

Canada provides an example of an effort to protect the reputation and market share of higher education institutions in the global education marketplace. The Canadian government has funded the development of a consumers' guide, based upon extensive research into the literature relating to quality in technology-assisted distance learning. The project aims to produce *Consumer-Based Quality Guidelines for Learning Technologies and Distance Education*. The guide is designed to be applied to education and training products (entire programmes and individual courses) at any level which are delivered by 'technology-assisted distance learning', which is defined in the guidelines as 'where the learner is in one location and the provider of the learning is in another and technology is used to make the link'. In this context, the quality of the education and training products and services is defined in terms of what makes them effective and efficient.

Underpinning the guidelines is the belief that all learning products are a combination or system of inputs and resources, processes and practices, and outputs and outcomes. While all are important, 'from the consumer's point of view, the outcomes are the most important, then processes and practices and finally inputs and resources that have gone into the design, production and delivery of the learning product/service'.

The guidelines list the desirable features of a high-quality course or programme and are structured to reflect the hierarchy of concerns described above, starting with quality outcomes:

- Acquired content skills and knowledge should:
  - be relevant
  - be transferable
  - be specific for the purpose (e.g. work or higher learning)
  - blend traditional education and applied technology skills.

- Necessary learning skills are acquired for:
  - course/programme completion and success
  - lifelong learning
  - self-directed learning management.

- Completion takes the form of credit or credentials that are:
  - recognised by professional accreditation bodies and employers
  - recognised by other educational institutions
  - of the same value whether acquired through on-site or distance learning
  - transferable within programmes and institutions, locally, nationally and internationally.

- Return on investment of the learner's time, finances and energy meets expectations for:
  - accessibility as and when needed
  - objective benefits and utility
  - effectiveness: subjective achievement of personal goals
  - efficiency: best use of resources
  - customer satisfaction with all course/programme elements.

The draft guidelines are available at www.futured.com.

To achieve the output standards listed above, the provider must have in place systematic quality processes and practices for student management systems in the areas of pre-entry counselling, admissions, registration and orientation of students, assessment and recognition of prior learning, and the accurate and secure management of student records. They should allow for learner involvement in decision making and provide assistance for students with the technologies being used.

National governments in many of the advanced industrial economies have not been slow to embrace e-learning, recognising the potential presented by the global market for education to secure new revenue to offset high infrastructure and development costs and at the same time to further their ambitions to trade in other economic sectors. The advantages presented to learners in developing countries by the opportunity to access scarce, top-quality expertise anywhere in the world and to gain access to curricula that embrace a broader spectrum of knowledge than any one institution might accomplish (Mason 1998) must be offset by the danger of the emergence of a new cultural imperialism. The globalisation of content facilitated by the new communications technologies leads to a potential loss of cultural diversity and richness. In the domain of quality assurance, global access makes the application of standards and performance measures even more problematic. If standards are relative to the context, to the needs of the students and to their approach to learning, they will be disparate. If, as Tait (1997) asserts, 'no quality assurance system can be transplanted from one institution to another across organisational, social and cultural boundaries', how can local cultures, institutions and educational approaches retain their voice in a globalised world? The Canadian approach of researching global best practice and deriving national benchmark standards in key domains which can be applied both to local courses and to those offered by remote providers may offer a useful model which could be applied by policy makers in other jurisdictions.

The role of accrediting agencies

National quality assurance agencies have also published guidelines to meet the needs of their constituent institutions which are engaged in the delivery of open and distance learning. Examples include those produced by the Quality Assurance Agency of the UK in 1999 (www.qaa.ac.uk/public/dlg/append1.htm), which are based upon generic guidelines on quality assurance procedures developed originally for programmes delivered face to face, published in 1996, and the NZAAU's guide *External Quality Assurance for the Virtual Institution* (Butterfield *et al.* 1999). In Australia, where open and distance learning at university level is provided on a very wide scale through dual-mode institutions, and where the development of technology-mediated flexible learning resulting from the convergence between distance and face-to-face modes of delivery is well advanced, all institutions and programmes are audited according to a single set of benchmark standards irrespective of the mode of delivery (McKinnon *et al.* 1999).

In the USA there is no national academic audit agency, and accreditation is a voluntary activity undertaken usually at the regional level among groups of institutions. In the global virtual education market, students continue to seek assurance that the programme they are studying is accredited by a reliable agency or that it bears the insignia of an institution or group of institutions, whose names are synonymous with excellence. The development of consortium arrangements for the delivery of online courses and programmes is mirrored by greater collaboration in policy development across accrediting regions and states. For example, the *Guide to Best Practice for Electronically Offered Degree and Certificate Programs* has been developed by the Western Cooperative for Educational Telecommunications, an arm of the Western Interstate Commission for Higher Education (WICHE) spanning fifteen western states in the USA (www.wiche.edu/telecom/accrediting – best practices.pdf). This project takes as its starting point the fact that well-established essentials of institutional quality found in regional accreditation standards are applicable to the emergent forms of learning. Taken together, they reflect the values which the regional commissions foster among their affiliated colleges and universities:

- That education is best experienced within a community of learning where competent professionals are actively and cooperatively involved with creating, providing and improving the instructional programme.
- That learning is dynamic and interactive, regardless of the setting in which it occurs.

- That instructional programmes leading to degrees having integrity are organised around substantive and coherent curricula which define expected learning outcomes.
- That institutions accept the obligation to address student needs related to, and to provide the resources necessary for, their academic success.
- That institutions are responsible for the education provided in their name.
- That institutions undertake the assessment and improvement of their quality, giving particular emphasis to student learning.
- That institutions subject themselves voluntarily to peer review.

These general statements of good practice offer a comprehensive guide for institutions contemplating the move into technology-mediated learning to the range of quality issues involved. Yet again, the underpinning message to providers is clearly expressed: 'Methods change but standards of quality endure. The important issues are not technical but curriculum driven and pedagogical. The big decisions are made by qualified faculty and focus on learning outcomes for an increasingly diverse student population' (WICHE 2001).

(adapted from Hope 2001: 127–35)

ORGANISATIONAL STRUCTURE

Editors' note

As noted in Chapters 2 and 7, the development of new information and communication technologies, one of the drivers of globalisation, has brought into place a new set of actors in open and distance learning. In their analysis, the British team looking at borderless education identified seven different kinds of organisation, though without being able to quantify the scale of their work. In all cases institutions were actually or potentially able to operate across frontiers. Four groups of actors are dominated by private-sector agencies. The first are described as the *corporate universities* although the term is often misleading: 'The focus of activities in most – not all – corporate universities is not at a higher education level, subject coverage tends to be narrow, practitioners rather than academics act as tutors, and links to academic research are rarely a part of curriculum design and content' (CVCP 2000: 10). Alongside the corporates are the *for-profit institutions*, some offering accredited degrees and, as with corporate universities, often working in partnership with conventional universities. Among the bona fide institutions are the diploma mills and fly-by-night operators that are giving 'particular cause for concern to institutions and higher education agencies in the USA, South Africa and Central and Eastern Europe' (ibid.: 11–12). The corporates may be distinguished from *educational services* where 'contractors increasingly handle student enrolment, manage training and development and run student support systems. . . . Information technology companies are also large-scale providers of information technology training and education, offering both stand-alone courses and modules for delivery within higher education programmes' (ibid.: 13). A fourth category, which operates at school level as well as in higher education, consists of *media companies* offering support to learners. Companies with backgrounds in publishing, computers or broadcasting have moved into the provision of teaching either for individuals or for use within institutions.

Professional bodies have long operated across borders, seeking to maintain the same professional standards through the conduct of examinations and control of entry to their professions. In contrast, *educational brokers* are newcomers to the scene. Within national frontiers the Open Learning Agency in Australia and the University for Industry – Learndirect – in Britain act as brokers between institutions providing a complete or partial education service and the learner. Many of them have explored the possibility of working outside their host country as well as within so that, for example, a membership organisation such as the Open Learning Foundation in Britain has attracted overseas as well as British membership institutions. Finally, many existing *universities and colleges* have been vigorous, even aggressive, in exploring how open and distance learning can enable them to reach new audiences of students. This has involved a variety of arrangements including the franchising of courses overseas, direct enrolment of students, and the development of a variety of consortia.

These developments have been paralleled by the activities of international agencies with related concerns. Within the anglophone and francophone worlds, governments have set up international agencies dedicated to international cooperation in open and distance learning. The Briggs group, which drafted the first plans for the Commonwealth of Learning, defined its aims as 'to widen access to education, to share resources, to raise educational quality and to support the mobility of ideas, of teaching, of relevant research and of people' (Briggs *et al.* 1986: 60). The parallel francophone agency, CIFFAD (now Institut francophone des nouvelles technologies de l'information et de la formation), set out its objectives as follows:

a) to set in place a cooperative network between francophone institutions concerned with distance education;

b) within member countries to support the development of distance education through the sharing of information and both pedagogical and technical resources;

c) to offer technical and financial support to projects consistent with CIFFAD's aims and the criteria for their acceptance which it has laid down.

(CIFFAD 1991)

In practice, as time has gone on, while both agencies have continued to have a broad mandate in international education, the main emphasis of their work has been to support the development of distance education within individual countries with cooperative ventures playing a more modest role.

Regional actors have also played a part in international distance education, with the European Commission much to the fore. A series of European policy documents have argued that open and distance learning, and the use of telematics, can bring economic benefits to Europe by strengthening education and training. Technology-driven programmes – COMMETT, DELTA, EUROTECHNET and SATURN – have led to a suite of open and distance learning activities within the European Socrates and Leonardo programmes, devoted to promoting European integration and economic competitiveness. At least as important as the policies, the Commission's interest has led to their funding exemplary projects that typically involve a group of institutions working together across frontiers.

Many of the organisational issues faced by institutions working internationally are similar to those familiar from national activity. As suggested above, more difficult policy questions are likely to arise in relation to cooperation between institutions, student support, and quality assurance.

As noted in Chapter 2, the range of functions needed for open and distance learning has often stimulated cooperation between institutions. Most international cooperation has, however, been at the lower end of a scale of complexity, and limited to a sharing of information and occasional cooperation on materials development. As a result we have few well-established and well-documented partnerships on which to report. Stimulated by the work of CIFFAD, and its related agency Resafad, there have been some collaborative developments in francophone West Africa where regional and international resources were used to develop a course for headteachers in Burkina Faso. Here course development had an international dimension while materials were distributed and student support provided on a national basis. Similarly the Commonwealth of

Learning has supported the regional development of materials for science teaching in southern Africa, with student support being offered locally. The record of international cooperation between tertiary-level institutions is, however, mixed. Some schemes have closed down because of disagreement between the various parties, others because of government response to what was seen as inappropriate behaviour by an external institution. Effective cooperation may be necessary in a globalised educational world but remains difficult to achieve.

CONCLUSION: THE THREE-TIER AGENDA

The various reviews of borderless education, and of the impact of global-isation on open and distance learning, have made it possible to identify the major questions these pose to institutions and then to go on and ask about national and international policy in relation to them. Many of the decisions, on student support, quality assurance and organisational structure, turn on issues of resources and quality.

Decisions about resources are challenging, and at the time of writing many institutions are having second thoughts about their level of commit-ment. Following the euphoria of 2000, when the British government announced its e-universities, 'it is not just dot-com companies that have been asking themselves . . . what went wrong. Universities and companies that invested in e-learning have also had their fingers burned by rushing hopefully online' (MacLeod 2002: 10). The British Open University has closed down its American branch at a reported loss of £9 million; Columbia University cut back from a planned investment of £18.7 million; commercial publishers have withdrawn from borderless educational business (ibid.: 10–11). The scale and pace of development of the global campus remains unclear and difficult to predict. At the same time, it seems unlikely that universities, at least, will withdraw from the inter-national search for students, even if they try to do so through lower levels of technology; they will then face many of the same policy issues we have been examining here. Where institutions are exploring partnerships, or contemplating working overseas, they are likely, for example, to need protocols for the franchising of courses; balancing intellectual property interests against the free flow of ideas, regardless of the technological sophistication of the way they are teaching.

The national agenda also addresses resource issues but extends into issues of quality assurance or consumer protection. One set of resource issues concerns the development of national capacity to provide programmes in response to international demand. The British government's view was that the development of global educational activity was of such national significance that there should be government investment to kick-start it. Without some kind of central mechanism of this kind it is difficult for any one institution to locate and allocate resources for course development, or for a system of student support, in areas of work where the demand, and the importance of the subject area, are such that there is a case for investment on a national, regional or international scale but not on an institutional one. There are therefore supply-side issues about encouraging individual institutions to play a role in the global educational marketplace.

Alongside these there are, at least in some countries, demand-side issues about the extent to which national educational needs may now, more readily, be met through international enrolment. The existence of distance-education courses, deliberately designed for an international market, offers new choices to planners and students: they may now be able to study in-country, or to travel abroad to study, or to study abroad through distance learning. This new possibility is likely to be of particular importance for small states, and for highly specialist disciplines. One of the first courses designed for an international market was, for example, the University of London's Master's course in agricultural development, attracting students in relatively small numbers from a relatively large number of countries. The other major national issue is about the need to monitor or regulate cross-border enrolment where there will be a need to balance between protecting national consumers and promoting free access to education either within or across borders. Hong Kong, referred to above, has acted vigorously by legislating to regulate offshore enrolment. However, in many parts of the world, there are no measures to protect the interests of the uninformed student who cannot tell from an advertisement whether something is reputable or a degree mill.

There are then a series of issues that need to be resolved nationally but have international repercussions. Some of these are in the area of scholarship policy where, until recently, scholarships and fellowships have been available for conventional study abroad but not for enrolment on distance-education courses. A small handful of experimental projects is beginning to build up expertise in the modalities of providing scholarships for distance students. The Commonwealth of Learning has funded students on Indira Gandhi National Open University Master's course in distance education; the Canadian government has funded linked distance-education courses between Canada and the Caribbean; the Commonwealth Scholarship Commission of the United Kingdom has begun to support distance-education partnerships between British and overseas institutions.

It may also be appropriate to develop national policies in relation to fees for international enrolment, which balance institutional priorities with equity. (This would certainly seem appropriate if, for example, aid funds were used for the development of courses to meet international priority needs.) There may also be scope for a national, alongside an institutional, policy for supervising arrangements for academic recognition and transfer.

The international agenda reflects the national but goes beyond it. Education here reflects international realities and the growing recognition that the institutions of the nation state, or the structures of individual national institutions, do not fit with social needs. This general point was made by the Commission on Global Governance:

> Most governments accept responsibility for the provision of public goods such as policing and justice, financial stability, or environmental protection; to do otherwise would be to abandon essential functions of a state. The same responsibility applies – but is less readily acknowledged – at an international level. . . . The growing interdependence of the global economy and environment increases both the benefits of providing these international public goods and the penalties for neglecting them.
>
> (Commission on Global Governance 1995: 150–1)

The Commission did not refer specifically to education among these public goods but argued for an open system for trade and technology transfer, common standards and technical specifications and 'equity and social cohesion: through economic cooperation in its widest sense'. While that concern for equity is relevant to educational policy, we lack mechanisms of governance to guide or regulate the process of international educational activity.

At the level of international policy it is therefore difficult to work out the kind of structure and set of institutional arrangements that would be appropriate to defend the international interest in this area. The needs go beyond those that are already being met by UNESCO or the specialist agencies such as the Commonwealth of Learning or CIFFAD, or bodies such as the Association of Commonwealth Universities and regional associations. They range from broad questions of national identity and culture and the proper balance between local educational development and international sharing and exchange of learning to the narrow ones of protecting the interests of the uninformed potential student reading e-learning advertisements.

Globalisation, with its promise of sharing intellectual resources, can bring benefits to education. They will be maximised only if institutions, governments and the international community grapple with these issues in the interest of the public in general and the global community of learners in particular.

REFERENCES

Adelman, C. (2000) 'A parallel universe, expanded: certification in the information technology guild', www.aahe.org/change/paralleluniverse.htm> (accessed 7 July 2000).

Briggs, A. *et al.* (1986) *Towards a Commonwealth of Learning: Commonwealth Cooperation in Distance Education and Open Learning*, London: Commonwealth Secretariat.

Butcher, N. and Welch, T. (1996) 'A distance education quality standards framework for South Africa', Pretoria: Education, Media and Technological Services, Department of Education.

Butterfield, S. *et al.* (1999) *External Quality Assurance for the Virtual Institution* (AAU series on Quality Number 4), Wellington: New Zealand Universities Academic Audit Unit.

Carnoy, M. (1995) 'Education and the new international division of labour', in M. Carnoy (ed.) *International Encyclopaedia of Economics of Education*, Oxford: Pergamon Press.

CIFFAD (1991) *Bulletin d'information* 1.

Commission on Global Governance (1995) *Our Global Neighbourhood*, Oxford: Oxford University Press.

Committee of Vice-Chancellors and Principals (CVCP) (2000) *The Business of Borderless Education: UK Perspectives (Summary Report)*, London.

Craig, C. (2001) 'Globalisation and its critics', *The Economist* (A survey of globalisation), 29 September.

Cunningham, S. *et al.* (2000) *The Business of Borderless Education*, Canberra: DETYA.

Farrell, G. M. (2001) 'Issues and choices', in G. M. Farrell (ed.) *The Changing Faces of Virtual Education*, Vancouver: Commonwealth of Learning (accessible at www. col.org).

Gunawardena, C. and Duphorne, P. (2000) 'Predictors of success in an academic computer conference', *Distance Education* 21 (1): 101–17.

Held, D., McGrew, A., Goldblatt, D. and Perraton, J. (1999) *Global Transformations: Politics, Economics and Culture*, Cambridge: Polity Press.

Hope, A. (2001) 'Quality assurance', in G. M. Farrell (ed.) *The Changing Faces of Virtual Education*, Vancouver: Commonwealth of Learning (accessible at www.col.org).

McKinnon, K. R., Walker, S. H. and Davis, D. (1999) *Benchmarking: A Manual for Australian Universities*, Canberra: Department of Education, Training and Youth Affairs (DETYA), available at <www.detya.gov.au/archive/highered/otherpub/bench.pdf> (accessed 31 May 2001).

MacLeod, D. (2002) 'Distant dreams', *Guardian (Guardian Education)*, 2 April.

Mason, R. (1998) *Globalising Education: Trends and Applications*, London: Routledge.

Rossiter, D. and Watters, J. (2000) *Technological Literacy: Foundations for the 21st Century*, Brisbane: Queensland University of Technology.

Ryan, Y. (2001a) 'The provision of learner support services online', in G. M. Farrell (ed.) *The Changing Faces of Virtual Education*, Vancouver: Commonwealth of Learning (accessible at www.col.org).

Ryan, Y. (2001b) 'Higher education as a business: lessons from the corporate world', *Minerva* 39: 115–35.

Tait, A. (ed.) (1997) *Quality Assurance in Higher Education: Selected Case Studies*, Vancouver: Commonwealth of Learning.

Western Interstate Commission for Higher Education (WICHE) (2001) *Guide to Best Practice for Electronically Offered Degree and Certificate Programs*, available at <www.wiche.edu/telecom/accrediting-bestpractices.pdf> (accessed 31 May 2001).

Wilson, M., Qayyam, A. and Boshier, R. (1998) 'Worldwide America? Think globally, click locally', *Distance Education* 19 (1): 109–23.

Chapter 10

Governance, accreditation and quality assurance in open and distance education

Bernadette Robinson

Open and distance education has faced an ongoing struggle to establish its credibility and legitimacy, even when its quality is good. Its success in achieving these has varied among countries and institutions. Much doubt has been cast on its quality, especially in contexts where it is new or it faces a history of poor-quality provision. A new dimension of concern is raised by current global trends in electronic delivery, cross-border provision and international partnerships and franchises. For these reasons, attention to its governance, accreditation and quality assurance is essential in establishing good practice, standards and reputation. Success in establishing the status and value of open and distance learning programmes depends on the policy and actions of governments, national or regional bodies and individual institutions, together with effective articulation among them. Aligning policies, regulations and practices presents considerable challenges, whatever the context. This chapter examines three interlinked and overlapping areas of endeavour: governance, accreditation and quality assurance. It identifies key trends and issues for planners and policy makers faced with the need to assure the quality of open and distance education.

GOVERNANCE IN OPEN AND DISTANCE LEARNING

In many countries today education of all kinds operates in a rapidly changing policy and regulatory environment. The past decade has seen a shift from an emphasis on 'government' (usually interpreted as the state ruling and controlling through institutions and regulations over a given territory) to 'governance',

> the control of an activity by some means such that a range of desired outcomes is attained . . . a function that can be performed by a wide variety of public and private, state and non-state, national and international, institutions and practices.
>
> (Hirst and Thompson 1995: 422)

Governance activities generally relate to the funding, regulation and provision or delivery of educational services. The state's role in relation to the public sector and education is being redefined, changing from one of carrying out most of the work of education itself to determining where the work will be done and by whom. The change from a state-controlled to a state-supervised model is apparent in many education systems (Dale 1997, Hargreaves 1997) and helps explain, in part, the increased emphasis on accountability in educational provision. This trend is driven largely by the state, though globalisation and market forces exert a growing influence. Globalisation and targets of education for all have turned the attention of individual countries to international standards and market forces have created new problems, impelling reforms and legislation in response. The growing marketisation of education as a commodity with choice by consumers and competition by providers (Bridges and McLaughlin 1994, Le Grand and Bartlett 1993) is engendering a tightening in the regulation of education and greater scrutiny of standards and performance.

The shift from government to governance (and the ensuing debate) started in Western countries but is also emerging more globally, as Streeten (1996) and Mok (1997) illustrate in the context of Asia. The nature of governance is changing too in education systems around the world, from China to America. In his study of governance, Rhodes (1997) argues that the type of governance practised in Weber's ideal bureaucracy is in the process of deconstruction, with new forms arising. These bring more actors and voices into the policy process and transfer control to bodies other than the government or state. This is highly visible in countries where decentralisation policies are being implemented and where the costs of education at all levels are being redistributed to its beneficiaries, from basic education to higher education. However, some analysts (e.g. Dale 1997) conclude that the process of decentralisation has actually strengthened the role of the state in the control of education and that parallel trends of centralisation and decentralisation are occurring. Issues arising from the transition from government to governance revolve around accountability, the maintenance of control and steering capacity in education systems, the power relationships between the different stakeholders or partners, the human resource capacity and needs of stakeholders for training in governance and the management of standards. In addition, particular issues for distance education are whether or not it is adequately represented in policy dialogue and process, and the appropriateness and adequacy of the controls and standards set for it.

Models for the governance of education vary widely, shaped by the specific traditions, history and the degree of bureaucratic organisation in any context. Actors include the state, the educational institutions and providers, the market, the community, learners, employers and professional associations, to varying degrees in different countries. Learners tend to come low down in the list of actors, though this is changing with the growth of market forces and consumer protection legislation (still woefully lacking in many countries). Whatever the model of governance, planners and policy makers face new challenges in finding effective mechanisms for the governance of educational programmes which cross national boundaries and legislation – an aspect of particular relevance for offshore courses, international partnerships, applications of information and communication technologies (ICT) and distance education.

This, then, is the broad context in which open and distance education operates. It is characterised by increasing demands for accountability, a shift in the state's role from provider to supervisor or regulator or enabler, the transfer of some functions of governance from state to stakeholders in parallel with greater specification of requirements and standards, growing stakeholder involvement in the governance process, an expanding marketisation of education within and between countries, and a huge increase in the provision of open and distance learning, often by those new to the field. Out of this context, what challenges and issues arise for planners of distance education? Where do policy makers and planners begin in reviewing or improving the governance of open and distance education? The following section indicates the scope of the questions to be asked.

Strategic questions for policy makers and planners

Although contexts will vary, policy makers and planners need to ask strategic questions of the following kind in reviewing or planning good governance for open and distance education.

1   What *forms of governance* already exist? Does the governance of open and distance education need to align with these forms or create new forms? Is it organised as a separate system or integrated within the governance of the institutions which provide it? Which forms or mechanisms are crucial for establishing the credibility of open and distance education? Where is governance located (central authorities, local institutions, voluntary associations)? Where does responsibility for the governance of cross-border programmes lie?

2   Is the *policy basis* for open and distance education adequate for its governance and regulation? Does it need revising and developing? Are the desired outcomes for the role of open and distance education clearly defined in policy documents and plans? Are there regular opportunities for bringing key stakeholders into the policy process? Does the policy accommodate cross-border programmes or does it need reworking for this?

3   What are the *principles* which underpin the governance of open and distance education? Are they explicit and reflected in the mechanisms and activities which regulate open and distance education and ensure its quality? Are the principles congruent with those of open and distance learning in this particular context and with policy for it? Will cross-border programmes be required to fit with the stated principles in some ways?

4   Are the *arrangements* for governance appropriate and up to date? Do they work effectively, ensuring that acceptable levels of quality are achieved? What up-to-date evidence and information sources are available about their effectiveness? Do the arrangements need revision or amendment? When were they last reviewed? Do they reflect current policy goals? Are they appropriate for open and distance education as currently practised in the country? Are they appropriate for the governance of cross-border programmes?

5   Are the *different forms or types* of open and distance education provision accommodated sufficiently in the arrangements for governance? Do new arrangements need to be made for the regulation of new developments (e.g. franchises and partnerships with overseas providers, ICT-based programmes, international or offshore provision and the compatibility of accreditation arrangements)? Is policy and/or legislation sufficiently responsive to the rapid changes and trends generated by these developments?

6   In the arrangements made, are the *responsibilities* of agents or stakeholders clearly defined (providers, accrediting bodies, professional associations, unions, ministry departments, inspectors, assessors and providing partners)? Are mechanisms in place to ensure that these responsibilities are carried out? Is there clear definition of the functions of governance to be performed by public and private, state and non-state, national and international, agencies or institutions? Is there consensus on them by the stakeholders involved? Are the rights and entitlements of students or users made explicit?

7   Is there sufficient *articulation* between the policies and between the policies and the roles of implementing agencies (the ministry, the institutions, the accreditation bodies and others)? Is there a review cycle which monitors this periodically and provides opportunities for amendment when needed? How and by whom will coordination be achieved? Is responsibility for the governance of open and distance education appropriately located in government or ministry structures? Does its current location present any problems for implementation of policy? How does the policy articulate with that governing or adopted by overseas providers or recipients of programmes?

8   Do the arrangements accommodate a range of *differences in institutional missions*? If so, how? How far is a generic model of governance

appropriate? Is it flexible enough to support a diversity of provision? Does the diversity accommodate cross-border provision or reception of programmes?

9 Is the *accreditation system* effective? What role does it play? How will it ensure the credibility of open and distance education? Does it operate at an institutional or programme level? Are there too many or too few accreditation agencies at work? What sanctions and rewards apply to programme providers as a result of the work of the accreditation agencies? How are accreditation agencies monitored? Is there a single overseeing accreditation agency? How will accreditation as a regulatory mechanism be guided, monitored and developed? How does it accommodate cross-border programme delivery? Is there adequate training for those conducting accreditation activities? How can it be ensured that they understand the practices of open and distance education?

10 Are mechanisms in place for *reviewing and monitoring* the arrangements for governance? Are those responsible for policy development and regulation of provision well-informed about current practices, performance levels and new developments? Do the mechanisms need to take account of international arrangements in accreditation and governance (such as those developed by international organisations or regional agencies)?

11 How will *quality assurance* be used as part of the governance of open and distance education, for in-country and offshore programmes? Where will responsibility for it lie? What form will it take? Is a national framework needed? If a federal structure is in place in the country, how will equivalence of standards and a common currency in qualifications be achieved? How are standards for quality set? What force will they have? Have systems and standards for quality assurance been clearly defined and communicated to all concerned? Are clear guidelines provided? Have these been developed with input of stakeholders' groups? Are the guidelines and existing arrangements adequate for cross-border provision and franchised programmes or do they need further attention?

12 What is the intended balance in existing arrangements between *external control and self-regulation*? Is it appropriate for both in-country and cross-border programmes? Are the rationale and goals desirable and achievable? What are the costs and benefits in present arrangements? To what extent is standard setting centralised or decentralised? Where should the balance lie? What kind of auditing takes place and with what purpose? Who has responsibility for this? Is quality assurance and adherence to standards required (mandatory for institutions) or recommended?

13 Do the arrangements for governance and quality assurance provide

adequate *protection for students* and enquirers? Are they likely to create confidence in them and in others (employers and funders, ministries and government, professional associations and the public at large)? Is the necessary information freely available? Do the arrangements have real force? What mechanisms for complaint and appeal exist? Do all of the arrangements and information provided work equally well for cross-border students and programmes? Do additional arrangements need to be made for these?

14   Is the mode of governance and its mechanisms *clearly visible and demonstrable* to all involved and to the public at large? Is there a communication strategy in place to ensure this? Is communication with overseas partners clearly established?

Goals, forms and mechanisms of governance

The general goals of open and distance education are similar to those of other educational providers: the operation of a well-functioning system which provides well-designed, relevant programmes and enables learners to complete them successfully, to defined standards, at lowest possible cost for the quality provided. In addition, open and distance education has two further goals: parity of standards with other providers and parity of esteem for the qualifications earned and the means of earning them. Some institutions and governments may also have goals of social equity in their provision of open and distance education.

Parity of standards and esteem are not always achieved easily. The problem is illustrated in the following two examples from Malaysia (similar examples may be found in other countries too). The Legal Profession Qualifying Board of Malaysia grants graduates of open and distance education programmes only partial recognition of the equivalent award earned or imposes additional requirements. The Board of Engineers of Malaysia differentiates between degrees earned on campus and through open and distance education, considering the distance-education qualification to be of restricted value and requiring six years' work experience before these graduates can sit their professional assessment examination compared to four years' work experience from on-campus graduates (Gan 2001). In these cases, the different status of the distance-learning programme is determined by professional associations. In others, government regulations maintain the distinction, for example, where teachers studying through distance education are successful in the same exit examinations taken by college-based students but are not allowed to proceed to further formal study as are college-qualified teachers. Solving problems of parity involves several actions: demonstrating high comparable standards, or, where no equivalent programme exists, creating sets of criteria for demonstrating the achievement of good quality, negotiating recognition of programmes by professional associations or employers, disseminating persuasive but sound evidence on the value of programmes and distance learning and gaining the support of significant stakeholders. Changing attitudes or perceptions is difficult but is part of the equation for establishing the value of distance education, provided the evidence supports the claims.

Forms of governance

The forms of governance for open and distance education differ widely, as they do for more traditional kinds of education. They demonstrate to varying degrees the presence or absence of a national authority responsible for formulating policies on standards and quality assurance; the use (or not) of national accreditation boards to validate institutional awards; the balance between centralised external control and self-regulation; the role of funding as a tool in regulating provision; the use of formal quality-assurance systems and their status as optional or mandatory; and the extent of government intervention and inspection. Some countries have a strong policy basis for open and distance education, expressed in documents and law, but these are in the minority. In many others, the reference to open and distance education in policy documents or the education law is brief, general in nature, and neither developed further in detailed strategy or plans nor reflected in structures or mechanisms for its governance. In some cases, the governance of open and distance education develops on a piecemeal basis and policy tries to catch up later, trying to reduce undesirable inconsistency in quality and standards. This raises issues at both institutional and national level, as the experience of Malaysia again serves to illustrate:

> All universities in Malaysia are moving quickly into the distance education market, each following a different path in planning and implementing distance education programmes. While some are adopting a carefully charted decision-making and planning process, most seem to follow a rather ad hoc process of implementation. There is a need now for each institution of higher learning to assess the situation and recognise that some innovations and changes have to be made at institutional, and even the national level, to avoid unnecessary competition and lend more credibility to the distance learning courses they offer both on and off campus.
>
> (Gan 2001: 197)

Pressure to review or improve the governance of open and distance education seems to come as much, if not more, from changes in the environment (other parts of the education system, or the consequences of international or offshore or ICT programme provision or even complaints in the press and media) as from timely or anticipatory internal review and development processes by ministries or authorities.

In some cases, issues of governance arise from the location of open and distance education within the administrative structure. For example, responsibility for programmes provided through distance-teaching universities may be placed with the department of non-formal education within a Ministry of Education rather than the Department for Higher Education (as was the case in Vietnam). This can lead to perceptions of the distance-education provision as marginal to the mainstream or of lower quality and its lack of representation in some key decision-making bodies. It may also place the open and distance learning programmes under an inappropriate set of regulations for its role and governance.

Different models of governance operate for national and federal states. In Australia, for example, there is no central national body responsible for the governance of distance education, and responsibility is delegated to states and integrated with campus-based provision. Responsibility for the management of distance education, its academic standards, resource allocation and infrastructure is distributed through individual states, the Technical and Further Education (TAFE) Colleges and the universities, an arrangement described as 'one of the great strengths of the Australian system because it means that the standards and services of distance education are those of the existing and mainstream systems rather than separate and marginal institutions' (Latchem 2001: 340). The degree of integration in this case makes separate governance for conventional and distance education inappropriate to an extent, when set in the context of a 'blended' or 'flexible' educational provision which combines both forms. However, in other countries with federal structures but different distance-education histories, differences in state regulatory frameworks and standards can act as obstacles to the transferability of qualifications and credit and to the achievement of credibility and quality in open and distance education. Some now seek a common currency of exchange through the development of modular programmes and shared frameworks of accreditation while at the same time attempting to retain their autonomy.

Mechanisms of governance

Mechanisms used in the governance of distance education include policy, legislation, market forces, voluntary professional associations, the allocation and conditionality of funding, accreditation and quality-assurance systems.

Legislation as a means of regulating distance education has been used since at least the 1940s (e.g. in Norway, Denmark, Germany, France) and, in some cases, separate bodies have been established to exercise state control (Karow and Storm 1975). In the case of Norway the legislation shows the shift of emphasis over time from external control to self-regulation (see Box 10.1). Much legislation on distance education has dealt with private or commercial provision as a separate area and has not applied to distance-education provision from public institutions. The main aim in the legislation has been to protect consumer interests, through requirements for the contractual terms and sales methods as well as for professional and pedagogical quality (accreditation of courses and curricula, qualifications of staff and inspection schemes). In public institutions, distance education has generally been subject to the regulations applying to the institution or category of provision in general, especially in the implementation of quality assurance for higher education, though in terms of self-governance, the degree of autonomy for the distance-teaching universities has often been less than that for traditional universities.

Box 10.1 Evolution of regulations and accreditation in Norway

The first law on correspondence schools in any country was passed in Norway in 1948 as a means of regulating the quality of the many correspondence schools in existence at the time. This law set up a Correspondence Schools Council to assist the Ministry of Education, Research and Church Affairs in supervising correspondence schools. An amendment of this law in 1969 required the correspondence schools to gain accreditation. Thus private institutions had the responsibility for carrying out correspondence education and the public authorities monitored the quality. These laws and the required accreditation of schools had a positive impact on the quality and development of correspondence education in Norway. The accreditation scheme ensured that:

- each course was evaluated by independent consultants who also advised on changes for improvement before a course could be put on the market;
- the time limit of accreditation (three to five years) ensured the currency of courses and services;
- the correspondence schools were inspected and required to provide reports on specific aspects of operation (marketing, tutoring, turn-around times for assignments and so on) and statistics on their performance.

Training activities and practical handbooks were part of the relationship between the correspondence schools and the Correspondence Schools Council.

The good quality achieved by independent or commercial providers of distance education in Norway resulted from two factors:

1   the follow-up, supervision and economic support provided by the authorities;
2   the willingness and ability of the individual institutions to cooperate and to carry out systematic quality improvements through research and development work.

Although this Act concerning Correspondence Schools was effective, it was repealed in 1968 in order to improve it, to modernise the legislation in line with changes taking place in distance education (including developments in media and technology) and to overcome some limitations. These limitations lay in achieving objectivity in the appraisals made, the use of external consultants who were unfamiliar with distance education, the underuse of the skilled, competent internal staff in the process of appraisal, too much attention to external consultants' appraisals at the expense of attention to student needs, too narrow a focus on learning materials at the expense of other relevant aspects, and too little scope for quality improvement as part of the process.

The new legislation was based on two conclusions drawn from experience: distance education should be regulated as a form of adult education; and the accredited institutions, in collaboration with the authorities (the Ministry of Education), should take responsibility for their own quality assurance. As a consequence, the public regulation of distance education in independent or commercial institutions was incorporated into the Norwegian Adult Education Act of 1993 and the Correspondence Schools Council was discontinued. The responsibility for ensuring the quality of the learning materials, teaching and implementation of study programmes was delegated to the individually approved distance-education institutions. The Ministry of Education requested the Norwegian Association for Distance Education (NADE) to provide guidelines for quality standards for distance education and, to do this, NADE appointed a Standing Committee on Quality. NADE, formerly the Norwegian Association of Correspondence Schools, was established in 1968. A Code of Ethics for distance education was part of its founding charter.

Source: based on Ljoså and Rekkedal 1993

One advantage of using legislation as a way of regulating quality, particularly in relation to commercial providers, is that it can carry some force if applied effectively, and can raise standards overall. Although it may be argued that good-quality distance education exists in some countries which have little legislation for it (thus questioning its necessity), in others where low-quality distance-education providers abound and self-regulation is weak, legislation offers a way of removing or improving them.

It can also regulate provision within an education sector in line with policy, as may be seen in countries where open and distance education has been used for national development purposes. It provides a means of targeting quality improvements (for example, where a government proposes to fund only those programmes which offer a component of student support according to specified standards), though institutions (especially universities) might experience this intervention as interference with their autonomy. The disadvantages of legislation are that it may set minimum standards as the goal to be achieved, engender an attitude only of compliance to external requirements, specify requirements that are too restricting to allow self-development by an institution, become quickly out of date as distance education evolves new forms and fail to have force in controlling poor-quality providers.

One recent focus of legislation has been the regulation of offshore programme providers as education becomes increasingly global in its recruitment and provision. The case of Hong Kong illustrates this (Jegede 2001). In June 2000, there were 550 programmes available in Hong Kong from out-of-country (non-local) providers, offering more than 60,000 places. Some programmes were delivered from overseas institutions, others through partnerships with Hong Kong institutions or agents. Inevitably, there was wide variation in the quality of provision and value of awards. To deal with this situation and protect Hong Kong consumers, the government of Hong Kong passed the Non-Local Higher and Professional Education Ordinance (June 1997) which required a rigorous registration process for any award-bearing non-local programmes offered in Hong Kong. The body responsible for conducting registration, the Hong Kong Council for Academic Accreditation, was the only independent statutory accreditation authority in Hong Kong. Its remit was, among other things, to ensure that degree programmes offered in Hong Kong achieve internationally recognised benchmarks or standards. A different solution is proposed in Morocco, where in 2002 the government aimed to legislate against all programmes run in collaboration with overseas universities, phasing them out altogether in an attempt to regulate the sector by eliminating collaborative programmes, often of poor quality, and encouraging the growth of domestic providers.

Market forces

It is sometimes argued that legislation to regulate distance education is not necessary because market forces will do the job of removing poor-quality provision. In some countries market forces are the only means of regulation together with very general consumer-protection legislation. Where commercial provision is expanding rapidly to meet social demands for education unmet by public-sector provision, the regulation of distance education has not yet caught up with expansion of provision. Market forces can be effective up to a point, especially where providers (including public institutions) offer choice and compete in a buyer's market. In this circumstance institutions or providers are likely to pay greater attention to the quality of their own (and competitors') provision and to seek public endorsement for it. But even when competition forces out low-quality providers, the process takes time and individual learners suffer. Providers should assume responsibility for assisting potential students to make informed choices (one reason why the provision of adequate pre-registration information and advice needs to be part of quality assurance frameworks). Experience so far indicates that planners need to beware of the assumption that market forces result in improved quality, as the following illustration from India shows:

> Today every third university in India offers distance education programmes. Unfortunately, however, this is often because distance education is a seller's market. A number of private institutions, and industry, have entered education and training because they find it convenient to seek the collaboration of a university for the purpose of certification so that the question of validity does not affect marketing and sales. In the process, the classical functions of the university, namely prescribing curricula, developing courses and setting standards have been appropriated by market-savvy private enterprises. Universities also find this arrangement convenient. It is easier to give away certificates and degrees without taking on the responsibility of framing curricula.
>
> (Kanwar and Pillai 2001: 283)

Voluntary professional associations

Quality has also been regulated by associations of providers who agree voluntary standards and accept a code of ethics. Such associations have sometimes offered a 'kitemark' or seal of approval to organisations or providers after assessments conducted by the association and have the power to withdraw this too. Regulation by associations has operated at both national and international levels (e.g. the British Association of Open Learning, the Norwegian Association of Distance Education, the Canadian Association for Distance Education (whose mission is to foster excellence) and the Association of European Correspondence Schools). Some associations have established accrediting schemes; for example, the National Home Study Council in the USA established a crediting commission which was approved by the federal government. Voluntary associations such as these have worked with governments or ministries to varying degrees, in some cases setting the standards for governments to apply (as was the case in Norway), and bring a strong force in self-regulation. In other cases they have had little impact on the sector other than to act as a loosely organised professional association. While the notion of self-regulation is an appealing one, its track record as an effective mechanism of governance is poor in a number of countries and the scope for providers to opt out of self-regulatory associations weakens its force.

Controlling through funding

One mechanism which creates much debate is the regulation of quality through funding allocation in the public sector, especially in higher education. Funding is linked increasingly to performance, with governments rewarding institutions which perform well ('well' being defined in terms of economy, efficiency, cost-effectiveness and employability of graduates) and penalising those which do not. The control of funding is also used to shape and regulate the provision of open and distance education overall within an education sector. For example, in New Zealand, a shift in government funding policy tying institutional funding more directly to student numbers has led to unintended as well as intended results: increased competition between institutions, the growth of private commercial providers, the rationalisation of programmes to fit both market needs and, the most financially destructive option, the avoidance of high-risk options in programme provision and discouragement of experiment with innovatory programmes (Prebble 2001).

ACCREDITATION

Accreditation has been used as an instrument of governance more in some countries than in others, though it is currently gaining new attention as a form of international educational currency. Accreditation means different things in different countries and there is some confusion surrounding the term, but essentially it represents a promise that a provider will deliver the quality of education it claims to offer. More specifically this means that the institution operates on a sound financial basis and has enough funding to ensure course delivery, an appropriate programme of study and learner support, qualified teachers, adequate facilities and equipment, approved recruitment and admission policies, and truthful claims in its promotion of programmes of study.

Accreditation of educational programmes (a set of courses which lead to a degree or award) has its roots in the USA where it has been the main form of regulation since the early twentieth century. Institutional accreditation grew out of the activities of associations of institutions which together created shared standards. These standards then became prescriptive and required the reporting of largely quantitative data about fixed characteristics. It eventually became clear that this approach did not take account of the diverse nature and missions of institutions or qualitative aspects of them. As a result the standards were changed in the 1930s to accommodate more qualitative dimensions of quality, the diversity of institutional missions and educational objectives. These same issues are still live ones and solutions are still being sought in the USA and elsewhere.

The process of accreditation has been described as one by which

> an institution of post-secondary education periodically evaluates its own educational activities, in whole or in part, and seeks an independent judgment that it substantially achieves its own educational objectives and is generally equal to comparable institutions or specialised units. Essential elements of the process are:
> 1. a clear statement of educational objectives;
> 2. a directed self-study focused on these objectives;
> 3. an on-site evaluation by a selected group of peers;
> 4. a decision by an independent commission that the institution or specialised unit is worthy of accreditation.
>
> (Young 1983: 21)

Accreditation is intended to guarantee levels of performance and quality in order to create confidence in the educational community and the public at large. It can apply to the operation of the whole organisation, or to a programme, or across a whole profession. However, a major issue in accreditation systems is the status and credibility of the accreditation agency and, in some cases, information about these (their status, role, funding, constitution, powers) is difficult for some would-be students to obtain or interpret.

Common elements of accreditation models are summarised in Table 10.1. They show a mixture of input and outcome elements. For some time the main emphasis was on inputs, based on the assumption that outcomes would follow automatically if adequate inputs were in place. However, realisation that this does not necessarily happen has shifted attention to the outcomes of an education system as well as to the quality of the processes.

Limitations

Some of the limitations of accreditation as an instrument of governance are illustrated from the context of the USA where

> accreditation, higher education's primary method for assessing itself, has been criticized for doing little more than tallying library books and faculty credentials at a time when education is undergoing a radical

Table 10.1 Common elements in accreditation models

1 The programme	2 Antecedents	3 Transactions

General
  – Mission
  – Philosophy
Content
  – Substantive knowledge
  – Intellectual skills
  – Professional skills
	Students
	  – Prior knowledge
	  – Entry requirements
	  – Pastoral care
	  – Other guidance
	Faculty
	  – Qualifications
	  – Experience
		Teaching
		Learning
		Research
		Operational
		  – Fair practice
		  – Equal opportunity

4 Outcomes	**5 Assessment**	**6 Physical aspects**

Immediate
  – Graduation criteria
Intermediate
  – Certification
  – Entry to profession or qualifying
    course
  – Competence or licence to practise
	Programme
	  – Internal
	  – External
	Students
	  – Assessment methods
	  – Assessment criteria
		Resources
		  – Financial
		  – Facilities
		  – Equipment
		  – Supplies
		  – Intellectual (library, audiovisual,
		    computing)
		Personnel
		  – Administrative
		  – Clerical and other support
		  – Technical
		  – Faculty (academic, clinical, student
		    support)

Source: based on Liston 1999: 39–40

transformation. The accreditation process, in which institutions study themselves and then are examined by a team of outside reviewers, has been called cumbersome, expensive, secretive and outdated – sometimes by the accrediting agencies themselves.

(McMurtrie 1999: A41)

The nature of external review and quality assessment in accreditation can present problems for distance education since the approaches and indicators tend to be based on the practices, organisation and expectations of traditional institutions and face-to-face teaching. Problems include the emphasis on the tangible and traditional elements in accreditation models (some of the input elements in Table 10.1), the limitations of reviewers from traditional institutions in understanding how teaching and learner support are provided and how distributed organisational structures and resources function in open and distance education, and the meaning of 'site visits' in learning systems where students do not attend a campus. These can put the validity of the judgements of external assessors in doubt. Accreditation review approaches and requirements need to be revised or reinterpreted when applied to open and distance education. However, documentary evidence for analysis can be greater and more easily available for inspection in open and distance learning systems which function through written exchanges between tutors and students and feedback on coursework, or whose record-keeping systems play an important role in managing a complex operation. Electronic websites too provide permanent records of interactions between tutors and students, and tutors and their managers.

QUALITY ASSURANCE

As is evident, issues of governance, accreditation and quality assurance overlap. Quality assurance refers to the systems through which an institution demonstrates that conditions are in place for students to achieve the standards set in educational programmes. A quality-assurance system includes 'all those planned and systematic activities which provide confidence that a product or service will satisfy given requirements for quality' (HEQC 1994). While quality-assurance practices exist for programmes at all levels (non-formal and basic education, vocational and professional training), quality-assurance systems in higher education have received the most attention and become most formalised. However, descriptions of quality-assurance systems and mechanisms give little indication of the contentious political and educational issues often involved in establishing and operating them.

International trends in quality assurance

From the early 1990s onwards many governments have intervened directly to introduce new quality-assurance policies and practices, particularly in higher education. Some ministries have set up their own formal evaluation centres or committees to conduct external reviews of quality, while others have set up independent bodies. In some cases these have taken the form of a single national agency, in others, separate agencies responsible for different regions or types of institution (as in the Netherlands, Mexico and Romania). In some countries, control of quality lies wholly with institutions; for example, in Germany the definition of 'quality' has been determined by universities and staff, not by students (Bargel cited by Baumeister 1997: 16), though this is under pressure to change. Some governments have linked assessment of quality to the funding allocation for universities (as in Argentina and the United Kingdom), resulting in increased competition between universities for resources, a redirection of academic effort towards generating funding and an inevitable ranking of institutions' success in assessment outcomes.

The scope of quality-assurance systems varies widely too. Some (as in Scotland and England) monitor teaching effectiveness while others (as in Hong Kong) focus on management processes. Some rely heavily on accreditation systems for ensuring quality (as in the USA). Others include the quality of research productivity, either of individual scholars (as in Mexico) or of whole academic departments (as in the United Kingdom). Quality-assurance systems are beginning to develop for the international delivery of courses. However, as Liston (1999: 22) warns, 'the global pursuit of quality assurance auditing of institutions and accrediting of programmes provides evidence of more mistakes made than lessons learned'. Action is often taken in retrospect, after the problems have arisen.

Some common international trends in quality assurance are evident. There has been an increasing formalisation of quality-assurance activities, especially for higher education, making them explicit and more often externally validated. Activities relating to quality assurance within institutions and the creation of job roles devoted to it have increased. More organisations and agencies designed specifically for quality-assurance purposes have been established. In developing new quality-assurance systems, familiar and traditional academic review processes have been incorporated into new formal systems, though concepts and practices on quality management have been adopted from the corporate world too. Wide-scale cultural borrowing among countries is now evident, together with an international discourse on quality assurance and plans for international quality agencies. Regional networks and plans for trans-national arrangements are growing.

Overall, there has been a growing attention to internal self-audit alongside external assessment of quality, though strong tensions exist between the two (see Table 10.2 for the positive and negative impacts). Finally, there

Table 10.2 Internal and external regulation of quality

	Internal or self-regulation	External regulation and assessment
Positive aspects	Fits with or fosters a culture and tradition of self-regulation if embedded in everyday systems and practices. Can heighten ownership of quality and standards by a provider. Provides an organisation with increased self-knowledge if well done and can support organisational learning. Can encourage reflective practice. Can act as vehicle for staff development. Can complement external assessment or form the basis of it.	Engenders public and peer confidence in the institution or provider. Provides external reference points or benchmarks for standards and performance. Assists change and development when needed. Can provide confirmation of an institution's internal review systems and conclusions. Can provide new perspectives and awareness. Can validate achievement. Provides a way of assessing quality across a system or sector.
Negative aspects	Can embed and sanction poor practice in an organisational culture. Can lead to insularity without some external reference points. Can become out-of-date in its approach without new input. Can become a token or mechanical exercise if not well led, responsibly conducted and leading to change and quality improvements where required. Can be biased and partial.	Can prove burdensome, bureaucratic and time-consuming to the extent that it interferes with 'real work'. May divert institutional effort, becoming an end in itself. Can lead to quality assurance becoming a special or occasional exercise, only for external assessment purposes. Can generate high costs, financial and human, disproportionate to the value gained. May add little value to institutions which already have effective self-regulatory systems. A single rigid approach can fail to take account of an institution's individual and distinctive mission and achievements. May impose inappropriate changes. Can be misappropriated as a political tool.

is increased availability of public reports on institutional quality and more transparency of process in many countries, in turn generating debate on criteria, processes, standards and the value of rankings.

Out of experience so far, some have voiced a concern for a focus on educational values and more intangible, difficult-to-measure outcomes. Barnett (1992), for example, has argued for the distinctive nature of educational quality which he describes as having emancipatory goals, transforming the learner and highlighting the difference between 'customer' or 'consumer' and 'learner' as a consequence. He has warned too, as have others, against a preoccupation with creating indicators as measures of quality, on the grounds that they tend to measure only the measurable and not always the more elusive but worthwhile aspects.

Does the use of formal quality-assurance systems lead to improved practice? Some researchers claim that it does. For example, one survey (Brennan *et al.* 1997) found that, as a result of quality-assurance requirements and external review reports, universities in the United Kingdom had taken positive action to initiate improvements, especially at the departmental level. However, some of this impact was arrived at as a result of the internal institutional reviews which preceded the external review. These internal reviews raised awareness about quality assurance, informed staff about their own institution's practices and promoted ownership of the quality-assurance activities. As a result of this experience, some internal review practices became embedded in the routine and regular conduct of work, rather than being one-off activities done only in preparation for an external review.

One feature of quality assessment so far is the very high costs and time burdens of heavily bureaucratic systems – a warning for planners. The costs to governments and institutions can be very large, as the experience of the United Kingdom has shown. An illustration of the time and effort involved comes from the Open University where more than 2500 reports about university departments were prepared for the national Quality Assurance Agency for Higher Education during the assessment period 1992 to 2001. The balance between the costs and benefits of formal quality-assurance systems raises some uncomfortable questions. For example, out of a very costly and demanding quality-assurance regime in the United Kingdom, the number of unsatisfactory institutions or departments is very small. This raises questions about the relative cost-benefits of the exercise. Improvements in institutional ratings over time also suggested that they had learned to play the quality game and were able to present the evidence required as much as reflecting real improvement.

Global agendas for quality assurance

A more global agenda for quality assurance has grown with increases in cross-border programmes and international partnerships, especially in higher education. At the time of writing, at least seven major initiatives worldwide are in progress, to develop structures for international accreditation systems, recognition of qualifications and acceptance of international quality-assurance agencies. All the bodies involved are acting independently and include UNESCO (Global Forum for Quality Assurance, Accreditation and Recognition of Qualifications), the Organisation for Economic Cooperation and Development, the European Commission, the International Association of University Presidents and the International Network for Quality Assurance Agencies in Higher Education. The rationale for this appears to be a mixture of anxiety about protecting home provision, a wish to benefit from market opportunities and a counter-initiative to the World Trade Organisation's inclusion of education as a global market in the General Agreement on Trade in Services, since the latter would negate some national regulatory systems.

To avoid some of the confusion arising from the multiple meanings of accreditation, these initiatives propose various voluntary schemes of 'quality labels' (for programmes, qualifications, institutions and bodies providing accreditation and quality-assurance approval). This approach is seen to offer a solution to emerging problems in international education (even if its achievement will be a painful process of negotiation and agreement). However, the notion of labelling and categorisation of educational programmes in these ways rings alarm bells for some educators. The new quality labels would be granted either after desk exercises or after inspections by new international agencies. An informed observer concludes that the first will probably result in only limited guarantees of quality and standards, and the second may be forced to use 'lowest-common-denominator approaches to avoid getting into diplomatic hot water. They thus run the risk of becoming window-dressing exercises devoid of any real attempt to tackle the difficult and serious business of assuring academic quality and standards internationally' (Williams 2002).

Quality assurance in open and distance education

Quality assurance in open and distance education reflects international trends and is often subject to the same kinds of regulation, especially if provided by a campus-based institution. It serves several purposes: to satisfy the need for accountability for funds used; to ensure that defined standards will be reliably achieved and that awards have credibility; to inform decision-making when setting standards or redefining goals; to demonstrate good practice; to improve quality and standards in programme provision, service delivery, operations, student learning and institutional performance; to provide reference points, internal and external, past and present, for judging performance; to provide evidence of achievement in relation to competitors; to gain public confidence; and to ensure that learners receive the programmes and services as promised in pre-programme information and at registration.

However, distance education has the following organisational differences which need to be addressed in quality-assurance arrangements:

- More parties, stakeholders, specialists or sites involved in the development and delivery of a course or programme.
- More separate activities, roles and players to be coordinated.
- Longer chains of communication (from course developer to student, from plan to product, from central campus to local support centre).
- Larger-scale programmes, often provided over a wide geographical area.
- More detailed planning of production and budgets in advance of programme presentation.
- A greater number of administrative tasks (e.g. record keeping, or monitoring local centres and tutors, or in supporting course production), often distributed between different points (central, local, regional) and partners.
- More diverse target audiences, with differing needs to be met and provision to be made.
- In some cases more electronic transactions.
- More complex arrangements for the assessment of practical work and its delegation to local or workplace agents and partners.
- A distributed organisational structure in some cases, either in materials creation or teaching arrangements or in learner support.
- More frequent collaboration with other institutions or agencies for the delivery of a programme or course, together with reliance on partners.
- A different interpretation of what constitutes teaching (e.g. the separation of roles in providing learning content, tutoring and assessment).

Accommodating these differences in quality-assurance systems has been essential in establishing the credibility of open and distance learning. However, even within dual-mode universities (those offering campus-based and distance-education courses) achieving the credibility of distance-education programmes has not been automatic. For example, in New Zealand, the wider university community remained sceptical about standards of the distance-education programmes for a time after their introduction. Massey University sought to overcome this doubt by demonstrating that the distance-education version of each course remained identical to its conventional face-to-face version in critical ways. The same examinations were set and taken at the same time (though logistically complicated and expensive to do) and student awards or transcripts did not indicate the mode by which the qualification was obtained (they have equal value). Some providers in other countries too have found that only when acceptance and recognition of standards has been established in relation to conventional provision has it been possible to move to more appropriate arrangements for the quality assurance and quality assessment of distance education.

Institutional planning for quality assurance

While detailed procedures for managing the quality of course production and accreditation may be in place within an institution, there is sometimes no institution-wide plan covering other aspects of quality such as learner support or staff development. In some cases national bodies may offer a framework to guide this in order to reduce institutional variation or the neglect of quality assurance. In India, for example, the National Assessment and Accreditation Council (NAAC) was established in 1995 to plan and implement schemes for ensuring quality in higher education together with the Distance Education Council (established in 1992 within the Indira Gandhi National Open University) to do the same for distance education (Koul 1997). One advantage in making institutional plans for managing quality in open and distance education is that many of the customary practices (in developing good-quality materials, in using student feedback, in monitoring learning-support systems and operational systems) provide an existing basis for system building. Quite often, the task is to systematise practices which are *ad hoc* or piecemeal and reformulate them into a coherent institution-wide approach (as Robertshaw (1997) described of the Open University of Hong Kong in the 1990s).

Organising and managing quality in open and distance learning is essentially about managing its standards (operational and academic, internal and external). Providers often need to reconcile different sets of standards: internal (in-house best practice) and external (perhaps a requirement of national quality councils or agencies). In general, standards in education are subject to continual reinterpretation and renegotiation between stakeholders (governments, national councils, professional bodies, institutions, employers, the public, teachers and managers, local tutors, accrediting bodies, parents and students, donors and other agencies). This means that a review of the standards themselves at regular intervals needs to be a part of the plan for assuring quality.

In planning an institutional policy and strategy for quality in distance education, planners and managers need to ask themselves the following questions:

- What goals in quality and standards are we seeking to achieve as an institution? What levels of quality do we currently achieve and in what aspects? Where are we weakest? What are the critical areas and functions we need to focus on?
- What aspects of quality should we focus on? What should be our underpinning principles? What approaches to quality management should we take?
- What kind of policy do we need to formulate? How should this fit with our institutional mission and values? What factors in the external environment (national policy, regulations, requirements of professional associations, competitors' standards, identified market needs, educational trends, funding provision) should we take account of? What are our goals? Are they appropriate?
- What do departments and units in the institution need to do to align themselves with the chosen goals? What are their current goals and standards of performance?
- What procedures for assuring quality and standards do we need to put in place for the different areas of work, products and services that constitute our provision of open and distance learning? What already exists?
- What criteria and indicators will we use to judge the achievement of the standards we define? What evidence will we need in order to demonstrate our achievement of standards?
- What information systems do we need to support the activities of quality assurance? What already exist?
- What mechanisms should we put in place for identifying and dealing with gaps in quality?
- Who will be responsible for managing quality throughout the institution?
- Which external agencies do we need to interact with in relation to quality?
- What do we need to do in order to operate a cycle of continuous improvement?
- Where do we begin? What have we already got in place?

General features of good practice in managing quality assurance at an institutional level include the following:

- Allocation of responsibility for quality assurance at a senior level.
- Cultivation of ownership and responsibility for managing quality at all levels.
- Coordination of quality policy, initiatives and practices.
- Design of systems and practices which align with, but are not dominated by, external requirements and standards.

- Guidelines widely disseminated and understood so that all concerned share the same picture.
- Staff development and training in relation to quality practices and policy.
- Establishment of monitoring processes which feed back into activities for improvement in policy and practice.

Obviously, the kinds of structure for managing quality will depend on the size and nature of an organisation. Those for a large distance-teaching institution will be different organisationally than for a small-scale project, but the underlying principles are similar.

CONCLUSIONS

What emerges from experience so far is that the arrangements for controlling the activities of providers and users in open and distance education are both common (good practice is recognisable across contexts) and context-specific (arising from particular traditions and circumstances). Demonstration of good quality is essential in establishing the credibility of open and distance education but in many cases so far, attention to quality assurance is less than it needs to be, sometimes covering only parts of an institution's activities. In some countries, policies and quality assurance frameworks are lacking or inadequate. Pressure for improvement in these is increasingly coming from the expansion of international and offshore programmes, and the need for countries to initiate new internal legislation, for these may have beneficial backwash effects on the regulation of open and distance education, control of standards and consumer protection overall. However, approaches which concentrate on the measurable at the expense of educational worth and value are likely to be counter-productive in the longer term.

REFERENCES

Barnett, R. (1992) *Improving Higher Education: Total Quality Care*, Buckingham: The Society for Research into Higher Education and Open University Press.

Baumeister, H-P. (1997) 'Germany's place within the international discussion of standards and quality in open and distance learning: some unsystematic deliberations', in A. Tait (ed.) *Quality Assurance in Higher Education: Case Studies*, Vancouver: Commonwealth of Learning.

Brennan, J. L., Fredericks, M. and Shah, T. (1997) *Quality Assurance in Higher Education: A Legislative Review and Needs Analysis of Development in Central and Eastern Europe*, London: European Training Foundation, Quality Support Centre.

Bridges, D. and McLaughlin, T. H. (eds) (1994) *Education and the Market Place*, London: Falmer Press.

Dale, R. (1997) 'The state and the governance of education: an analysis of the restructuring of the state–education relationship', in A. H. Halsey, H. Lande, P. Brown and A. S. Wells (eds) *Education: Culture, Economy and Society*, Oxford: Oxford University Press.

Gan, S-L. (2001) 'Malaysia', in O. Jegede and G. Shive (eds) *Open and Distance Education in the Asia Pacific Region*, Hong Kong: OUHK Press.

Hargreaves, D. (1997) 'Restructuring: postmodernity and the prospects for educational change', in A. H. Halsey, H. Lande, P. Brown and A. S. Wells (eds) *Education: Culture, Economy and Society*, Oxford: Oxford University Press.

Higher Education Quality Council (HEQC) (1994) *Guidelines on Quality Assurance*, London: Higher Education Quality Council.

Hirst, P. and Thompson, G. (1995) 'Globalisation and the future of the nation-state', *Economy and Society* 24: 3.

Jegede, O. (2001) 'Hong Kong', in O. Jegede and G. Shive (eds) *Open and Distance Education in the Asia Pacific Region*, Hong Kong: OUHK Press.

Kanwar, A. S. and Pillai, C. R. (2001) 'India', in O. Jegede and G. Shive (eds) *Open and Distance Education in the Asia Pacific Region*, Hong Kong: OUHK Press.

Karow, W. and Storm, U. (1975) 'Criteria for the evaluation of distance teaching courses by state authorities', in E. Ljoså (ed.) *The System of Distance Education. Proceedings of the 10th ICCE International Conference*, Malmö: ICCE.

Koul, B. N. (1997) 'Quality assurance practice and principles: the case of Indian distance education', in A. Tait (ed.) *Quality Assurance in Higher Education: Case Studies*, Vancouver: Commonwealth of Learning.

Latchem, C. (2001) 'Australia', in O. Jegede and G. Shive (eds) *Open and Distance Education in the Asia Pacific Region*, Hong Kong: OUHK Press.

Le Grand, J. and Bartlett, W. (1993) *Quasi-Markets and Social Policy*, London: Macmillan.

Liston, C. (1999) *Managing Quality and Standards*, Buckingham: Open University Press.

Ljoså, E. and Rekkedal, T. (1993) *From External Control to Internal Quality Assurance*, Oslo: Norwegian Association for Distance Education.

McMurtrie, B. (1999) 'Assessing the group that assesses accreditation', *Chronicle of Higher Education* 12 (XLVI): A41–2.

Mok, K. H. (1997) 'Retreat of the state: marketisation of education in the Pearl River Delta', *Comparative Education Review* 41 (3): 260–76.

Prebble, T. (2001) 'New Zealand', in O. Jegede and G. Shive (eds) *Open and Distance Education in the Asia Pacific Region*, Hong Kong: OUHK Press.

Rhodes, R. A. W. (1997) *Understanding Governance: Policy Networks, Governance, Reflexivity and Accountability*, Buckingham: Open University Press.

Robertshaw, M. (1997) 'Developing quality systems in the fast lane: the Open University of Hong Kong', in A. Tait (ed.) *Quality Assurance in Higher Education: Case Studies*, Vancouver: Commonwealth of Learning.

Streeten, P. (1996) 'Governance', in M. G. Quibria and J. M. Dowling (eds) *Current Issues in Economic Development: An Asian Perspective*, Hong Kong: Oxford University Press.

Williams, P. (2002) 'Get label conscious', *The Times Higher Education Supplement*, 5 April.

Young, K. E. (1983) 'The changing scope of accreditation', in K. E. Young, C. M. Chambers, H. R. Kells and Associates (eds) *Understanding Accreditation*, San Francisco, CA: Jossey-Bass.

Part IV

Outputs

In order to make allocation decisions about expenditure on open and distance learning rather than on conventional education, or to choose between expenditure on different components within open and distance learning, the planner needs guidance about effectiveness and costs. Often it is necessary to compare different approaches to open and distance learning in order to meet the educational needs of different audiences or for different purposes. Chapters 11 and 12 examine these themes. A common thread running through both is the shortage of well-founded data on which to base such decisions. The problem is partly conceptual: there are major difficulties in comparing the outputs of conventional and distance education when its purposes and audiences often differ markedly. These are compounded by inescapable difficulties of measurement as soon as one moves from crude measures of examination results or graduations. In part the difficulties reflect the shortage of good research. In part, the question is too broad: open and distance learning is not a single system, as easily defined as a primary-school classroom with a teacher and black-board, but an umbrella term for a range of very different systems. In part, too, it matches uncertainty about the links between systems or processes of education generally and outputs measured in economic terms. Even in conventional education the relationships between education and economic growth, for example, are too complex for there to be simple answers to questions about the comparative benefits of investment at a particular level of education in any single instance.

We can seek answers to the planner's question by asking about the outputs of open and distance learning in relation to society in general, to the workforce in particular, and to individual learners, and then go on to ask about its costs. We may seek but not find. If the broad purpose of open and distance learning is to widen access to education, in response to a political view about the role of education in society, we will find some answers to questions about effectiveness by examining the reach of distance-education programmes but economic analysis will be of limited value in taking us further. Restricting ourselves to economics, the late

Charles Carter cautioned against too narrow an analysis in suggesting that the most cost-effective system of education was likely to be one that embraced both conventional and distance education. In practice we find few robust answers to questions about the value of open and distance learning for society in general. There is evidence, examined in Chapter 11, on its effectiveness for workforce education and training where the results for teacher education and for some programmes of higher education suggest it has a legitimate place as an educational technique. Similarly we can establish that some individual students benefit from programmes of open learning, gaining qualifications and moving on to better jobs; individuals may be voting wisely with their feet and purses when they enter open and distance learning. On cost-effectiveness there are just enough data to demonstrate that there can be circumstances in which open and distance learning has an economic advantage.

An examination of the links between the nature or form of open and distance learning and its outputs takes us back to process. Chapters 11 and 12 both look at the links between distance-education methods and outputs, emphasising the need for careful trade-offs by the planner. Measures to increase effectiveness, through strengthened student support or greater investment in materials' development, are at the same time likely to increase costs, and so perhaps to narrow audiences. But the equations between cost and effectiveness, when measured in terms of completion rates, will be heavily influenced by measures to increase the retention of students within the system. Cost, quality and access may pull in three different directions. The pleas in Chapter 11 for more research on outcomes, and in Chapter 12 for more informed financial planning, are designed to help the planner here; the planner's solutions, in terms of educational and management design, are likely to be found in the issues examined in Part III. Quality depends on process.

Chapter 11 looks at the evidence on outputs in basic education, for teacher training and in tertiary education. Chapter 12 concentrates on costs, exploring the financial choices that have to be made by planners, and putting them in the context of the purposes of open and distance education and the evidence we have of its effectiveness.

Benefits for students, labour force, employers and society

Reehana Raza

The ultimate test of policy is in its outcomes, and the education sector is no exception. Policy makers looking to institutionalise open and distance learning (ODL) institutions, or improve existing ones, will look to justify their decisions by reference to the benefits they can generate for individuals and society as a whole. In the current discourse on economic growth and development, differing levels of knowledge acquisition are seen to be a key part of the explanation of why countries travel different economic trajectories (World Bank 1998). The contribution of education is not only in those areas which we are familiar with – productivity and innovation – but is also now emphasised in non-market areas, such as democratisation and human rights (McMahon 1987, 1999). If this is true, then decisions regarding systems of education provision are critical, especially in relation to their effectiveness. Moreover, as ODL institutions can play a key role in the context of non-market benefits – especially due to their potential ability to reach those on the margin – assessing their effectiveness becomes important in a policy context.

The arguments for ODL are well known – its cost advantage, its flexibility, and its ability to reach communities at a distance. These potential advantages, not the evidence of its effectiveness, have been the drivers for its growth in the past three decades. Little is known about the outcomes in open and distance learning. This is not because there are no benefits – rather the evidence is mixed. The problem is more about the difficulty of measuring outcomes. We discuss this first before moving on to review the existing evidence on outcomes in open and distance learning by sectors: basic education, teacher education and higher education.

MEASURING OUTCOMES

What outcome to measure and for what purpose is a common starting point for those looking to measure effectiveness in education. This is particularly sensitive in the context of ODL because of the clientele it serves. Due to its method of delivery, ODL reaches an audience not usually catered to by conventional education. Its clientele tend to be students on the margin. It is likely that ODL students have fewer prerequisite qualifications; many of them may be returning to education after a number of lapsed years; they are more likely to be disadvantaged in terms of their learning environment; in addition, many may be studying part-time. Relative to students in conventional institutions, these students start with more handicaps. For these reasons, certain proponents of ODL argue that, because of these obstacles, traditional means of measuring outcomes used in conventional education are inappropriate. (Indeed within conventional education, there is also a debate about what outcomes provide the most appropriate measure.) Despite this, most outcome measures are similar to those used in conventional education. This is partly because the need remains to compare ODL institutions with more conventional providers and partly because sensitised measurements of outcomes are difficult to carry out.

There is also a question about the level at which outcomes should be measured. Outcomes can be examined in terms of private gains acquired by the student, family or employer or in terms of social gains enjoyed by the labour market and society as a whole. For the most part within the context of ODL, studies have looked at the former rather than the latter. This is mostly because of a lack of systematic data on ODL which can be used in conjunction with other existing data to examine the social impact of these institutions. Often, especially in the developing-country context, comparable national data are also not available.

The crudest way of looking at outcomes is to examine the output of the system, using indicators such as graduates, examination results or course completions. Criticisms of this approach are twofold. One is that this method does not separate out the innate differences in students in terms of their ability, as well as other differences in their socio-economic backgrounds. Second, the method takes no account of the benefits that students acquire despite not completing a programme or a course of study. This latter argument holds particular weight in the context of open and distance learning because of the low completion rates and because of the particular characteristics of ODL students who, regardless of completing, can be expected to have gained something through participating in the learning process. Others argue that a more appropriate way of measuring outcomes is to take a value-added approach. Here the focus is on the measurement of outputs in terms of the net gain in skills that is acquired because of the educational experience itself (Lockheed and Hanushek 1988: 22). The impact of an educational intervention can take a number of forms. There are of course behavioural and cognitive gains brought on by the educational intervention. Alternatively (a by-product of human capital theory) there are the income gains brought on by the improvements in labour productivity and economic growth. The more recent emphasis on educational externalities in the areas of civic responsibility suggests that other gains could also be measured in terms of increased voter participation, for example, or a decrease in crime rates.

Having decided on the chosen outcome, there are major conceptual problems which impede measuring outcomes. We have already mentioned the difficulty of attributing cause to effect, especially when the cohort entering varies with respect to ability and socio-economic background. This problem, although potentially soluble through a value-added approach, first assumes that we can measure for these differences before the educational intervention occurs. Even if this were possible, it does not detract from another criticism which is that there may be a natural maturation process which may explain the gains rather than the educational process itself. Linking cause and effect in the labour market is equally difficult for similar reasons. Differentials in income may have less to do with the educational experience than the ability to access networks or may reflect the educational institutions' ability to screen the more able members of society. In the context of ODL, the latter may have less applicability given the open-door policy of ODL institutions. A further problem in measuring cause and effect relates to the lag factor involved in examining when the effect takes hold (Solomon 1987). To gauge effect properly would require extensive tracing which has its own methodological problems.

Ultimately, however, outcomes of ODL that are measured have more to do with what is possible than what we would optimally like to measure. A number of practical problems impede researchers working in this area. The first set of problems relate to data collection and management. Data-management systems in many of these institutions, particularly in developing countries, are not set up in a way that makes it easy to measure outcomes. First, many institutions do not yet maintain computerised databases or are at the very early stages of establishing computerised data systems. Even if databases are maintained, they are manned by a few skilled people who are working at full capacity. Researchers demanding data often only add to the workload of these people, with differing implications for access. Lastly, the particular characteristics of ODL students – the longer period they have for completion and their tendency to become dormant for long periods – complicate data management. One tendency evident in the South Asian open universities has been that data on enrolment and examination have been maintained separately. Only recently have attempts been made to integrate them, allowing administrators (and researchers when they have access to data) to trace students from the cradle to the grave.

The second set of problems for researchers relate to access to data. Data on outcomes are highly sensitive for administrators of these institutions who are then called upon to justify them. Governments are also sensitive to outcome results as ODL institutions have played a key role in relieving the pressure for education by enrolling a large number of individuals not accommodated within the conventional system. Figures which indicate their failure could be politically sensitive (Perraton 2000). Consequently, it is often in the interest of administrators and civil servants to discourage researchers from having access to the data. The poor data-management systems and poorly staffed units highlighted above only exacerbate the problem.

The third set of practical problems that confront researchers relate to those trying to carry out comparative work or work which requires data from a number of institutions. This presents its own set of problems which have been summarised by Rumble (1997). They include:

- *Quality of data*: There are three issues that curtail the comparability of data. One is the fact that different ODL institutions use different methods of data collection. A related problem is the fact that definitions on which data are collected vary between different institutions. Finally, not all variables are collected by all ODL institutions, so that comparisons across the board cannot occur. Issues of comparability are particularly problematic in the context of costing exercises, as methods on which accounts are maintained vary significantly.
- *Differences in institutions*: Another issue that complicates comparisons of ODL institutions is the fact that they vary considerably in terms of teaching methods, the level of student support, regulations governing student admission and progress, technology, the way in which staff are hired, and in particular the balance between permanent core staff and those hired on a casual basis and the balance of tasks (research, teaching, consultancy and so on) that staff are involved with. The subject mix of these different institutions also complicates comparisons.
- *Variation in outputs*: In comparing outcomes, a key concern is whether the outputs produced by differing institutions are of similar quality. In the context of ODL, are the institutions producing comparable graduates? Are the graduates valued equally on the market?

Each of these features makes the task of measuring outcomes more difficult.

WHAT KIND OF STUDIES DO WE HAVE?

Despite these constraints, researchers within and outside these institutions have carried out a large number of studies. Many are of variable quality and can be questioned on the soundness of their methodology. Most research is qualitative in nature. Studies tend to be course or programme specific, small-scale and non-replicable in nature, making it difficult to extrapolate from their results to broad-based policy conclusions. Consequently there is a need to balance the important qualitative research that is being carried out within ODL with more quantitative studies if possible which use sound sampling techniques. However, this is not always easy given the constraints researchers face. Even aggregated data on simple completion rates are extremely difficult to gather. For the most part, the evidence we have on ODL is based on programme evaluations, some aggregated statistics from student evaluation units, and analysis carried out on the basis of in-depth case studies. As a broad taxonomy, we first summarise the crude measures that are given in existing studies in terms of completion, graduation and examination results. Then studies are examined for what they reveal about the impact of educational innovation.

BASIC EDUCATION

Perhaps the area where we have the least information on outcomes is with respect to ODL and basic education. Basic education is used as an alternative to formal primary education or to support primary education as well as providing junior-secondary education. The attractiveness of ODL for basic education is obvious. As a method of provision, it addresses some of the major constraints facing those attempting to reach education for all (EFA) targets in developing countries. It is a means of providing education for those in existing employment, both adults who have failed to attain any basic education, and children, who, because of economic imperatives, are forced to work rather than attend school. In addition, due to its method of delivery, it can provide basic education to a range of isolated areas which are likely to have a larger proportion of those individuals who have been unable to access or have had insufficient basic education.

With respect to enrolment, basic education through open distance learning has acquired a certain level of legitimacy. For instance, almost all the E-9 countries have large-scale institutions linked to ODL and basic education. Indonesia has a sustained programme in primary education. For secondary education, Brazil and Mexico have led the way with long established programmes, and South Asia's open schools in India and Bangladesh have recently entered the fray (UNESCO 2001: 57–8). Where outcomes are concerned, the programmes in Mexico and Indonesia seem to indicate that these programmes can be highly successful. The Mexico *Telesecundaria* programme, for instance, has an enrolment of 817,000 and a pass rate of 93 per cent (UNESCO 2001: 41). In 1997 to 1998 the programme reached 15 per cent of the total junior-secondary population and was providing an alternative to those who have little choice in the rural areas (Perraton and Creed 2000: 67). In Indonesia, the open schools were being integrated into the main framework for basic education provision before the financial crisis in 1998. Even by 1996 to 1997, enrolment in the open schools for junior-secondary level was at 197,000 and graduation rates were around 92 per cent (Edirisingha 1999: 5).

However, other evidence from South and South East Asia and Africa is not conclusive. Where enrolment is concerned the figures are good and indicate that ODL is effective in reaching students. Further, ODL has been successful in providing opportunities to many marginalised groups. It is with respect to outcomes that we know little. For instance, the National Open School in India had an enrolment of 400,000 in 1998 to 1999 with a completion rate of 43 per cent. Thailand, which has the oldest programme outside Latin America, and with the largest enrolment (2,547,664), has a completion rate of 39 per cent. Zambia and Malawi, although with much lower enrolment, also had a relatively poorer graduation rate of approximately 35 per cent (Edirisingha 1999: 5). Indeed, even in terms of enrolment, some goals are not being reached. Africa has seen a decline in its junior-secondary enrolment and the Asian enrolments are not reaching expected targets (Perraton and Creed 2000: 67–8). (Data on the enrolments and costs of open schools are also discussed in Chapter 12 and figures shown in Table 12.2.)

However, as Yates (2000: 237) notes, 'Reaching audiences is not the same as teaching them, and teaching a student is not the same as supporting individualised learning'. Given that ODL is perhaps the only hope for many who have been left out of the education process it is the quality of delivery which is of concern. There is evidence that certain techniques in basic education can pay dividends in terms of transferring skills. Tests of learning gain show that some methods work in transferring knowledge and can also encourage students to remain in school (Perraton and Creed 2000: 68). For instance, techniques that use mass media in school training, notably educational television and interactive radio (IRI), seem to work in complementing existing systems. The evidence suggests that these methods can help children learn effectively and can support curriculum reform (Yates 2000: 238, Perraton 2000: 32–3). In South Africa, for instance, there was a 20 per cent increase in test scores for those who were subject to IRI. Similar scales of achievement were reported for earlier IRI schemes (see Edirisingha 1999, Jamison 1982). However, in-school programmes in ODL lose out in terms of costs and sometimes of political support. For these reasons they become difficult to sustain (Perraton 2000, Yates 2000). Where outcomes in open schools are concerned, there is very little evidence besides that which relates to crude outcome figures. In short, we have some evidence based on crude outcomes for the effectiveness of open schooling and for the schools' success in terms of reaching their audiences, but little beyond these crude measures. Where technologies have been used to support conventional schooling there is evidence of effectiveness, but always at increased cost.

Where cost and scale efficiencies are concerned, there may be inherent contradictions between internal effectiveness and external efficiency. Yates (2000: 237) notes that recent academic discourse suggests that scales required for cost-efficiency are incompatible with the need for the local context and individual attention required for literacy. Thus whereas ODL may offer a solution to the particular education needs of the masses who have been left out of the education process, the costs that may ensure effective delivery may make it unfeasible. There may however be niche areas where these conflicts do not arise. One instance is refugee populations which are large in number but located on one site, and another is the case of scattered or nomad populations (ibid.).

TEACHER EDUCATION

As in other areas of ODL, getting to grips with outcomes in teaching teachers is fraught with lack of good data. There are four different ways in which distance education is used for teachers' education: initial professional education, continuing professional development, curriculum reform and teachers' career development. What can we say about skill development for teachers through ODL? In terms of reach, distance education has been very successful particularly in the developing world. Indeed the south has led the way in using distance education to train teachers in order to fill that gap of supply and demand in the post-colonial period (Creed 2001: 11). In Mongolia, for example, distance education has reached more then half of all the primary teachers in the country, while in Burkina Faso, distance education reached a quarter of all headteachers. Reach does not extend only to the number of teachers, but also to the range of educators involved in the process of teaching (Perraton *et al.* 2002: 13–14).

However, the data on reach tell us little about outcomes except to indicate the perceived legitimacy of the method of provision (Perraton 2000). Other figures are required which give us some idea of outcomes in terms of completion rates or examination results. Although imperfect, they do offer us some measure to gauge results. In training teachers the evidence is that ODL has been more successful than in other sectors (Robinson and Latchem 2003). For instance, in Perraton's (2000: 80–1) overview of ODL experience in teacher education, he provides a summary of outcomes in a number of teacher-education projects. Eight of the summarised projects (nine in total) have data on completion rates; all but one has a pass rate of over 50 per cent and five have pass rates in the 80 percentile. Another particularly impressive statistic relates to an early programme in Tanzania. Here, out of the 45,000 teachers recruited, 38,000 went on to acquire their qualifications (ibid.: 64–5). The authors identify the pay incentives offered to students on completion as a key element of the success. This somewhat rosy picture is countered by some recent research conducted by Perraton *et al.* (2002). These case studies, where data existed, suggest poorer completion rates – 55 to 64 per cent for Nigeria, 15 per cent for a Certificate in Guidance in India, although the results are much better for Burkina Faso and the British Open University. In spite of this, Perraton *et al.* (2001: 30) note that these low completion rates 'indicate some inefficiencies in the system or flaws in programme design since these drop-out rates are high in relation to the average rate for other distance education programmes'.

Another area where there are some crude figures is examination results. Based on the earlier set of case studies, it was found that the programmes studied could achieve examination pass rates of 50 to 90 per cent. As the authors note, this cannot be linked automatically to teaching capacity, but does indicate that distance education can be successful in transferring knowledge about an academic subject.

Moving beyond crude figures, what do we know about the effectiveness of distance education in training teachers? Robinson (1997: 130–3) has suggested one way of looking at effectiveness. She suggests gauging outcomes in terms of (1) knowledge about practice, (2) knowledge applied to practice, and (3) demonstration of knowledge and understanding through performance. However, such detailed studies are rarely conducted. Generally evidence is incomplete. To some extent the results on examinations indicate that knowledge about practice is effectively transferred through distance education. Other studies on Indonesia and Sri Lanka also support this (Nielsen and Tatto (1993) quoted in Perraton and Creed 2000). With respect to change in practice and outcome there are only a handful of studies mostly based on the Tanzania and Zimbabwe experience. Perraton *et al.* (2002: 14–15) note that 'Evidence from these large scale projects to expand teacher supply was re-assuring . . . students' classroom practice stood up comparatively well.' This however can only be a tentative conclusion at best, since we have very little research findings on how the knowledge acquired actually impacts on students' learning. Similar paucity of evidence however also exists for conventional teacher education (ibid.: 13–16).

If longevity of staying in a profession has implications for outcomes, then training of teachers through distance education may be extremely positive. The experience of the Open University is that teachers trained through the university remain in the profession for longer (40 per cent of newly trained teachers in England leave the profession within three years). Although hard evidence from other countries does not exist, such results are confirmed informally, which may reflect the fact that teachers trained on the job are less likely to move on completing their course than those who go away to college.

HIGHER EDUCATION

Data on graduation rates at the tertiary level of ODL are scarce. In a recent overview of the first three decades of ODL, Perraton (2000: 98–117) provides some of the most comprehensive statistics on graduation rates for the open universities. The evidence is clearly mixed. As he notes, there are successes such as the Chinese experience with more then 80 per cent of graduates completing their courses in the 1980s. However, more generally, the evidence is less than inspiring. He has data for a total of thirty programmes in ten institutions. Of these, thirteen programmes or almost half have graduation rates of less than 20 per cent. Out of the rest, two have pass rates of above 50 per cent with China being the clear outlier. Where the statistics relate to the Bachelor of Education Programmes (BEd) – University of South Africa (UNISA) and Bangladesh Open University (BOU) – the pass rates seem to be relatively higher. In all, Perraton (2000: 102) concludes that (1) shorter courses have higher completion rates, as do postgraduate programmes; (2) completion rates for degree programmes are little above 10 per cent which indicates that ODL institutions in higher education are failing to meet the aspirations of a great number of their students and providing inadequate numbers of graduates for their respective economies; and (3) student drop-out, rather then failure, explains these poor graduation rates.

Yet these statistics, although they are the best that we have, are extremely limited in what they reveal. This is partly because the data are relatively old (collected when these institutions were relatively young) and partly because they are aggregated across many courses and across years. Evidence from the British Open University (UKOU), which has the most extensive experience of trying to measure outcomes of ODL, and conversations with practitioners, suggest that outcomes can vary across a number of variables, including the type of course, its level, the type of student, and the year the course has been presented. Woodley and Parlett (1983), in another early study based on wastage rates (students who withdrew and failed) in undergraduate courses in a given year in the university, suggest that outcomes are better in lower level courses, and courses in the social sciences. With respect to students, the UKOU study indicated that female students, students between the ages of 30 and 39, students with more educational qualifications and those in professional occupations and alternatively housewives were more successful in completing their courses. Similar types of study in the context of other ODL institutions would be very useful for policy makers, since it would give them an idea of who the true beneficiaries of ODL are as well as some information on who drops out. One small-scale study by Gamaathige and Dissanayake (1999) on the Open University of Sri Lanka's (OUSL) experience in their foundation programme in social science is very revealing. This course is also indicative of the openness of the system, as it is an entry-level foundation course whose only requirement is that students be able to read and write in the vernacular language. The study attempts to correlate background characteristics of students against those students who complete and those who do not complete. The study's main conclusion is as follows:

> Students who enrolled in the study programmes in its first three academic years were largely males (66%) aged between 18–35 years (6%) had passed GCE (O/L) Examination (70%), rural based in terms of residence (60%) and the medium of study was Sinhalese (76%). Although the majority of students attracted to the course belonged to the above category, the study shows that those who had completed the study programme were predominately aged between 36–55 years (45%) living in urban areas (56%) and followed the study programme in English medium (50%) as compared with the overall percentage of completion (34%).
>
> (Gamaathige and Dissanayake 1999: 77)

Clearly then the implications in this case seem to be that the institution is effective in reaching its target group but, as in the case of other ODL institutions, it seems to be failing those very students who are arguably its main clientele.

A recent study by Reddy (2002) offers the most comprehensive figures on pass rates (wastage rates) in Indira Gandhi National Open University (IGNOU) for different years and across all programmes. The study is unique as it offers a complete picture of pass rates across all academic programmes for an ODL institution. Reddy's analysis of IGNOU broadly supports Perraton's (2000) initial conclusions about which programmes tend to be more successful. Average pass rates by type of degree seem to support his conclusion that postgraduate and certificate programmes have relatively higher pass rates than the bachelor or diploma programmes.

However, the scale of the data warns against simplistic conclusions. For instance, the detailed data on postgraduate programmes indicate that this group can be subdivided into two. At one extreme are the more successful programmes which are the Masters of Distance Education (MADE) and the Masters of Library and Information Sciences (MLISc) while at the other extreme are the Master of Business Administration (MBA) with a pass rate of 1 per cent and the Master of Computer Science (MSC) with a pass rate of 2.3 per cent. In addition, shorter courses need to be differentiated. Certificate programmes with a minimum period of six months and a maximum period of two years do have a higher completion rate. However, diplomas courses which are slightly longer in length – a minimum of one year and a maximum of three years – have a disproportionate fall in their pass rates. The difference may not relate only to the length of a course, but also to the actual design of the programmes themselves. These pass rates suggest that conclusions about motivation and success may also have to be rethought. There is a perception that more professional programmes are likely to attract more motivated students, resulting in higher pass rates. The data here seem to be contrary. On the one hand, the evidence from the Certificate in Computing and the Postgraduate Diploma in Computer Applications seems to support this. However, professional courses at the bachelor's and master's level indicate otherwise. Both the Master of Business Administration and the Master of Computer Application, as do the Bachelor in Computer Application and Bachelor of Commerce, have very low pass rates, indicating that these programmes do not necessarily result in self-screening by students. Shorter professional programmes clearly seem more successful. The reasons for this could be threefold: shorter courses are likely to seem more attainable given their shorter time horizon; more often than not, shorter courses feed into degree programmes providing an incentive to complete; compared to the master's programmes, shorter courses are likely to be less technically challenging for the self-learner at this lower level.

Two studies provide an insight into the impact of ODL – one based on the experience of students at the UKOU and another based on the experience of IGNOU students. Woodley's (n.d.) study of UKOU graduates notes that because most of their students are studying part-time and come from diverse backgrounds, conventional ways of looking at the impact of the effectiveness of education do not apply. For instance, given that most students are working while studying at the UKOU, purely looking at first-destination employment after they finish their degrees is not sufficient, since UKOU students may be achieving promotions while studying. Alternatively, changes in employment while students are enrolled cannot be attributed purely to the UKOU experience, as it may reflect experience acquired previously on the job. Further, given the diversity of the student body, outcome changes cannot be measured purely in terms of career changes. Consequently, other measures need to be considered.

Woodley's (n.d.) study is based on a sample of 3046 graduates with a 71 per cent response rate. With respect to career advancement, approximately 24 per cent of the respondents indicated that taking the UKOU course led to a salary increment; 17 per cent stated that the UKOU course had led to a new occupation. Almost 36 per cent of the respondents indicated that taking the course had implied a change within their existing occupations in terms of promotion to a higher grade, a more specialist job in the same occupation, or a change of specialisation within their occupation. More interesting are the results which suggest a significant shift out of existing occupations, particularly for those employed in manual employment and at the lower end of the non-manual strata. For example, 63 per cent of those employed in secretarial occupations shifted out, as did 61 per cent of those employed in industrial plants and as machine operators. In terms of non-career outcomes, three out of four students indicated that taking the UKOU course had great or enormous benefit, with women benefiting disproportionately. A subsequent study by Woodley and Simpson (1999: 4–5) on rates of return also suggested that, while graduation from the university was likely to be associated with increased earnings, the increase was greater for women than for men.

The other set of studies that look at outcomes after graduation are Gaba's (1999, 2002), which examine the experience of IGNOU graduates in the job market. Gaba (1999) sampled 1755 (with a 24 per cent response rate) students who had successfully completed IGNOU's BA and BCom programmes. As with the UKOU almost three-quarters of IGNOU's students were in some kind of employment before enrolling. Of those respondents who indicated that their main reason for joining the course was to get a job, 24 per cent were successful; of those who desired promotion, 28 per cent achieved one; approximately 36 per cent of those who joined IGNOU in order to pursue higher education did so. Overall, the largest share of those who were sampled continued in higher education. Clearly some of the aspirations of students at the onset of joining IGNOU were met.

In terms of the importance of the IGNOU experience for career change, the evidence is not very clear. The pre-employment pattern and post-employment pattern of those surveyed (ibid.: 15 and 21) indicate that 74 per cent of IGNOU students were in some kind of employment before joining IGNOU. After graduation, the percentage in employment (whether full-time or part-time) fell to 23 per cent, with a large share of students (33 per cent) staying in higher education and another 32 per cent occupied in the 'other' category. These figures, showing lower employment after graduation, are not so contrary if one examines the stated objectives of these students *before* they enrolled at IGNOU. Indeed these objectives are quite revealing in terms of suggesting that individuals, even in developing countries, pursue education for other than purely economic reasons. Out of the students surveyed by IGNOU, 43 per cent enrolled to continue in education; 14 per cent enrolled to get a job; 10 per cent enrolled for promotional purposes while 6 per cent enrolled for social reasons. In light of this, the outcomes after graduation are quite positive. However, the micro-analysis of juxtaposing each individual student's objective against his or her outcome is not so encouraging. For instance, out of the students who wanted to get jobs, only 13 per cent were able to do so. Similarly, of those who wanted to continue in higher education, only 36 per cent were able to do so. This does suggest that these figures are masking a mismatch between expectations and opportunities, part of which is a level of underemployment.

Student evaluations on the IGNOU experience were positive. Most (64 per cent) felt that the IGNOU degree was more useful than a degree from a formal institution. Of those who gained employment (n = 41), the majority felt that the IGNOU degree had helped them in getting a job, with 39 per cent feeling that it played a crucial role. Gaba (2002: 108–9) supplements the student survey with an employer survey based on seventeen employers who advertised in Indian papers during July and August 2001. Here, contrary to the positive response of students surveyed, 67 per cent of employers felt there was no interaction between distance-education institutions and industry with only 8 per cent of employers saying they would hire students from the ODL system.

CONCLUSION

At the broadest policy level there are two observations that may be made about outcomes in ODL: first, that although our evidence is patchy at best, there is some evidence that ODL can generate benefits for its target audience, and second, that more evidence on the outcome of ODL needs to be gathered in order for better policy decisions to be made. More specifically, what conclusions may one draw for policy makers?

First, open and distance learning can be successful in reaching a range of students who have been marginalised for either economic or geographical reasons. Here there is no doubt. However, as has been noted above, reach is not sufficient and a key area of failure is effective delivery of programmes. This is revealed by the disjuncture between enrolment and graduation rates. Open and distance learning institutions can deliver education effectively. The evidence may be more in the exceptions than the rule as many institutions have, in contrast, disturbingly low graduation rates. However, the focus needs to be on ways of ensuring effective delivery because of the strength of open and distance learning in reaching the unreachable. The onus on policy makers is to ensure that this method of provision which services the most vulnerable groups in society is helping to reduce the inequality gap rather than contributing to it.

Second, the evidence seems to be that ODL is more effective in certain areas. The evidence here seems to highlight that ODL is more effective in providing inservice training to teachers, for instance; that IRI and ETV have been successful in delivering basic education to in-school programmes, and that shorter courses at the tertiary education level are more successful. In keeping with this, policy makers need to direct resources to those areas where the returns to investment will be higher, rather than allowing the unlimited expansion of these institutions and their programmes.

Third, in these times of shrinking public budgets, the preoccupation with efficiency in education is often at the cost of effectiveness. Indeed, the effective interventions may not be the most efficient. As Lockheed and Hanushek note (1988: 21), to look at efficiency in purely cost terms, excluding how changes in resources affect outcomes, is a disservice to the idea of efficiency. For policy makers attracted to ODL because of its cost advantage, the warning is that a focus on reducing costs, without considering the loss in value-added, is unlikely to be cost-effective in the long run.

To bolster outcomes and improve policy making, the key contributing factor is more research, as noted above. The research agenda needs to include the following: (1) encouraging and improving systems of data management and institutionalising evaluation and research in ODL institutions; (2) continuing to collect data on outcomes in such measures as enrolments and graduation rates; (3) carrying out systematic research into the value-added of these education interventions, whether in terms of non-market or market implications as well as cognitive and behavioural changes generated by this experience; and (4) to understand which particular variables contribute most to the effectiveness of these institutions.

REFERENCES

Creed, C. (2001) *The Use of Distance Education for Teachers*, Cambridge: International Research Foundation for Open Learning.

Edirisingha, P. (1999) 'Reaching the unreached through distance education: costs, outcomes and sustainability', UNESCO Regional Seminar on the use of simple modern media for rural education, 12–16 December.

Gaba, A. K. (1999) *Distance Education and the Job Market: A Case Study of IGNOU Graduates*, New Delhi: STRIDE.

Gaba, A. K. (2002) 'Employment prospects of distance education in India: a case study on IGNOU graduates', *University News* 40 (4): 106–10.

Gamaathige, A. and Dissanayake, S. (1999) 'A comparison of some background characteristics of students who have completed and not completed the Foundation Programme in Social Science', *OUSL Journal* 2: 65–79.

Jamison, D. (1982) 'Radio education and student repetition in Nicaragua', in J. Friend, B. Searle and P. Suppes (eds) *Radio Mathematics in Nicaragua*, Stanford, CA: Institute for Mathematical Studies in the Social Sciences, Stanford University.

Lockheed, M. E. and Hanushek, E. (1988) 'Improving educational efficiency in developing countries: what do we know?', *Compare* 18 (1): 21–38.

McMahon, W. W. (1987) 'Externalities in education', in G. Psacharopoulos (ed.) *Economics of Education: Research and Studies*, Oxford: Pergamon Press.

McMahon, W. W. (1999) *Education and Development: Measuring the Social Benefits*, New York: Oxford University Press.

Perraton, H. (2000) *Open and Distance Learning in the Developing World*, London: Routledge.

Perraton, H. and Creed, C. (2000) *Applying New Technologies and Cost Effective Delivery Systems in Basic Education* (Thematic study for Education for All 2000 Assessment), Paris: UNESCO.

Perraton, H., Robinson, B. and Creed, C. (2001) *Teacher Education through Distance Learning: Technology, Curriculum, Evaluation, Cost*, Paris: UNESCO.

Perraton, H., Creed, C. and Robinson, B. (2002) *Teacher Education Guidelines, Using Open and Distance Learning*, Paris: UNESCO.

Reddy, M. V. L. (2002) 'Students' pass rates: a case study of Indira Gandhi National Open University programmes', *Indian Journal of Open Learning* 11 (1): 103–25.

Robinson, B. (1997) 'Distance education for primary teacher training in developing countries', in J. Lynch, C. Modgil and S. Modgil (eds) *Education and Development: Tradition and Innovation*, Volume 3: *Innovation in Delivering Primary Education*, London: Cassell Education Press.

Robinson, B. and Latchem, C. (eds) (2003) *Teacher Education Through Open and Distance Learning*, London: Routledge.

Rumble, G. (1997) *The Costs and Economics of Open and Distance Learning*, London: Kogan Page.

Solomon, L. C. (1987) 'The range of educational benefits', in G. Psacharopoulos (ed.) *Economics of Education: Research and Studies*, Oxford: Pergamon Press.

UNESCO (2001) *Distance Education in the E-9 Countries*, Paris: UNESCO.

Woodley, A. (n.d.) 'The experience of older graduates' (mimeo), Milton Keynes: Open University.

Woodley, A. and Parlett, M. (1983) 'Student drop-out', *Teaching at a Distance* 24 (3): 2–23.

Woodley, A. and Simpson, V. (1999) 'Learning and earning more? Measuring "rates of return" among mature graduates from part-time courses' (mimeo), Milton Keynes: Open University.

World Bank (1998) *World Development Report: Knowledge for Development*, New York: Oxford University Press.

Yates, C. (2000) 'Outcomes: what have we learned?', in C. Yates and J. Bradley (eds) *Basic Education at a Distance*, London: Routledge.

Chapter 12

Costs, effectiveness, efficiency

A guide for sound investment[1]

Neil Butcher and Nicky Roberts

Sadly – despite many claims to the contrary – sound and rigorous financial planning is often omitted in new projects and institutions seeking to harness the potential of distance-education methods. The most problematic aspect of this omission is not analysis of the current or short-term running costs of a distance-education programme or institution; many (but by no means all) planners have a handle on these dimensions of distance-education practice. Far less common, though, is rigorous planning for the long-term sustainability of a programme or institution. Obviously this is problematic in any context, but it is of particular concern in contexts where financial resources are very constrained, which is usually a feature of distance-education programmes in developing countries.

Some financial problems are beyond the control of financial planners. For example, in many countries, even modest course fees are beyond the reach of many potential learners. Similarly, national communication systems (roads, telecommunications, postal services) are often not sufficiently reliable or pervasive to meet the requirements of distance education. Beyond this, though, there are many other problems that arise from ineffective financial planning. The following common features of struggling distance-education programmes are symptomatic of weaknesses in financial planning:

- face-to-face tutorial support is seen to be crucial to learner success, but too expensive to implement;
- there are few reliable and sustainable strategies for making ongoing investments in the design and development of course materials;
- professional development for educational and administrative staff members is sporadic and limited, resulting in insufficient skills among personnel to sustain distance education systems;

---

1 This chapter draws heavily on the work of Don Swift, who worked at the South African Institute for Distance Education (SAIDE) between 1992 and 1997. It is dedicated to his memory and to the extraordinary legacy he left behind.

- administrative systems either do not exist or are highly under-developed;
- innovation in distance education relies heavily on unsustainable sources of funding, particularly donor funding.

This chapter explores ways to avoid the symptoms of weak financial planning. It outlines key concepts and approaches to financial planning for distance education. It then explores some key mistakes that have been made in financial planning in different contexts.

SOME KEY CONCEPTS

While there are numerous approaches to costing distance education, each of which is tailored to specific institutional requirements, many of them have common features. As an introduction to our discussion on costing distance education, we offer a short explanation of approaches to costing distance education by focusing on a few pertinent concepts.

Differentiating between effectiveness and efficiency

In considering sound educational investment, it is essential to distinguish effectiveness from efficiency. Cost-effectiveness is used as a term distinct from cost-efficiency. For the purposes of this chapter, the latter is about 'cheapness' of educational provision – usually expressed in terms of per-student costs – while the former represents striking the optimal balance between cost, student numbers and educational quality, a balance which will be entirely different for different educational contexts. In many ways, the concept of cost-effectiveness represents the balancing act that constitutes open learning. There is no magic formula that leads to cost-effective education; rather, cost-effectiveness needs to be measured on an ongoing basis in relation to changing contextual requirements.

The difference between actual costs and notional estimates

Many approaches to costing distinguish between actual and notional costs. *Actual costs* are an accurate reflection of what an item or activity costs at a specific time. Such costs can be accurately calculated only retrospectively, as there are various factors (that are in themselves dynamic) which determine actual costs at a specific time. *Notional costs* on the other hand reflect an average sum of what an item or activity is likely to cost. Notional costs are considered in estimating expenditure when projecting forward in planning (therefore needing to take into account the likely effects of inflation). The actual cost of buying a *Super DX e-180 VHS* videocassette in South Africa in November 2000 may be R13.99 (US$1.85). An appropriate notional cost for financial planning in 2001, which factors in the likely impact of inflation, may therefore be R15 ($2). These differences may seem obvious, but the process of extrapolating notional costs from historical data is often ignored in financial planning processes.

The difference also becomes critically important in planning broader resource usage. To illustrate, we will look at the issue of how much time learners spend on different learning tasks (the *hours of learning*). This concept is important, as it has a direct impact on the use of all resources (human and otherwise) in any education system. *Actual hours of learning* refers to the amount of time a specific student spends engaged in an educational course. This can seldom be accurately predicted, and thus requires careful measurement for specific students to give an accurate reflection of the time they have spent on a particular course.

Despite the impossibility of predicting accurately how long different learning activities will take, it is critical to estimate *notional hours of learning* during planning processes because this estimate affects all other resource and financial planning (in particular, it strongly influences personnel costs). In such exercises, educational planners seek to estimate the average time that the average learner would spend on a particular course. Although such estimates can never be entirely accurate, they are crucial to effective planning. Moreover, they can become increasingly accurate over time by measuring actual hours of learning across a range of students and using these measurements to revise future estimates. Likewise, establishing means of comparing actual and notional costs is an important component of improving financial planning processes and ensuring that financial planning processes are sufficiently detailed and accurate to be useful.

Fixed and variable costs

One of the most common distinctions made in costing approaches is between fixed and variable costs. *Fixed costs* refer to actual or notional costs of an item or activity that remain constant when other variables (such as student numbers) change. *Variable costs* are dependent on other factors. They change as student numbers or the level of activity change.

The most obvious example of a fixed educational investment in distance education is that of course design and development. This cost remains constant no matter how many students are added to a course. By contrast, the process of producing and disseminating these course materials may be considered to be variable, as it is likely to increase in direct proportion to increases in student enrolments. Some costs will vary according to different parameters. For example, the cost of running tutorial sessions will increase as new groups of students are formed, rather than as individual students enrol.

Some costs may share characteristics of both fixed and variable cost. For example, investments in designing administrative systems for distance education are generally regarded as fixed (although the costs of running the administration are obviously not). However, when a distance-education system expands beyond a certain size, additional fixed investments will be required to redesign the administration (cf. Rumble 1997).

Direct, indirect and overhead costs

When considering the costs of a distance education course, the *direct costs* are all those costs associated with a specific course. These include items such as course materials, educator and tutor time, and student administration, as well as costs of course design, coordination and learner support. Indirect costs are course-related costs that are not specific to that course alone. Students may, for example, make use of a telephone help-line or a venue that is used for other courses and by other students. Although these costs are related to an individual course, they are also distributed across several courses and are therefore referred to as indirect costs. Where indirect costs are summed or simply allocated as a percentage of direct costs, these are referred to as overhead costs. The exact definition of *overhead costs* varies within different approaches to costing. Most frequently, overhead costs are used to distribute costs common to all courses within an institution without having to calculate unit costs for each element. These might include costs associated with office and building infrastructure (repair, maintenance and rental), electricity and water, gardening, cleaning, security and so on. Such costs are necessary to run an educational institution and are distributed accordingly as indirect costs or overheads.

Unit costs and cost centres

Various *units of analysis* are used to measure costs in distance education. For example, an appropriate unit of analysis for course materials may be a book or a page. The unit cost is the cost associated with one unit of analysis. The unit of analysis selected will depend on what the financial planner is seeking to cost. Thus, if one were seeking to compile a broad budget for a new distance-education course, one might select a unit of analysis that incorporated all costs associated with designing and developing a study guide. For more micro-level planning, one might break this down into smaller units of analysis such as design of a single graphic, copy-editing of a single page, or desktop publishing of a single page.

In developing costing approaches and models, a series of unit costs are frequently clustered or grouped around specific areas of activity or items.

Costing is calculated according to agreed categories such as costs associated with a course, with a department, or with a student. Costs may also be grouped according to function, such as by teaching and learning strategy, course design, course materials production, or dissemination. Such groups or categories of costs are referred to as *cost centres*. Different institutions develop different approaches to costing and therefore use various cost centres.

Cost drivers

According to Rumble (1997: 27), 'a *cost driver* is anything that, following a change in its volume, causes the overall costs to change'. It is anything that influences costs, and can drive costs in either direction: up or down. Depending on which aspect of distance education is being considered, there are different cost drivers. In the example of course materials, one cost driver for the costs of producing course materials (per page or per book) is the number of students. Increases in student numbers will drive up overall costs associated with producing, storing and distributing course materials. However, it may also help to reduce the unit costs of this activity, as certain economies of scale will start to take effect with increased student numbers.

Cost drivers are the factors or variables that influence costs described above as *variable costs*. Identifying appropriate cost drivers or factors that will influence overall costs is essential to making cost-effective financial decisions. It is therefore essential to examine costs drivers over different periods and to consider the effects they will have both in the short and long term.

Personnel costs

Personnel costs refer to all costs relating to the time spent by people on specific activities (whether these people are employed on a full- or part-time basis or employed as subcontractors). These would include functions such as course design, course or programme coordination, instructional design, tutoring, mentoring and counselling, student assessment, invigilation, moderation, administration, tutor coordination, and research, as well as a host of others.

Capital costs

Capital costs are used to reflect an initial purchase of equipment, infrastructure, or items that have a useful life of more than one year. Capital costs are generally not considered to be recurrent. This is the commonly used approach in accounting but obviously most capital investments have various related costs that are recurrent and therefore should not be considered once-off investments in this way.

Rigorous financial planning takes into account all costs related to a capital investment such as repair, maintenance, insurance and depreciation costs that will recur over several years. For example, the capital cost of purchasing a photocopying machine may be, say, R20,000 (US$2500). This can be considered a capital expense in its first year, but has several related recurrent costs. Ongoing repair, maintenance and insurance will be necessary, and the capital investment will also be depreciated over, say, five years. Taking these recurrent costs into account in financial planning allows for capital items to be used optimally and to be replaced when necessary.

UNDERSTANDING THE LOGIC OF DISTANCE-EDUCATION COSTING

The financial logic of introducing distance education has, in many ways, been a response to education systems that are in crisis because they are pushing against the ceiling of capacity of their teachers to manage the learning of incoming students. The methods of what became known as distance education offered some hope that the productivity of education systems could be raised. Distance educators have also long held that the quality of educational experience for students can also be improved by proper use of those methods. This is because they introduce greater flexibility into the system, enabling students to study in ways and places and at times that best suit their personal circumstances. By such methods, institutions can reach students who would not otherwise be drawn into education systems. Finally, they also support, and encourage, highly desirable system developments towards internally generated quality assurance and accountability.

However, it has become a dangerous piece of conventional wisdom that distance education is less expensive than traditional contact education. There are many ways in which that is not the case. At present, many education systems in the developing world are looking to distance education because it seems to offer cost-efficiency benefits. However, consideration tends to take the form of asking, 'Is distance education cheaper than contact?' as if distance education were a set of social arrangements as standardised as conventional education.

Research on comparative costs has not been undertaken on a sufficiently consistent or comprehensive basis. Some studies have looked at institutional costs, others at public expenditure costs, and still others at total economic costs. Some have examined recurrent costs but neglected capital costs. The accumulated research literature on the cost-efficiency/effectiveness of distance education (e.g. Dhanarajan *et al.* 1994) does suggest two fundamental conclusions. First, distance-education institutions are usually more cost-efficient than conventional institutions, particularly when they enrol large numbers of students on each course in order to reap wide economies of scale. Second, distance-education institutions *can* be more cost-effective than conventional institutions when they offer high-quality learning materials and tutorial support to students, thereby securing satisfactory retention and graduation rates. Conversely, if they do not achieve satisfactory retention and graduation rates they may well be much more expensive.

In distance education, major expenses are incurred in designing courses – particularly if they involve the use of relatively expensive media and technologies. This is potentially a bottomless pit of expense, since it is always possible to add more person-power or to seek more expensive media and technologies, but this need not be the case. Many good courses have been designed with relatively small amounts of person-power. However, the world of distance education contains many times more bad courses than good. A broad generalisation that has fairly high reliability for distance education is that the quality of the course (in terms of subject matter and pedagogy) is related to the level of investment in its design.

Taking time to design

Perhaps the first danger that politicians and educational planners face is grossly to underestimate the amount of person-power needed to design one hour of student study time. Bedazzled by the cost-efficiency claims of distance educators, they conceive of distance education as merely another, less expensive, type of school and proceed to plan its costs in similar ways. Instead, the budget for distance education should be built up from a detailed costing of the design and presentation costs of each of its proposed courses. The first stage involves considering the level of investment to be made in the design of each course. While this decision involves an enormous amount of rule of thumb and guesswork, it is a necessary process for initial decision-making because so much depends on the media mix, level and type of subject matter, and the kinds of competence aimed for in the course. Some crude generalisations are likely to bring recognition of reality, if not firm agreement, from those involved. At higher education first-year level (perhaps the most challenging), the figures in Table 12.1 provide some indication of the kinds of investment required.

No matter how far a particular institution may diverge from these figures, two core agreements would be likely to emerge. First, at the lower part of each of these ranges, the quality of teaching (i.e. capacity to bring success to students) will be related positively to investment in design time. Disagreements may enter about the strength of the relationship at the top end, with returns to additional investment drying up beyond a certain point. It may be that an additional twenty hours after the first fifty might

Table 12.1 Material development times

Time taken to design one hour of student study time	
Print	20–100 hours
Audio	20–100 hours
Video	50–200 hours
Computer-based instruction	200–300 hours
Experiments	200–300 hours

Source: Swift 1996

only bring a small improvement, raising the possibility that it should have been invested more profitably in some other part of the system. Second, there is a point at the lower end beneath which it is not worth going – the likely failure rate, and/or poor quality of exit performance, make it unlikely that the investment will be justified in comparison with face-to-face provision. Falling below that lower figure runs the risk of an inadequately prepared course which must be compensated for by excessive amounts of teaching person-power in its presentation, or a high failure rate, or a lowering of exit performance standards, or, most likely, all three. Unfortunately, large amounts of distance-education practice internationally appear to have been pitched below this level.

A further complication in the ultimate budget for design of a course follows from real or accidental decisions about the proportion of hours of the course allocated to each medium in the course. Each is likely to make up a very different weight of student study time and may not necessarily play a proportionate role in equipping a student for success.

Finally, design time itself is not a stable quantum. It is worth considering that, in each medium, and in the course overall, different combinations of expertise may have different effects on student performance. For example:

Course Team A	%	*Course Team B*	%
Academic	95	Academic	50
Editor	5	Instructional Designer	20
		Media Specialist	20
		Editor	5
		Designer	5

All other elements being equal, it is reasonable to assume that, if the two teams put in the same total amount of design time, Team B will produce a more successful course.

Costs of design are incurred regardless of the number of students who study the course. Low unit costs then follow only if large numbers of students study it successfully and the person-power devoted to presenting the course is substantially lower than in face-to-face settings.

The costs of teachers in traditional institutions are related directly to student numbers. Even more importantly, their magnitude is so great as to make all other aspects of variable costs relatively trivial. (For example, the cost of teachers' salaries in schools in South Africa is around 80 per cent of all costs. In higher education, it is lower but not substantially so.) Distance education therefore changes the production function of education by substituting cheaper management of students' learning for the expensive process of applying teacher time to it. This creates potential for lower costs per student, *provided* that large numbers of students can take the expensively designed course and that the resulting unit cost advantage is not eroded by the lower success rate that is likely to ensue.

In successful distance-education systems, as much attention is given to presentation or teaching of courses as to their preparation. Where they are well resourced and judiciously deployed, high-quality materials and learner-support systems can bring substantial benefits in improved completion rates and thus enhanced cost-effectiveness. That is how distance-education institutions can be more cost-effective than conventional institutions.

COMPARATIVE COSTS

Care needs to be taken in using measures of effectiveness that are appropriate to distance-education institutions. Most, and particularly those concerned with lifelong learning, aim to ensure that as many students as possible attain their various learning objectives, whatever they may be. In some cases this is a degree, but in other cases it may be a certificate or diploma, a single course credit, or a short updating course successfully completed. Graduation is therefore not the only successful outcome of study.

Higher education

While we have more information on higher education than on other sectors, this is often difficult to interpret. Some distance-education institutions operate an open admissions policy and are committed to offering higher education to those who lack traditional entry qualifications. Success rates for those students are inevitably lower than for students qualified and selected for entry to conventional universities. Nevertheless, institutions with such policies may be adding more value in personal and social benefit than the conventional universities.

Regrettably, measures of cost based on units of education achieved other than degrees and on concepts of added value are not yet widely used. This leaves only less satisfactory measures such as cost per registered full-time equivalent year of study. Such calculations greatly favour distance-education institutions because their very much lower course pass rates are not brought into the equation. On the other hand, calculations based only on successful graduations favour conventional institutions because distance-education students who are satisfied with partial completion of a programme are ignored and their costs charged to graduations. Nevertheless, even on this limited criterion of success, distance-education institutions with high-quality materials and tutorial support score well (although those without score very badly).

Early studies of the British Open University (OU), for example, indicated that it produced graduates at something over half the cost of other universities. A study undertaken by the Department of Education and Science in 1981 found that a three-year full-time equivalent degree at the OU cost £4890 compared to an average of £8550 in other universities. A four-year full-time equivalent degree cost £7984 at the OU and £11,842 elsewhere. The differences were even greater when calculated in terms of public fund costs (£4356 compared to £10,801 for a three-year full-time equivalent degree) and total economic costs (£7116 compared to £17,843) (Department of Education and Science 1981). The differentials have narrowed somewhat since 1981 because the proportion of underqualified students entering the OU has increased and unit costs in other universities have fallen – but a more recent calculation put the cost of an OU graduate at less than two-thirds that of a full-time graduate in other universities (Horlock 1984).

A further study, undertaken by the Department for Education and Science in 1991, compared the cost of OU degrees with part-time degrees offered by three conventional institutions. It found that a three-year full-time equivalent degree at the OU costs less than 60 per cent of the average degree course of the other universities. These are impressive statistics, but they are not unique. Other distance universities with similar teaching systems achieve similar rates. For example, the Allama Iqbal Open University in Pakistan, which is modelled on the British Open University, achieves costs per graduate that are 45 to 70 per cent of the cost of conventional universities (Perraton 1994: 21). The Open Learning Institute of Hong Kong made heavy use of existing distance-teaching materials from the OU and elsewhere and married these with highly resourced student support arrangements. As a break-even institution, it was required to charge students the full cost of their courses. Its graduates paid about one-third of what a similar degree of the University of Hong Kong costs (Swift and Dhanarajan 1992).

There is another variation on the question of returns to investment in distance education. Few distance-education specialists in Australia would accept a general argument that distance education is cheaper than residential, because in Australia it is not. This is because, in general, the methods are used for other purposes than cheapness and, inevitably, on small numbers. The most precise study of costs in which outcomes were identical was conducted at the University of Southern Queensland (USQ) in comparing the cost of its distance-education and residential output. The conclusion was that they were broadly comparable. The advantages of adding distance education to conventional provision were *political*, in the sense that a wider clientele of students was being served, *institutional* in that a small institution was able to increase its size giving both general-ised cost-efficiency benefits and greater weight on the higher education institutional battlefield, and *educational*, in that use of distance-education methods across all fields encouraged pedagogical quality. Some income and staff development benefit was also derived from offshore registrations in Asian countries.

The studies of the British Open University and the University of Southern Queensland (USQ) elucidate only some of the benefits of the range of distance-education methods because neither institution uses all of them. Each also dealt with only a specific range of possibilities among the clientele (Taylor and White 1991). The USQ had small numbers of students on a large number of courses: two important causes of high costs. The OU has an open entry policy; very expensive course-design strategies; a short (thirty-two-week) studying year; a slow registration procedure, and for most of its life has been restricted in the numbers it was permitted to enrol. In these ways, the cost-efficiency of its degree structures, particularly in science and technology, has been retarded.

The course production methods of the two institutions are almost at the two extremes of expensiveness – the OU spending up to £4 million (US$6 million) to prepare a course equivalent to one-eighth of a four-year honours degree while USQ spends a small fraction of that amount. In summary, the OU, despite limitations on its numbers set by government policy and challenges to its teaching system of open entry, was large enough (in course registrations), with a small enough number of courses, to produce a particular level of cost advantage (up to 40 per cent cheaper) over its competitors. The USQ had no chance of achieving similar numbers and therefore the expensive course was not an option; nor was it likely to obtain a cost advantage over conventional delivery.

Studies also reveal, however, that distance-education institutions which do not invest in high-quality materials and student support systems achieve much lower completion rates and therefore lower cost-effectiveness rates than the OU and, indeed, than conventional universities. In the early 1990s, for example, the International Correspondence School in the USA was providing materials but no student support and taking no action to monitor student progress. Completion rates were less than 15 per cent. The conse-quences of low completion rates can be catastrophic to cost-effectiveness if the most challenging criterion of graduation rates is used as the sole measure of educational value-added. A study of data supplied by the ten largest distance-education universities illustrates the point. Daniel found that these 'mega universities' taught their students at between 10 and 50 per cent of the average cost of the other universities in their countries (Daniel 1995). However, they were less likely to bring their students to the point of graduation. Where graduation rates are an important aspect of the higher education system, that cost advantage is diminished by the ratio of the difference between the two forms.

Other education sectors

The same financial challenges exist when transporting the logic of distance education into sectors other than higher education. Internationally, there has been growing interest in introducing open schools. (As used here, an open school refers to an educational institution operating in the spheres of primary and/or secondary education, providing courses and programmes predominantly through use of distance-education methods.) While there are varying motivations for the introduction of such schools (discussed further below), a common motivation when such projects are aimed at younger learners as an alternative to mainstream schooling is usually to reduce the cost of providing education. Evidence from around the world suggests that open schools tend to succeed in this regard, as Table 12.2 illustrates.

Again, however, these comparative costs should be read in combination with several of the other points made in this chapter. They do not, by themselves, create an argument in favour of introducing distance-education methods, as the educational implications of this need to be weighed up against any likely financial efficiencies.

RELATIVE FINANCIAL BENEFITS

There is ample evidence that the methods of distance education can be used to increase the productivity of education systems. *Prima facie*, the evidence and the logic of analysis seem indisputable. However, two kinds of argument, one educational and one macro-economic, can introduce doubt. The educational argument asserts that any dilution of the intense personal interaction between educator and learner will weaken the quality of the learner's experience. Even if many more students are taught, even if they achieve the exit performance levels of the old system, something will be lost. Few would disagree with this if two extremes are compared – an Oxford personal tutorial relationship with a correspondence course – but one is not possible and the other is not proposed. In between, we are left with the educator's responsibility for managing the highest quality learning experiences for as many people as possible at the lowest cost.

Table 12.2 Costs of some school equivalency projects

Country, project, date	GNP per capita at date of study		Student numbers	Cost per learner	Comparative cost
	Current US$	1998 US$		1998 US$	
Brazil, Bahia State, Madureza, 1976	1410	3793	8000	$418 per student following three courses	Higher cost per student than alternative
Brazil, Minerva, 1977	1410	3793	118,118	$49 per student following group of courses for one year	Costs 65% of private sector alternative; no evidence on cost per successful student
India, National Open School, 1990	360	449	40,885	$44 per student p.a.	Cost 63% of cost of government school
South Korea Air Correspondence High School, 1976	980	2636	20,000	$171 per student p.a.	Cost per student 24% of alternative; cost per successful student 29%
Malawi Correspondence Study Centres, 1978	150	404	2884	$399 per student; $2794 per examination pass	Cost per student 62% cost at day school; cost per pass 81% higher
– 1988	160	220	17,000	$107 per student; $378 per pass	Cost per pass reduced to 34% of day school rates

Mexico Telesecundaria, 1975	1160	3514	33,840	$589 per student	Cost per student 76% of alternative
– 1981	3170	5684	170,000	$927 per student	Cost per student 9.5% higher than alternative
– 1988	1860	2563	>400,000	$441 per student	Cost per student 32% of alternative
– 1997	3680	739	767,700	$562 per student	
Zambia Correspondence Study Centres, 1981	600	1076	11,800	Cost per student in range $102–291	Cost per student 7–21% of day school

Source: Perraton 2000: 126–7

Experience elsewhere demonstrates that the quality of distance education can be as good as the best conventional teaching. In Britain, where the quality of higher education provision is being assessed by peer review according to a set of common criteria, OU provision was judged 'excellent' (the top rating) in almost half of all subjects assessed, putting it in the top twelve of 120 higher education institutions (Swift 1996).

The second, macro-economic argument is to do with the minutiae of economic costing. Well-established, large-scale distance-education institutions are easily capable of producing equivalent educational outputs to those of traditional institutions whether expressed in certificates obtained or, even less difficult, per full-time equivalent year of study. However, they often do so partly by taking advantage of the historic investment in people and facilities of the wider system. To the extent that any educational gain brings cost benefits that are distributed in favour of the distance-education institution, calculations that do not take this into account will be biased. For example, do the charges made by traditional institutions for use of their classrooms, laboratories, accommodation and ancillary staff represent true cost or marginal cost? If the latter, they could be said to be subsidising distance education. This kind of question, however, has relevance only in interinstitutional comparison. All would agree that the *system* benefits because output is increased from the same quantity of historical investment in expertise and capital equipment.

Equally difficult to quantify will be the returns to lifetime earnings of degrees by distance education. To the extent that distance-education students are in a much wider age range, they could be said, as a group, to have a lower working life expectancy. If many of them are in employment it may also be difficult to ascribe future earnings to the act of graduation. Traditional analysis of returns to investment tends to assume a fully causal link. On the other hand, because most distance-education students are studying part-time while in employment, they continue to contribute to the gross national product, paying taxes and (probably) paying a higher proportion of the costs of their education in fees. These environing arguments may be ignored for present purposes. They either work in favour of the cost–benefit advantage of distance education against residential education or they bring system benefits. As lifelong learning gains a hold around the world, the economic advantage of distance education over so-called full-time residential education will begin to be demonstrated.

National needs

One implication of the foregoing analysis is that distance education offers a very much wider and more detailed range of alternatives to the educational policy maker or planner than does traditional education. This wide range, unfortunately, includes not only unconscionable amounts of failure, but also excessive and unproductive expenditure. Measurement of cost-efficiency and effectiveness is therefore key to assessment of an institution's performance.

There is a further implication, which is well illustrated at the level of higher education. Quite the most crucial policy difference between distance-education institutions of economically developed countries and those in the developing world is that the latter are important elements in provision for *traditional university entrance cohorts*. In developed countries their functions are usually seen to be those of extending second-chance opportunities and enhancing the lifelong learning capacities of the system. Consequently, their responsibilities may be expected to be very different. Table 12.3 outlines differences between distance-education universities in industrial and developing countries.

For this reason, while international institutions may have much to offer on a wide range of techniques, strategies, systems and philosophy it is essential to consider separately the nation's policy in funding a given institution or programme. For example, a relatively rich country may fund a distance-education university for second-chance and personal enrichment purposes. In this case, the institution performs functions marginal to

Table 12.3 Some contrasts between distance education universities

Industrialised countries	Developing countries
Curriculum may well be vocational, interest-directed, flexible, non-traditional, experimental.	Curriculum must be that thought to be necessary for school leavers.
Curriculum may range broadly.	Curriculum should concentrate on subjects of national need.
Graduation rates and speeds are less important than other, more general educational objectives.	Graduation rates and speeds are of primary importance.
Student support may assume maturity of students and infrastructural support for independent learning.	Student support in all its aspects will be crucial in early years of study.
Student counselling may concentrate on use of the learning system.	Student counselling may play an important part in directing student careers.
Cost per unit of educational output may not be important.	Cost per unit of educational output must be important since other forms of education are underfunded.

those of mainstream education. Graduation rates, and the subjects within which graduations occur, may not be of particular importance. The general contributions to adult education, to flexibility of the system and to the satisfaction of the electorate are looked upon as proper returns to use of tax revenue. At the same time, because students are adult, perhaps already qualified, and pursuing personal or economic interests, it is also possible to countenance low graduation rates depending upon the cost of the various units of output. It would be difficult to imagine a developing country substantially funding distance education with any of these functions as primary objectives or even acceptable consequences.

Similar differences may be found when exploring the development of open schools. Many countries around the world, when faced with problems of learner access to conventional schooling systems, have implemented some form or other of open school as a response to these problems. However, the reasons for establishing such systems are many and varied, depending on the context in which they are implemented. The correspondence school in New Zealand, for example, was established in 1922, while the open school in India is over twenty years old. Reasons for establishing such schools have tended to revolve around accessibility to traditional schooling. In the two examples mentioned above, part of the motivation to establish the school was to provide access to students in remote farming communities (New Zealand) and access to large numbers of students which the mainstream schooling system could not absorb (India). Our financial analysis has illustrated the potential of such approaches for reducing costs per learner (even per successful learner), but this of course needs to take into account the various dangers of introducing distance education simply because it may reduce cost.

SOME COMMON PROBLEMS

In our final section, we focus attention on some common problems and difficulties that often accompany implementation of distance education in the developing world.

Building a financial planning culture

The most obvious problem which tends to arise is that some educational planners continue to believe that, because education is theoretically an endeavour in the public interest, some amorphous entity (often referred to vaguely as government) should cover the bill regardless of what it may be. As a result, financial analysis is frequently absent, resulting in widespread systemic inefficiencies across both distance and contact education provision. More importantly, though, it has meant that, in several cases, decisions to introduce distance-education courses and programmes are not based on any sound financial argument, but rather on a vague notion that distance education is cheaper than the alternative.

Where financial planning is done, it has tended to focus narrowly on the direct costs of a course or programme, rather than on understanding the full direct and indirect costs necessary to sustain both the educational intervention and the educational provider itself. At its worst, such financial planning is integrated with the *laissez-faire* attitude outlined in the previous paragraph, with educators in many systems routinely omitting their own costs as part of their financial plans. At a systemic level, it is often reflected in the absence of systematic financial planning templates that take account of indirect costs and institutional and administrative overheads within financial plans. Usually, these errors of omission are symptomatic of a culture of financial dependence, in which institutions that have received funding regularly from a guaranteed source (usually government finance) have not been required to engage seriously with strategies to ensure their own financial sustainability.

A key problem, related to this and faced by many educational planners, is that of knowing whether courses and programmes are generating more income than expenditure. Careful analysis of all associated costs of a course or programme is the only meaningful way to overcome this problem. Our experience is that the only meaningful way to achieve this is to begin by developing a thorough map of what students will be expected to do. All education involves a set of teaching and learning strategies. It is possible to group these strategies into three related categories:

1   *Contact strategies*, which refer to all time spent in synchronous or asynchronous communication between educators (e.g. facilitators, tutors, lecturers or mentors) and learners. Contact strategies include face-to-face sessions, as well as other communication strategies such as telephonic support, e-mail and internet chat, and video-conferencing. The key cost driver of contact strategies is the ratio of learners to educators.

2   *Assessment strategies*, which refer to activities designed to enable educators to evaluate student learning or progress. Educator time on assessment strategies will be affected by the number of assessment tasks, the complexity of those tasks (as increasing complexity usually requires additional time spent on assessment), and the number of students working together (assessment tasks completed by groups of students reduce the overall number of tasks requiring assessment, but may increase the time that has to be spent assessing each submission).

3   *Independent study strategies*, which refer to all student time spent in course-related activities that do not directly involve educators (other than in design of those activities).

These distinctions are essentially arbitrary, but are designed to estimate student notional hours of learning (how many hours each student is expected to put in to complete the course successfully) and the resulting staff workload. From this base, it becomes relatively simple to calculate a full range of associated costs, including specialised costs of course design and development. It also becomes possible to compare accumulated costs with projected income, and thus to determine whether or not proposed curriculum strategies are financially viable.

Distance-education planning, however, introduces the need to project costs over time and student numbers. This is because distance education is predicated on the logic that up-front investments in design and development of courses and administrative systems will be amortised over time and large student numbers. It is therefore not reasonable to expect a distance-education programme to generate more (or at least as much) income as expense in a single year. However, such financial sustainability needs to be achieved over a cycle of a number of years. Without undertaking such calculations, it becomes impossible to establish when – if ever – new courses and programmes will break even financially, hence making it harder to make effective financial decisions on whether or not to implement initial design and development investments.

It is important to note here that such planning does not assume a need for all income to be generated from students. (See Chapter 6 for a discussion of the options.) There are several other potential sources of income, including governments, donor agencies and businesses. The important point, though, is that the *educational* viability of any distance-education programme will definitely be undermined if income does not at least match full expenditure.

Avoiding the income trap

When financial analysis is undertaken, it often focuses narrowly on unit costs (that is, the cost per individual student). Such analysis depends for its persuasiveness on demonstrating declining student costs as economies of scale are achieved. This often ignores macro-economic analysis to assess whether or not the total sums of money that such educational activity will require exist in the educational economies for which new distance-education programmes are being planned. This problem is most serious when it creeps into national policy planning, and it has undermined the viability of many distance-education programmes around the world.

Developing countries share at least one common problem: there are more urgent social problems to solve than the time or resources to solve them. Faced with so many urgent problems, it becomes very difficult – some would argue almost impossible – to establish priorities, as focusing on one course of action over another often involves taking decisions that may be construed as ignoring fundamental human rights or even – at its most extreme – leading to loss of life (through poverty, disease, unemployment, and other core social problems). This makes it increasingly tempting to want to solve all problems together, as prioritisation simply forces decisions that are too difficult to take.

Often, distance-education planning succumbs to the pressure of this problem. Persuasive arguments about reduced unit costs prompt investments in large-scale new programmes aimed at providing almost immediate solutions to major problems. The following example illustrates this financial logic:

> Graduating a single student at a traditional contact institution is, say, costing $5000. If we invest in a large-scale distance-education programme – using earmarked government funding or money from a donor agency – we can reduce this unit cost to, say, $2000 (and still provide a quality experience, as this will incorporate extensive learner support).

Regretfully, such logic is usually seriously flawed by inadequate analysis of real income streams. It requires an additional element of analysis, which might run as follows:

> Our analysis is based on a current reality in which 100 students are enrolled for the contact programme, thus leading to a total cost of $500,000. To achieve the economies of scale we have planned, we need to enrol at least 1000 students. Thus, although our unit costs have declined, we need to expect total expenditure to increase to $2,000,000, a fourfold increase.

In many instances, income analysis will reveal that there is simply no way to accommodate this increase in total expenditure. We have witnessed several examples where omissions of this type of planning have led to diversions of income away from small, but sustainable, interventions into large, unsustainable interventions. As income streams dry up, the large-scale intervention is forced to cut back on certain crucial investments, most notably ongoing course design and provision of adequate learner support. At the same time, the smaller intervention has also been rendered unsustainable. The net consequence is an increase in the kinds of social problem outlined above as education delivery becomes undermined.

One source of this problem is that planners often seek to understand institutions and systems considered to be successful in other contexts. While this is a sensible approach to understanding different models and conditions for success, it runs the risk that successful models are assumed to be appropriate within a different local context. Regretfully, experience demonstrates that such expectations are rarely fulfilled. Again, the only meaningful strategy is to undertake rigorous financial planning on a case-by-case basis.

Perpetuating current patterns of expenditure

On the flip side of the above problem is that of perpetuating financial inefficiencies. In many cases, establishing distance-education institutions and programmes perpetuates existing patterns of educational expenditure rather than challenging them. Very often, their establishment has been motivated by intrinsic weaknesses in the mainstream, contact system, which policy makers have seen requiring years of structural change before large-scale improvements will become noticeable. Thus distance education provides a handy, reasonably quick institutional solution to problems of educational delivery, which can operate largely outside of mainstream systems and hence not be slowed down by the pace of these structural changes. On the face of it, these appear then to be structures of particular interest and relevance to developing contexts. There is, however, a very real danger implicit in this, namely that such expediency retards further the pace of change in mainstream systems. Better financial planning – particularly at national level – can go some way towards avoiding these problems.

CONCLUSION

Perhaps the best generalisation that can be made about the methods of distance education in relation to cost-effectiveness is that they provide tools for designing and building high-quality systems for facilitating learning that are sensitive to the specific needs of students. Their cost-efficiency and effectiveness depend primarily on the number of students who can be recruited to each of their courses and the quality of their teaching materials and student support systems. Other factors have a bearing (for example, whether fees are set at levels that discourage recruitment and retention, and whether courses are designed from scratch or bought off the shelf), but these are the fundamental conditions for success. Distance-education institutions that have been able to fulfil these conditions satisfactorily have been able to demonstrate higher levels of cost-efficiency and cost-effectiveness than comparable conventional institutions.

REFERENCES

Daniel, J. S. (1995) 'Open universities and the knowledge media: new opportunities: new threats', Conference paper delivered at the ninth annual conference of the Asian Association of Open Universities, 3–5 December, Taipei, Taiwan.

Department of Education and Science (1981) 'Average recurrent unit costs of the Open University and conventional universities', unpublished paper.

Dhanarajan, G., Ip, P. K., Yuen, K. S. and Swales, C. (eds) (1994) *Economics of Distance Education: Recent Experience*, Hong Kong: Open Learning Institute Press.

Horlock, J. H. (1984) 'The Open University after 15 years', *Proceedings of the Manchester Statistical Society*.

Perraton, H. (1994) 'Comparative cost of distance teaching in higher education: scale and quality', in G. Dhanarajan *et al.* (eds) *Economics of Distance Education: Recent Experience*, Hong Kong: OLI Press.

Perraton, H. (2000) *Open and Distance Learning in the Developing World*, New York: Routledge.

Rumble, G. (1997) *The Costs and Economics of Open and Distance Learning*, London: Kogan Page.

Swift, D. (1996) *A Conceptual Analysis of the Costs of Distance Education*, SAIDE concept paper, unpublished.

Swift, D. and Dhanarajan, G. (1992) 'Cost-effective distance education: a Hong Kong strategy', unpublished working paper, Hong Kong: Open Learning Institute.

Taylor, J. C. and White, V. J. (1991) *The Evaluation of Cost Effectiveness of Multi-media Mixed-mode Teaching and Learning*, Canberra: Australian Government Publishing Service.

Part V

Conclusion

Chapter 13

Framing policy for open and distance learning

Helen Lentell

Open and distance education is becoming an increasingly significant policy choice for developing countries if policy papers from international organisations such as UNESCO and the World Bank are to be taken seriously. Open and distance learning holds out the promise of increasing accessibility to education and training and enabling the best use of limited educational resources. Similarly, it is playing a growing role in the OECD countries with, as has been seen in Chapters 2, 9 and 10, increasing activities by the private sector. But a clear policy for open and distance learning is often lacking. Recent publications from UNESCO and the World Bank, for example, are informative on global trends in open and distance learning but silent on policy and strategy (Murphy *et al.* 2002, UNESCO 2002a). Like many other declarations and conference reports before them, they tend to provide a general argument for open and distance learning, rather than an articulation of specific strategies for implementing its methodologies, the theme of this book.

It is possible that this absence of specificity reflects what Unterhalter *et al.* have suggested is confusion and uncertainty about the relationship between open learning – as a philosophy of education, in which special value is given to certain underlying principles, in particular 'learner centredness', 'flexibility of learning', 'the removal of unnecessary barriers to access' and 'the recognition of prior learning and experience' – and distance education as a delivery strategy (Unterhalter *et al.* 2000). Robinson has, in contrast, developed a more persuasive argument. She argues that the gap between rhetoric and reality will remain until distance educators have assisted policy makers in translating high-level and general statements into concrete policy that can be implemented. She argues that distance-education practitioners need to identify ways in which they can aid policy- and decision-makers by providing them with information and understanding about open and distance learning if they are to develop and implement policies that support it (Robinson 1998). For, as a recent UNESCO news item trailing its study of basic education delivered via distance and open learning in five of the E9 countries identified, 'educational policy makers in the E9 countries are unlikely to commit themselves to any initiative, large or small, on the basis of inadequate information about costs and effectiveness' (UNESCO 2002b).

Policy in the context of planning for open and distance learning may be taken to be an 'implicit or explicit specification of courses of purposive action being followed or to be followed in dealing with a recognized problem . . . and directed towards the accomplishment of some intended and or desired set of goals' (Hough 1984). From a policy perspective the factors that national educational policy makers have to consider in this context remain fairly consistent, and were clearly identified by Dodds and Youngman some years ago. They are:

- The rationale for the development of distance education and its priority in relation to other options.
- The perceived needs for distance education and the appropriate levels of provision, namely secondary, tertiary, and adult basic education.
- The direct costs and opportunity costs of investing in distance-education provision and the potential cost–benefits.
- The appropriate institutional arrangements and the capacity for developing and maintaining an effective distance-education system in terms of the recurrent resources, management capability, trained staff, materials production, student support and (information) communications infrastructure.
- The status of distance education and the acceptability of its qualifications within the national system of educational credentials.
- The possibilities for international cooperation in developing and sustaining a distance-education system.

(Dodds and Youngman 1994)

This book has been designed to help with that articulation of policy, and central to its argument is the belief that the ordered framing of policy is likely to help the cost-effective and educationally sound expansion of open and distance learning. There are, however, many countries which have not yet developed a well-articulated national policy but in which open and distance learning practice is demonstrating clear achievements and benefits. Botswana provides an example: while it has no national distance-education policy, the government has given serious consideration to the role of distance education as a viable alternative vehicle for increasing access to education in Botswana. The National Commission on Education in 1993 acknowledged the potential of distance education to increase access to education in a cost-effective manner and recommended that government 'expeditiously develop the potential of distance education'. But as yet Botswana lacks a formally articulated national policy framework for the provision of distance education. Nhundu and Kamau have argued:

The existence of a policy framework underscores a government's commitment to distance education and allows for the marshalling of resources needed to support and accelerate the provision of distance education programmes. In order that distance education is not marginalized and relegated to the periphery of the education system, national policies should present distance education as a national initiative that is integral to, and contributes to, national planning developments. The policy should seek to integrate distance education within the formal education system and provide it with the necessary resources and political support that reflects government commitment to the new policies.

(Nhundu and Kamau 2002)

In commenting on distance education developments in the SADC region, Lawrence notes that to ignore proper educational policy frameworks and development principles 'merely reduces educational planning and development to piecemeal and ad hoc interventions leading to under-performance, ineffective strategic planning and non-sustainable delivery' (Lawrence 2001). Botswana has made progress partly because of a national decision to put resources in this area and partly because institutional development has resulted in the development of de facto policies. Thus, while not criticising the relatively unplanned and incremental approach used in Botswana, the case for formal development of national policy remains. Issues of governance and quality assurance, of appropriate and egalitarian funding policies, or of access by education to technologies, for example, discussed in previous chapters, depend on national policy frameworks and are often outside the capacity of a single institution.

It may be that the absence of national policy and frameworks reflects the lack of knowledge and skills among national and institutional policy makers – a view held strongly by the developers of a recent online course for distance education policy makers in southern Africa (Commonwealth of Learning 2002). On the other hand it was pointed out in Chapter 1 that the neo-liberal agenda has eroded the consensus that governments should plan centrally – so it is perhaps not surprising that in both the north and the south there is a remarkable absence of coherent, joined up, policy on implementing open and distance learning with the aim of achieving the policy priorities governments have identified for themselves, despite much genuflection directed at its supposed effectiveness and relevance.

Despite the lack of national policies and strategies for open and distance learning, organisations such as the Commonwealth of Learning, the World Bank and UNESCO have shown that open and distance learning is becoming increasingly significant worldwide as a serious element of educational and training systems in both developed and developing countries. Open and distance learning has extended its reach and application beyond open universities to schooling, work-based learning and skills training, thereby going beyond the formal educational provision of governments or government-supported institutions.

It is here – at an institutional and organisational level – that one can identify policy, or something akin to nascent policy at least. For the systems needed for open and distance learning seldom happen by chance, but are dependent upon careful planning and management. Unlike conventional educational provision, open and distance learning, because it is complex (involving many operational functions and specialisms), and often large-scale, invariably requires careful planning. In conventional classroom-based teaching teachers can plan on a day-to-day basis, and can tailor their teaching to reactions they perceive almost instantaneously. They can assume that their students are fairly homogeneous in terms of their age group and often their educational attainment. Not so with open and distance learning. Materials, which are costly to develop, cannot be abandoned lightly because they are inappropriate and are not working. In this sense distance education is an industrial process (Peters 1983), and as such requires clear policy, strategic planning and effective operational management.

It is true that the new information and communication technologies – especially those created by the emergence of the worldwide web – have made it possible for enthusiastic individuals, sometimes dubbed lone rangers (Bates 2000), to create their own web-delivered programme within a conventional teaching setting, bringing an apparent convergence of distance and contiguous methodologies. Lone rangers then promote, teach and generally manage these programmes. But costs are hidden and such a system is fragile; problems are almost bound to arise when these enthusiasts take a holiday, go on sabbatical or leave. If the decision is taken to expand this provision some central planning and institutional responsibility is necessary. It is for this reason that distance education is here referred to as having analogies to industrial processes and why policy and planning for open and distance learning must be concerned with the operational system.

This often makes the gestation period of a new open and distance learning system lengthy although, as Jegede and Okebukola note from their experience of Nigeria, nations wanting to transform and develop open and distance learning are in a hurry and need road-maps to guide them (Jegede and Okebukola 2002) What might a road-map look like? What are the sign-posts on the road? What are the critical issues in policy and planning for open and distance learning systems? They are:

- Identifying the target population and their needs.
- Choosing the type of system.
- Choosing the appropriate technology of delivery.
- Business planning and costing open and distance learning systems.

- Materials – developing or acquiring.
- Tutoring and supporting students.
- Recruiting and enrolling students.
- Assessing students.
- Managing and administering the open and distance learning system.
- Monitoring, evaluation and quality assurance.

This broad list indicates the areas of decision-making and demonstrates the range of decisions policy makers and planners have to address in establishing and maintaining open and distance learning systems. Table 13.1 identifies the kinds of issue to be resolved within each of these areas and shows why open and distance learning systems require lead-in times, often of a number of years.

The issues identified in Table 13.1 could be analysed at two levels. At the upper level are the range of issues on which policy decisions need to be taken within the framework of education and training policy generally. The purposes for which open and distance learning may be developed, the need to consider student and staff needs, and the various process issues discussed in Part III above, are all likely to be of concern for policy makers in the public or private sector, whose interests are much broader than open and distance learning. But then, at a finer level of grain, there are issues of implementation – just how should one train staff or arrange for quality assurance – that belong more clearly to individual distance-teaching institutions. In practice, planning and implementation are likely to be an iterative process. It is one that should be helped by an examination of the questions identified in Table 13.1 or in other practical guides to implementation (e.g. Rumble 1992, Perraton *et al.* 2002).

Missing from the above list is dealing with politicians who have short time frames or the flexibility needed to operate in highly fluid – perhaps even unstable – social, political, economic and religious environments. Colleagues working at the emerging National Open University of Nigeria could hardly have anticipated the burning down of their printers in Kaduna in 2002 during the 'Miss World' riots and the loss of their prospectus that was about to be published there. Nor could the emerging Open University in Britain have anticipated a national postal strike just at the moment they were to dispatch study materials to their first intake of students. And a general list cannot, of course, identify all the details of implementation that follow from policy, planning and decision making. In Nigeria, again, for example, the new university has adopted a policy of providing face-to-face sessions to tutor and support students, recognising that their students will benefit in terms of motivation and study support. This in turn means that the university has had to acquire 250 KVA generators and transformers for the first set of study centres due to the unreliability of mains electricity distribution ('This Day' 2003). Moreover,

Table 13.1 Crucial policy-making areas and some issues for distance education policy makers

Areas	Issues
Identifying target audience	• Educational purpose of the programme • Demography of learner population (e.g. age range, gender, employment) • Motivation for learning (e.g. vocational, academic) • Existing knowledge and/or skills of target learners (e.g. can study skills be assumed?) • Curriculum needs (e.g. is it defined by an examination or a professional body, academic knowledge, vocational skills?) • Market research
Type of ODL system	• Campus based, organisation based, individual based • Self-paced or programme based • Open access • Single, dual-mode, partnership service provider
Choosing the appropriate technology for distribution and materials and for interaction with students	• Print, audio/visual, web-based or a mix • Access implications of choice • Training implications of choice • Cost – including maintenance and sustainability

Business planning and costing	• Philosophy and objectives
	• Capital and recurrent costs:
	  – planning
	  – implementation
	  – maintenance and updating
	  – fixed and variable
	• Self-financing or subsidised?
	• Courses portfolio (e.g. length of study)
	• Course development and production process (e.g. team, individual, contract)
	• Course delivery:
	  – Enrolment
	  – Tutorial system
	  – Materials dispatch
	  – Assessment
	  – Record keeping
	  – Marketing
	  – Funding

Table 13.1 Continued

Areas	Issues
Materials	• Buy, make or adapt • Media choice and/or mix • Instructional design • Developmental testing • Production • Delivery • Updating • Storage
Tutoring and supporting students	• Tutor role and tasks • Tutor skills • Recruiting tutors • Induction and training tutors • Monitoring tutors • Marking and feedback • Face-to-face, telephone, online tutoring • Student counselling • Student guides and providing information to students
Recruiting and enrolling students	• Making course information available • Marketing • Diagnostic testing of potential students • Briefing students about ODL • Enrolment • Fee payment systems
Assessing students	• Methods to be used (e.g. exams, projects, thesis, and portfolio) • Summative or formative • Methods of submission and giving feedback (e.g. online or by paper correspondence) • Recording marks and student progress

Managing and administering the ODL system	• Operational issues, e.g.:
	  – Finance
	  – Student recruitment
	  – Enquiries processing
	  – Enrolment
	  – Materials development
	  – Materials manufacture
	  – Tuition and support
	  – Assessment
	  – Technology

continued

Table 13.1 Continued

Areas	Issues
Monitoring evaluation and quality assurance	• Who is the evaluation for? (e.g. politicians, managers, educational staff) • The level of monitoring (e.g. system level, course/programme level, individual tutor or individual learner) • Capability to act on findings of evaluation, monitoring and quality assurance • Quality assurance systems

Source: adapted from Freeman forthcoming

planning face-to-face sessions allows for a system of study material distribution where other distribution systems are unreliable.

Indeed it is because open and distance learning systems are complex that the literature on open and distance learning addresses costing as a crucial issue. But sadly, as Butcher and Roberts point out (Chapter 12 above), policy makers and planners may have some appreciation of the short-term running costs of distance-education programmes, but less of a grasp of planning for the long-term sustainability of a programme or institution. This is problematic in any context, they note, 'but it is of particular concern in contexts where financial resources are very constrained, which is usually a feature of distance education programmes in developing countries'. However, it is an instructive corrective to read that even in the private sector so frequently held up as clarions – even models of efficiency and effectiveness – the adoption of blended learning (online learning combined with classroom training) frequently turns into 'frustrating boondoggles, consuming far more money than anyone anticipated' because of poor planning: 'The bitter fruits of which often appear during the implementation of training, or long after substantial amounts of time, money and enthusiasm have been expended' (Troha 2002).

Table 13.1 as a road-map on crucial policy-making areas and issues does not intend to be exhaustive; there are clearly many more levels of detail, and policies to be developed and refined, as further questions follow from those issues that policy makers and planners have addressed. Beyond this, original decisions will also need to be revisited, as Perry's book on the establishment of the Open University in Britain clearly documented (Perry 1976). As noted in Chapter 2, the early thinking about the university placed great emphasis on television and played down the tutorial services which experience demonstrated needed to be developed and required resources. Perry developed an internal governance structure that seemed appropriate for the size of university originally foreseen but himself later saw it as unfortunately cumbersome for the university as it in fact developed and expanded. Nor does the road-map seek to be prescriptive in how policy makers should address these issues. Many solutions are country- and context-specific. Television is appropriate as a technology for open university education in China, inappropriate in many small states, and suitable for school or nonformal education only under particular local circumstances. Returning to recent developments in Nigeria gives us another illustration. A crucial policy area for all open universities will be the methodology for recruitment and enrolling of students. How do you get enrolment forms to potential students when there is no reliable national postal system and when 'we have to get the forms into every nook and cranny of the nation'? Solution: invite the banks to tender for the project and enforce on them that part of the winning of the tender means opening branches where they may not currently have them in order to provide access to the forms, thus providing a community service too. Out of the sixty-seven banks that applied, twenty-five met the criteria and guidelines ('This Day' 2003). Determining the criteria and guidelines for bank tenders may not immediately seem to be the obvious task of the chief executive of an emerging open university, but it is when one starts to address how to enrol students in the context of Nigeria.

This summary of the argument has concentrated on national and institutional policy but it is appropriate to identify the need for policy framing, and the opportunities for institutions to benefit from it, at two other levels: the regional and international. Authors have noted a number of regional initiatives, from those of the European Union to the two Commonwealth regional universities. In the Arab world, the scale of demand for virtual and open learning, and the scarcity of Arabic-language materials, are pushing for regional activity. Issues of accreditation may demand a regional solution especially for small states. Language policies may well go beyond national frontiers: decisions about the spelling of Sesotho and Sestwana, for example, are of significance for educators in Lesotho and Botswana respectively as well as in South Africa. There have, too, been important activities in staff training run on a regional basis, in some cases by one of the regional associations for open and distance learning. At the international level, there are obvious opportunities for policy-makers to share their experience but there are also issues that belong properly on an international agenda, as the existence of COL and CIFFAD testifies. Perhaps most important, the issues of credit recognition and transfer and the concerns for consumer protection, examined in Chapters 9 and 10, demand a global response. For the policy-maker in-country, or within an institution, the existence of an international dimension to key policy issues needs to be kept in sight.

The conditions of success for open and distance learning are many but can be subsumed under the chapter headings in the central three parts of this book, and demand attention to process as well as to inputs and outcomes. Sensitive policies towards learners and students are the core but these in turn demand well-thought-through decisions about organisational structures, teaching technologies and quality assurance. They will make sense only if sound decisions are taken about the raising and allocation of resources, and if the results justify continued investment of time and often money by students, and of resources and support by governments, colleges and supportive parts of the private sector.

Those of us who work in open and distance learning believe that it has a unique and crucial role to play in development. But this book has sought to argue that the contribution of open and distance learning – access to education and training and efficient use of scarce educational resources – will be lost if fundamental policy and planning issues at international, national and institutional levels are ignored.

REFERENCES

Bates, T. (2000) *Managing Technological Change: Strategies for College and University Leaders*, Thousand Oaks, CA: Jossey-Bass.

Commonwealth of Learning (2002) *Evaluation Report of the Course for Distance Education Policy-makers in Southern Africa*, Vancouver.

Dodds, T. and Youngman, F. (1994) 'Distance education in Botswana: progress and prospects', *Journal of Distance Education* 19 (1): 61–79.

Freeman, R. (forthcoming) *Planning and Implementing Open and Distance Learning Systems: A Handbook for Decision Makers*, Vancouver: Commonwealth of Learning.

Hough, J. R. (ed.) (1984) *Educational Policy: An International Survey*, London: Croom Helm.

Jegede, O. and Okebukola, P. (2002) 'The re-emergence of ODL in Nigeria and its use for transforming education for national development', paper presented at the Pan Commonwealth Forum on Open Learning, 'Open learning: transforming education for development', Durban, 29 July to 2 August.

Lawrence, M. (2001) quoted in 'South African distance education widens its scope as Technikon SA moves into Botswana', *Mail and Guardian*, 21 September.

Murphy, P., Anzalone, S., Bosch, A. and Moulton, J. (2002) *Enhancing Learning Opportunities in Africa: Distance Education and Information and Communication Technologies for Learning* (Africa Region Human Development working paper series), Washington, DC: World Bank.

Nhundu, T. J. and Kamau, J. W. (2002) 'From correspondence to open and distance learning: the Botswana experience', paper presented at the Pan Commonwealth Forum on Open Learning, 'Open learning: transforming education for development', Durban, 29 July to 2 August.

Perraton, H., Creed, C. and Robinson, B. (2002) *Teacher Education Guidelines: Using Open and Distance Learning*, Paris: UNESCO.

Perry, W. (1976) *The Open University: A Personal Account by the First Vice Chancellor*, Milton Keynes: Open University Press.

Peters, O. (1983) 'Distance teaching and industrial production: a comparative interpretation in outline', in D. Sewart, D. Keegan and B. Holmberg (eds) *Distance Education: International Perspectives*, London: Routledge.

Robinson, B. (1998) 'Developing open learning and distance education: some questions and issues for policy-makers', paper presented at IIEP Workshop on the Planning and Management of Open and Distance Learning, Bangkok: UNESCO/International Institute for Educational Planning.

Rumble, G. (1992) *The Management of Distance Learning Systems*, Paris: UNESCO/ IIEP.

'This Day' (2003) Lagos interview with Professor Olugbemiro Jegede, Director General of NOUN, 5 February.

Troha, F. J. (2002) 'A bulletproof model for the design of blended learning', available at http://www.refresher.com/!troha2.htm.

UNESCO (2002a) *Open and Distance Learning: Trends, Policy and Strategy Considerations*, Paris: UNESCO.

UNESCO (2002b) http://www.indev.nic.in/indev/profNewsItem.asp?id=300.

Unterhalter, E., Hoppers, C. O. and Hoppers, W. (2000) 'The elusiveness of integration: policy discourses on open and distance learning in the 1990s', in C. Yates and J. Bradley (eds) *Basic Education at a Distance*, London: Routledge.

Index